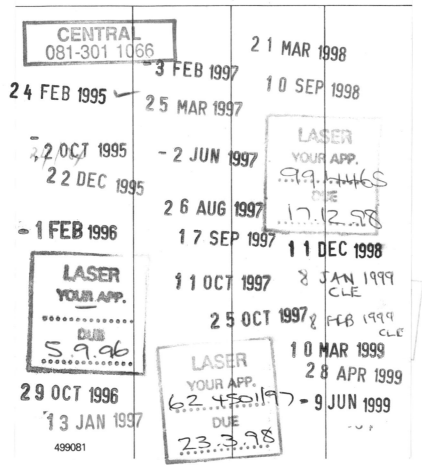

ADVANCED PROJECT MANAGEMENT

ADVANCED PROJECT MANAGEMENT

A Structured Approach

Third Edition

F. L. Harrison

Gower

First published 1981
Second edition 1985
Third edition published in 1992 by
Gower Publishing Company Limited
Gower House
Croft Road
Aldershot
Hants GU11 3HR
England

Reprinted 1993

ISBN 0–566–09100–3

Typeset in 10pt Times by Poole Typesetting (Wessex) Ltd, Bournemouth, Dorset
Printed in Great Britain at the University Press, Cambridge

CONTENTS

FIGURES

PART TWO

5   An Introduction to Project Planning and Control   95

TABLES

INTRODUCTION

Project management has been adopted by a wide range of organizations in industry, commerce and government to handle their many and varied one-off undertakings, i.e. projects. Unfortunately the problems involved in managing such undertakings mean that project management is an advanced and specialized branch of management. As a result, many projects take longer to complete and cost more than necessary because of a lack of professional skills and the use of inadequate methodologies.

There is a large amount of consensus both in the UK and the USA as to the reasons for the success or failure of projects and of project management. The principal factors leading to project failure have been identified as the following:

- Inadequate and inappropriate project organization structures, which lead to problems of authority, responsibility, communication and coordination.
- Inadequate planning and control methodologies and systems.
- The intergroup and interpersonal human problems and conflicts that arise in the flexible and complex organization of projects.
- A lack of integration of the organization, the work, the people and the management systems.

This book covers these critical areas of project management and is aimed to help the reader to make a success of project management and prevent the failure of projects. It is divided into three sections which concentrate in depth and at an advanced level on the following:

- An overview of project management and the project organization structure
- Modern methodologies of project planning and control
- Human behaviour in the project setting.

Since this book was first published, and in particular in the last five years, there have been significant developments in project management. Project management has been revolutionized by the increasing adoption of an integrated and structured approach to its organization, methodology of planning and control, and the human element.

Integration is critical in project work, and in fact is one of the prime reasons for the appointment of project managers and the adoption of project management. This integration applies to the organization, the planning and control methodologies, the information systems, and to the human system, that is it must be total integration.

The principal methodology for achieving this integration is 'structuring', both the structuring of the project and the structuring of the organization. This structuring not only provides a framework for integration but is also of assistance in the organization of the project, designing its management systems, planning and control, and man-management. In fact modern methods of management of projects depend largely on this structuring.

Thus this Third Edition of *Advanced Project Management* involves a complete re-write of the second edition, and an emphasis on structuring to provide a framework for total integration. Throughout the book it is emphasized that organization, project control and human behaviour are not separate compartmentalized areas of project management. These three systems interact and are interdependent, and therefore must be treated as an integrated whole. Each influences the other two systems and cannot be considered in isolation.

F.L. Harrison

PART ONE

Chapter 1

INTRODUCTION TO PROJECT MANAGEMENT

Projects and project management are taking increasingly important roles in industry, commerce and public sector organizations. A few years ago, project management was thought of as primarily applying to the oil, chemical, defence and construction industries. Today the application of project management has extended far beyond these industries and its old construction type emphasis, to many less traditional industries and to more intangible applications. Although the applications may be very different from the traditional application of project management, they are just as much projects and they can benefit from advanced project management.

Reasons for the widespread adoption of project management

There are primarily four reasons for the widespread adoption of professional and advanced project management today:

1. Management is recognizing that many of its organization's activities are projects and that the management of projects is different to the management of its other operations.
2. Market conditions are becoming more demanding and projects are becoming larger, leading to a requirement for more professional project management.
3. The rate of change facing industry is increasing and more undertakings are having to be treated as projects with tight time, cost and performance objectives.

4. The problems of integrating multiple disciplines in multi-company undertakings is making the adoption of project management critical to their success.

Many of an organization's activities can be regarded as projects

More and more managers throughout industry, commerce and government have begun to realize that many of their organizations' activities are projects and that their traditional general or functional-oriented approaches need to be changed to complete these projects successfully. These managers recognize the distinct nature and contribution of project management competencies and the need to employ the specialist management skills, organizational structures and techniques that belong to project management. Thus in order to complete these projects within their time, cost and technical performance objectives, these organizations are introducing project management.

More demanding market conditions

Market conditions have changed in the late 1980s and it is essential for any organization's survival that its projects are completed on time, to budget and that they meet their performance requirements. Projects involve large financial expenditures, and overspending on projects has seriously handicapped many firms. In addition, not only is time money, for example delays may lead to reduced cash flows in the early stages when income is desperately required, or interest payments are heavy, but also market opportunities can be lost.

The days when simple cost-plus forms of contract were in vogue, and schedule slippages and cost over-runs were the norm are over. Clients or internal project sponsors have become more demanding, more sophisticated and have higher expectations. Financial and market pressures demand that projects are finished in the shortest possible times and within their cost estimates. The days of *laissez-faire* planning and control of projects are also over; increasingly sophisticated systems of planning and control are available, are being used to manage projects and are being demanded by clients. In addition the human side of project management has become of greater importance, with a resulting need for skills in leadership, motivation, team-building and conflict management.

In order to achieve these objectives, professional and advanced project management is required to manage these undertakings. Even those firms who operate in the manufacturing and construction industries, where project management has been applied in the past are realizing that they can no longer rely on half hearted implementations of project management or their more traditional methods to manage project type work. They are facing increased demands for better project performance, and are having to adopt more advanced forms of project management.

An accelerating rate of change

The rate of change facing industry and commerce is accelerating and management by projects is one way for organizations successfully to cope with this change. The traditional forms of organization are well suited to dealing with relatively static, steady state situations, and to the performance of repetitive tasks or functions, where stability and continuity are important. Little of this applies to the situation facing many organizations today. The 1990s have ushered in a period of intense change, both nationally and internationally, which is increasing competition and the need for organizations to respond quickly to changing market demands. This has put a premium on the flexibility of strategies, organization structures and cultures, and has created challenges to organizations to respond rapidly to these changes, or cease to exist.

In order to cope with these demands many organizations are moving away from the traditional fixed pyramidal organization structures to flexible network type, project-oriented structures. They are using flexible and temporary project teams to implement change, or to deal with undertakings requiring sudden calls on management and technical resources to meet competitive demands. These organizations are being forced to 'projectize' many of their activities and undertakings in order to complete them quickly and satisfactorily. This is expanding the boundaries of the applications of project management into many new areas, particularly in the management of change. Project management is essentially the management of change.

The problems of integration

Projects are also becoming more complex, with an increasing number of specialized contributors required, necessitating the integration of many disciplines across organizational boundaries. More and more undertakings are involving multiple disciplines and/or multiple companies for their completion. If these undertakings are to be completed successfully, the individual disciplines and companies can no longer take a blinkered, parochial approach and be managed as separate entities. They are inevitably interdependent and interact, and therefore require integration into one project organization.

Project management provides the means for this integration, the forms of organization which span multi-discipline and multi-company activities, and the management systems designed to cope with this situation and the problems involved. Thus project management is being introduced by many organizations to handle multi-discipline, multi-company undertakings.

These factors are pushing firms to adopt project management seriously and to employ, or train professional project managers. The days when the person running a project was a straightforward technical specialist, say in design, research and development or construction are gone. Project managers have to combine a technical background with a business orientation, and the skills of general management, organization design, planning and control, and man-management.

There is an accelerating trend among organizations throughout the public and private sectors to manage at least part of, and in some cases all of their businesses as projects, and for the widespread adoption of project management as a specialist branch of management. This may be an explicit management decision, or it may sometimes be an implicit evolution which occurs without the organization consciously being aware of it. However, project management is an advanced and specialized branch of management that uses very professional skills and techniques. All too often projects fail because of a lack of recognition of these facts by senior management and a lack of these skills in the managers who endeavour to manage these projects.

Reasons for the success or failure of projects

The reasons for the success or failure of projects, and project management are many and varied, and a number of studies have been carried out to identify the principal factors. Before examining these, it is worthwhile to consider what constitutes the success or failure of a project. At first glance, a project that does not meet its time, cost and technical performance objectives would appear to be a failure, but this is not necessarily so. It is 'perceived' success or failure that is important and provided a project achieves a satisfactory level of technical performance, in retrospect it may be considered a success by the parties involved, despite exceeding its cost and time targets.

For example, a contractor may still make an acceptable profit on its part of the project, despite it being late and costing more than the original contract price. In addition, although the project cost more and took longer than the client originally conceived, the client may accept that this was unavoidable, was for good reasons, that it received value for money, and the project was still a commercial success. The criterion of success or failure is whether the project sponsor, owner, client and other parties concerned, including the project manager's parent company, are satisfied with the final outcome of the project.

Not all project successes or failures are due to the effectiveness or otherwise of project management. There are many reasons outside the project manager's control for failure of a project. For example, it may be that the contract was deliberately 'bought' with an unrealistically low price, or that the original cost, time and performance targets were set very optimistically and the project manager had no hope of achieving them. Another example would be where in order to obtain funds for the project, the initial funding requirements were minimized. Thereafter as funds committed are 'sunk costs', when costs appear to escalate, further funding is obtained, whereas if realistic estimates of cost were made at the funding stage, the project would not have gone ahead.

Thus in comparing projects and project managers, the fact that one project is completed on time and to budget and another is not, may not mean the first was better managed. It may be that in the apparent project failure the project manager had an impossible task and that by the exercise of a high level of management skills the delays and over-expenditure were minimized. In the other apparently successful project, the time and cost targets may have had 'fat' and they could be achieved with a very low level of managerial skill. Comparisons of relative project performance must therefore not be made simply on the achievement or non-achievement of their time and cost targets. It is the percieved success or failure by all the parties concerned that is important, and it must be viewed in the light of the circumstances affecting each project.

US experience

The major research work on the subject was carried out in the USA by Baker, Murphy and Fisher, who studied 650 projects.[1] They identified a large number of factors which affected the success of projects, the failure of projects and those which affected both success and failure, as shown in Figure 1.1. They also consolidated their findings and identified the following:

- The prime factors leading to project failure:
  Poor coordination
  Human relations.
- The prime factors leading to project success:
  Adequate and appropriate organizational structures
  Adequate and appropriate planning and control mechanisms.

UK experience

In the UK, two studies identified the factors leading to the failure of projects. Duffy and Thomas[2] identified the following reasons for the failure of projects:

- Part-time project management in the client, consultant, contractor and supplier organizations is an important factor in poor project performance.
- Inappropriate project organization is usually the key to an unsuccessful project. Here the roles and responsiblities in the project parties have not been clearly defined.
- Lack of direction and control in the project team often results in low productivity and a failure to meet delivery dates.
- On many projects consideration of an appropriate contract strategy is left until late in the project, when the full range of options available to the client cannot be considered.
- Often the scope of work is not defined adequately to those participating in the project.
- Frequently the level of planning is inappropriate to the scope of the project. Project stages are not clearly identified with agreed deliverables.

Factors affecting both success and failure

Goal commitment of project team
Accurate initial cost estimates
Adequate project team capability
Adequate funding to completion
Adequate planning and control techniques
Minimal start-up difficulties
Task (versus social) orientation
Absence of bureaucracy
On-site project manager
Clearly established success criteria

Factors affecting . . .

Failure	**Success**

Inadequate project manager:
  ● Human skills
  ● Technical skills
  ● Influence
  ● Authority
	Project manager commitment to:
	  ● Established schedules
	  ● Established budgets
	  ● Technical performance goals.

Insufficient use of status and progress
  reports
	Frequent feedback from the parent
	  organization

Use of superficial status/progress reports	Frequent feedback from the client
Insufficient client influence	Client commitment to:
Poor coordination with the client	● Established schedules
	● Established budgets
Lack of rapport with the client	● Technical performance goals
Client disinterest in budget criteria	
Lack of project team participation in decision-making	Organization structure suited to project team

Lack of project team participation in
  problem-solving
	Project team participation in determining
	  schedules and budgets

Excessive structuring within project team	
Job insecurity within project team	
Lack of team spirit and sense of mission within project team	

Parent organization stable, non-dynamic,
  lacking strategic change
	Parent commitment to:
	  ● Established schedules
	  ● Established budgets

Poor coordination with parent organization	● Technical performance goals.
Lack of rapport with parent organization	Parent enthusiasm
Poor relations with parent organization	Parent desire to build up internal capabilities

Project more complex than the parent has
  completed before
	Adequate control procedures, especially for
	  dealing with changes

Inability to freeze design early	
Inability to close out the effort	Judicious use of networking techniques
Inadequate change procedures	Minimal number of public/government
Unrealistic project schedules	agencies involved
Initial under-funding	Lack of excessive government red tape
New 'type' of project	Enthusiastic public support
Poor relations with public officials	Lack of legal encumbrances
Unfavourable public opinion	

Figure 1.1   Factors affecting the success or failure of projects
Source: Baker, Murphy and Fisher[1]

- Poor planning leads to underestimation of resources which inevitably leads to inefficiencies and delays.

- Cost growth occurs during project development due to poor change order control and an ever-expanding scope of work.
- Frequently the risks associated with the project are not identified and action is not taken to transfer or make contingency for the risk.

In the other UK study[3] of North Sea oil related projects, the principal areas in which shortcomings in project management contributed to increased cost and delays in the completion of projects were identified as the following:

1. The general management and logistics problems arising from the complex interactive nature of project work.
2. Lack of clear definition of organization structure, which causes problems of authority, responsibility, communication and coordination.
3. Inadequate planning, budgeting and control systems.
4. The intergroup, interpersonal problems and conflicts that arise in the flexible and complex organization of projects.
5. A lack of integration of the organization, the work, the people and the management systems.

Thus there is much consensus in these studies as to the reasons for the success or failure of projects and of project management. The following principal factors can be identified:

- Organization.
- Planning and control.
- Human factors.

Despite this, the emphasis of project management literature and training has been on the techniques used in project planning and control. Knowledge of these techniques is now much more widespread than five to ten years ago, yet 'techniques' are only one aspect of this function. On anything but the smallest project, the methodology used, and the management systems to back this up, have a much greater impact on the effectiveness of project planning and control, and indeed of project management.

In addition, most training carried out on human relations has tended to be generalized, that is, not specific to project management, and of a theoretical nature. It has thus tended to be of limited relevance to the harsh and specialized environment of the project management world.

Furthermore, relatively limited attention has been given to the design and implications of the form of the organization structure used in project work. It also tends to be a topic that the reader considers is not directly relevant and therefore skips over. Yet it has been established time and again that the form of organization structure used has a significant impact on performance on projects. It can influence performance in many ways, not the least of which is its effects on motivation, teamwork and conflict in the project setting.

Therefore this book is aimed to help the reader to make a success of project management and to prevent project failure. It thus concentrates on these three topics in depth and at an advanced level, and assumes that the reader is aware of the basic techniques of project planning and control.

The definition of 'project'

The main reason that these problems exist in the management of projects and that project management is an advanced and specialized branch of management is the complexity of this entity called a project. Thus it is necessary to understand clearly just what constitutes a project.

Surprising as it may seem, there is no standard, accepted definition of a project, although there is much commonality in the various text book definitions, for example

A project can be considered to be any series of activities and tasks that:

- Have a specific objective to be completed within certain specifications.
- Have defined start and end dates.
- Have funding limits (if applicable).
- Consume resources (i.e., money, people's time, equipment)[4]

A project can be defined as a non-routine, non-repetitive one-off undertaking, normally with discrete time, financial and technical performance goals.[5]

The official Project Management Institute (USA) definition of a 'project' is presented on page 4–3 of the *Project Management Body of Knowledge* (*PMBOK*):

Project: Any undertaking with a defined starting point and defined objectives by which completion is identified. In practice, most projects depend on finite or limited resources by which the objectives are to be accomplished.

Thus the simple definition of the 'basic' project could be taken to be: 'A discrete undertaking with finite objectives – often including time, cost and technical performance goals.' Although this defines the basic project, it does not necessarily mean that a project manager, or the specialized skills and techniques of project management are required. Every manager deals with many such undertakings in the normal course of duties. Thus this definition merely defines what could be termed a 'Stage 1' project.

The next stage in the definition of a project and the one that does necessitate the use of the project management concept is that these undertakings be of 'significant size, value, complexity and be under time pressure to complete'.

In the management of this 'Stage 2' project, significant benefits arise from the following:

1. Appointing one person as project manager, accountable and responsible for the management of the project and the achievement of its objectives.
2. A change of culture from operational or functional management to a goal-oriented project management culture.
3. The use of specialist project planning and control techniques.

Even with this extension of the basic definition of a project, many managers may query that this is sufficient to justify the statement that project management is an advanced and specialized branch of management requiring specialist skills and techniques. Some operational and functional areas of management, such as architecture or construction management, also use and benefit from these concepts.

The real difference between projects and other management activities that necessitates the use of advanced project management, arises as more amd more undertakings, because of their size and/or complexity, involve the 'integration' of the contributions of several groups, organizational units and/or companies. It is this integration requirement that crosses organizational boundaries which differentiates projects and project management from other areas of management and requires the specialized forms of organization, skills and techniques.

The genesis of the definition of a 'Stage 3' project is thus:

1. It is a discrete undertaking, that is, it has a start and a finish.
2. It has finite objectives, often including time, cost and performance goals.
3. It is of significant size, value and complexity, and is under time pressure for completion.
4. It involves the integration across organizational boundaries of groups, departments, organizational units and companies.

These factors define a project in which advanced project management is required to ensure its successful completion on time, within budget. This type of project requires a project manager and project management, and this project management is a separate branch of management, differentiated from other branches such as operations management, production management or even general management.

There are often two levels of project manager. There is the manager of the overall multi-discipline, multi-company project, that is, a Stage 3 project manager. For example in a building project, this project manager is concerned with integrating the client, architect and construction contractor companies into one project organization. There are also often Stage 2 project managers who are concerned with managing each individual company's contribution to the overall project. For example the client, architect and construction companies may each have their own 'project manager', who is less concerned with integrating across company boundaries, is concerned primarily with the individual company's success or failure and is not responsible for the project as a whole. They generally have multi-discipline, multi-company integration responsibilities, but only with their own company departments and their subcontractors and suppliers. They are primarily concerned with their own company's commitments and less with the overall project. Both Stage 2 and Stage 3 project managers will have many of the same problems, but it is the Stage 3 project manager who has the principal problems of integration across company boundaries, which necessitate an advanced and structured approach to project management. Both Stage 2 and Stage 3 project managers are required to manage such projects for the reasons outlined below.

The project manager

Without project managers, no one manager in the traditional department form of organization is entirely responsible for, and manages a project throughout its life. Emphasis by functional department managers is often given more to the technical success of the project, rather than to a balance of time, financial and technical success. Functional departmental managers tend to concentrate their efforts and understanding within their own departments. This often leads to tunnel vision, that is, they can only view a project within the narrow scope of their own function and cannot exercise judgement on the project as a whole.

The only common superior of the various groups, departments and organizational units of the principal company involved in a project is otherwise one of the senior general managers, and cannot carry out this role. The senior general management of a company cannot give the concentrated attention to any one individual project that is required for its effective management. This is particularly so in the multi-project situation, when a stream of projects is being handled, each in a different stage in the project life cycle. Thus there is a requirement for a Stage 2 project manager for the individual company.

These problems are accentuated in multi-company projects where, although each company may or may not have their own project manager, the following is often true:

1. There is no single point accountability and responsiblity for the overall project. No one individual, group or even company is accountable and responsible for all of the organizational units contributing to the project during its life cycle.
2. No individual, group or company thus attempts to integrate the work and the people from all the companies.

For example, in a building project, the owner is unlikely to have all of the skills and resources necessary to manage the overall project. At the same time, the architect and the building contractor may be concerned only with their own sphere of activities. Thus there is also the requirement in multi-company projects for the Stage 3 project manager. In many cases, one of the individual company Stage 2 project managers will carry out this overall project management role; in others it will be shared, leading to a dual management of the project.

Projects of significant size, value and complexity require to have vested in one individual, that is, a project manager, accountability and responsibility for integrating the management functions and activities of the many organizational units involved in a project. Without this there will be no effective management, leadership or integration of those involved in the project. This need for a project manager is even more critical when there are several companies involved in a project.

The project manager is responsible for the success of the project in terms of time, cost and technical performance. The project manager must provide the management and leadership neccessary to bind the people and groups from different departments and companies working on the project, into one managerial organization and team, and provide the drive necessary to ensure completion on time and within budget. This provides the individual accountability and responsibility for any one project, which is a prerequisite for the success of such undertakings.

Project management

The principal reason for the development of project management as a separate branch of management is that the traditional forms of organization and management techniques do not handle project work effectively. There is a need for specialized forms of organization, information systems, managers skilled in the techniques of project planning, financial management, control and the particular human problems arising in project work, because of the special characteristics of projects and the problems caused by them.
Project management can be defined as

The achievement of a project's objectives through people, and involves the organizing, planning and control of the resources assigned to the project, together with the development of constructive human relations with all those involved, both in-company and with the other companies involved.

Project management has evolved to be a general management-oriented and integrative activity, below the level of top management. As such, it can be used to train relatively junior managers in general management. Effective project management has been successful in handling the many planning, communication and coordination problems involved in project work. It has proved capable of integrating the various personnel and groups into one organization and, due to the nature of project work, of developing effective teamwork and commitment to the project's objectives. It is now widely accepted that some form of project management is necessary when large and complex undertakings are involved, and that its effectiveness can significantly influence the cost of a project and the time taken to complete it.

An advanced, specialized branch of management

Project management can be considered as another branch or specialized form of management, similar to production management, marketing management, etc. In a way it is, but in many ways it is far more than that. It does have its own range of specialized methods, systems and techniques, particularly in project planning and control. These in themselves would be sufficient to differentiate project management as a specialised branch of management. However, project management is more than that primarily because of the following factors:

Organization

The organization structures used are specialized, often complex and are designed to handle multi-discipline, multi-company undertakings. These structures often break many of the traditional rules of organization theory, namely:

- The organization has a hierarchical structure.
- Authority is based on the superior–subordinate concept.
- A subordinate can only have one superior.
- There is a division of labour based on task specialization.
- The span of control of a manager is limited.
- People are divided into staff and line management.
- There must be parity between a manager's responsibility and authority.

Human relations

The problems and challenges in human relations which face the project manager may be thought no different from those facing most managers, but in project management human relations problems are accentuated and accelerated. Project managers do not work in the usual superior–subordinate hierarchy and their responsibility typically exceeds their authority. Yet they must manage people who are not directly responsible to them and often outside their own company. They must also quickly build teams, or at least a cooperative working relationship, and must manage conflict which is generally held to be endemic in project work.

Culture

Culture as much as anything, differentiates project management from many other branches of management. Project management has a culture all of its own, which includes the following:

- Thinking globally and not parochially about one's own commitments.
- A total commitment to goals, including being:
  results-oriented;
  cost and time conscious.
- Accepting change as a way of life.
- Dealing with:
  flexiblity
  uncertainty
  complexity
  indefinite and inadequate authority
  temporary situations and relationships
  a high level of imagination.

Thus the areas where project management is differentiated from other branches of management and in which specialized skills, knowledge and techniques are required are as follows:

1. The organization of projects and project management.
2. The planning and control of projects.
3. Human relations.
4. Organization culture.

Organization structure

The conventional form of company organization divides the people in the company into groups of similar skills, interests, training and occupational specialization. Therefore one typically finds a company organized into departments, such as design, construction, purchasing, production, marketing and finance. Such a functional organization used in project work permits the efficient use of resources on several projects, as more or less people can be allocated to individual projects as required. It also increases the rate of development of professional skills by constant contact and interaction with colleagues in the specialism. The functional organization thus permits the efficient use and development of people on multi-project work.

This functional organization gives the company a horizontal dimension, into which it is divided by departments. Added to this there is a vertical dimension, with different levels, which represent varying degrees of authority. This hierarchical structure is the basic framework of the organization structure, and the superior–subordinate relationships are the lines in which authority flows from the top management to the lowest levels. This structure forms the traditional management pyramid, with the only focal point of power binding the organization together being the top management of the company or division. This is the typical company organization and it tends to lead to stable interpersonal and departmental relationships.

However, projects are essentially temporary undertakings for those concerned, with typical lives varying from three months to five years. They usually involve several departments of a company working together and in the majority of cases more than one company is involved in the work on any one project. Often these departments and companies are working on several projects at the same time, each at different stages in the project life cycle. Project work is therefore necessarily complex with respect to interactions and interdependencies between the groups, departments, organizational units and companies involved. This necessitates a complex organization structure which includes people from many different professions, backgrounds, departments and companies. An added complication is that these relationships and interactions are dynamic and never static. Typically at the start of a project, work emphasis may be on research and development; it then changes to design, purchasing and procurement, to manufacturing and/or to construction, to testing and commissioning and finally to operation. No single functional department or company is thus the most important over the whole life of the project and thus no individual departmental manager can assume the leading management role for the complete project.

The traditional form of functional pyramid type organization structure does not therefore handle projects effectively, tends not to meet time targets or schedules, and is operations-oriented and not project- or goal-oriented. It has severe difficulty in achieving effective communication, collaboration, coordination and control with several different departments and companies involved in a project. It cannot handle the dynamic, ever-changing relationships and the complexities involved in project work.

This is a particular problem in large projects where development, design, procurement and construction must often overlap to achieve the shortest possible project time. Effective communication and integration among different departments and companies is very difficult to achieve with the standard functional organization structure and yet lack of these factors is one of the common routes to failure. The traditional organization has no means of managing or coordinating a multi-company organization. It has no means of integrating different departments, at levels below top management, or clients, contractors, consultants, subcontractors, material and equipment suppliers into a single organization. Thus special forms of organization structure are required to handle projects and tie together these separate organizations into a single global project organization. They are very different from the traditional functional pyramid organization and must transcend the individual department, division or company, with in the extreme case hundreds of companies involved.

These specialized forms of project organization must cross group, department and company boundaries, and be very flexible. They are often complex, sometimes uncertain and usually involve imprecise authority and power relationships.

Project managers need to be able to design such organization structures and tailor them to each individual project. Although the project manager's parent firm's project organization structure may be established, the individual project's organization structure will involve a unique mix of other organizations and companies, and thus each project requires the design of an organization structure. An added complication is that on many projects, the organization structure will change through the life of the project, as the number of people, groups and companies involved changes. This is one of the factors that typifies the dynamic approach required in project management that differentiates it from other branches of management in which a more static situation applies.

Although the senior general managers of a company will from time to time restructure, that is, redesign the firm's organization structure, the relatively junior project managers may have to design an organization structure for every project in which they are involved. They also have to be able to manage such a necessarily complex organization and use it to integrate the activities of the many individuals, groups, departments, organizational units and companies involved in the project, and turn them into an effective team.

Planning and control

In the management of operations, work tends to be repetitive and there is an effective learning curve because of this. People carry out the same functions, week in and week out, and relationships and information flows are more or less permanent. Monthly budgets are staightforward measurements of variables, that change only slightly from period to period. Operational management can thus be viewed in the short term as a relatively static situation. This may not be the reality of the day-to-day operational situation, but the underlying concept is that of a static fixed organization carrying out repetitive work. Planning and control are important in the management of operations, but tend to handle a fixed labour force and fixed production facilities in this relatively static state of nature.

✗ None of this applies to project management. A project is by definition a unique, non-repetitive, one-off undertaking. There is a limited learning curve, as a project manager may carry out the various stages of a project only once every few months, or up to once every few years. Moreover, mistakes, errors, omissions, wrong or late decisions cannot be compensated for in the lifetime of the project. People's functions and roles are never the same, week in and week out, and are in a constant state of flux. Their relationships have to be established anew for each project, and vary throughout the life of the project. Project information systems have to be uniquely designed and established for every project, and monthly budgets deal with variables which change from month to month. Thus a project is always in a constant state of change and project management never deals with a static situation; the underlying concept is the management of a dynamic situation.

Furthermore, everything in a project has to be started from scratch. The scope of the project has to be defined, responsibilities allocated, work scheduled, resourced and budgeted uniquely. This project planning carries out many functions ranging from coordination and communication, to enhancing the power of the project manager and motivating the people to achieve the project's objectives.

A project is usually a large, complex, ever-changing dynamic entity, and it is difficult for mere human beings to envisage all parts of it and to know what is happening everywhere, and at all times. It is difficult to coordinate, is subject to many changes, and control is essential to enable the project manager to maintain a grasp of it, that is, to manage it effectively.

In project management, effective planning and control are not only important, they are critical to the success or failure of the project, and many, many projects have suffered delays and over-expenditure because of inadequate planning and control. However, project planning and control are difficult functions, due to such factors as the large number of activities, groups and companies involved, and the necessity of using specialist, normally computer-based methods. Although attention in the past has centred on the use of network planning techniques, such as the critical path method, or precedence diagramming, emphasis today in project planning and control is on the methodologies and systems used, as much or even more than on these techniques.

In the last few years, the major change in project management has been the increasing adoption of a structured methodology of project planning and control. This structured approach brings together the integration of computer-based information systems, earned value based performance analysis and stuctured, hierarchical, multi-level, two dimensional, rolling wave, distributed, but integrated project planning and control, with an emphasis on individual accountability.

It must also be emphasized that project planning and control is not simply the use of network methods, Gantt charts or other planning techniques. The project planning system is only one of the sub-systems of the total project management system that is concerned with planning and controlling the project. Effective planning and control involves many information systems carrying out such functions as work definition, estimating, materials management, design control, quality assurance, among many others.

All these systems are involved in the planning and particularly the control of a project, and furthermore it is critical that these systems are integrated into a single system, so that a change in one is reflected in the others. Without this integration, which also extends to the integration of schedule, resource and expenditure budgets, organization, and the human system, a project cannot be controlled and many projects have failed because of a lack of this integration. In the past, integration of systems was a difficult task, but today it is much more feasible with the widespread availablity and use of relational database packages.

Another factor which has changed is that whereas in the past, control analysis was essentially limited to backward looking variance analysis, the trend today is to use forward looking, earned value performance analysis, based on the US Department of Defense's C.Spec. methodology. Although this form of analysis, and the structured approach associated with it, has been around for a long time, it is only in the last few years that it has come to be accepted and used to any great extent in the private sector.

The adoption of this approach has been facilitated by the fact that many of the commonly used computer-based planning packages have adopted a structured approach to planning and include facilities for carrying out earned value analysis. These computer-based planning systems, the many other computer-based sub-systems and the relational database which ties them together into an integrated project management information system (IPMIS), are now essential to the successful planning and control of projects.

Human relations in the project setting

The project manager has to manage a complex organization requiring the work and contribution of many people from different professional backgrounds, different departments and different companies. Therefore even in the best of circumstances, the management of a project is a problem. It is a very difficult task to coordinate, communicate, provide leadership, motivate all the personnel involved, provide the necessary drive to achieve success, to plan, organize and control, that is, to manage a project.

A project manager's task is made more difficult by the fact that he or she acts as a junior general manager with normally ill-defined authority. Lines of authority or influence are grafted on to the existing pyramid structure, cutting across the normal lines of command and departmental boundaries.Project managers do not work in the usual superior–subordinate relationships but must manage their peers, juniors and superiors in other departments and companies who contribute to the project. Personnel in these organizations must work for two managers namely the project manager and their own parent department or company manager.

In the typical project organization, personnel and groups from several different functional departments, consultants, contractors and subcontractors must work together, but are generally not responsible directly to the project manager for pay rises, promotions or performance assessments and other line relationships. They have different loyalties and objectives, and have probably never worked together before and may never do so again. The one factor that binds them together is the project organization structure. The project manager must therefore deal with the human problems of developing a project team out of the diverse groups working on the project. This involves complex relationships with many other managers in these departments and companies, not just those directly employed on the project.

The temporary nature of the project organization means also that members of the project work together for a limited period of time and there is no time for interpersonal relationships to develop into a static state, as in usual operations management. Group performance is necessary from the very beginning of a project, as mistakes made and time lost at the start can never be recovered. In addition, the composition of the total management group on a project is constantly changing with new members joining it and the role of some older members diminishing in importance in time. It is further complicated by the fact that project managers must work under pressure to achieve cost, time and technical targets and their function includes applying pressure to the people and groups involved in the project.

Thus the project manager has a very difficult task and more problems in human relations than the typical manager. These problems arise out of the complexities and ambiguities of the forms of project organization used, such as dual subordination and inadeqate authority, and any interpersonal and inter-group problems are accentuated by the temporary nature of the project and the fact that many separate organizations are involved in one undertaking.

The temporary, complex and often loose nature of the relationships and authority patterns involved in project work, combined with the number of different departments and companies, whose objectives, management styles and cultures may differ, leads to human behaviour problems and a tendency for conflict between individuals and groups. Thus traditional management theory has to be modified in the management of projects.

The project manager requires skills in handling the human problems which arise because of the characteristics of projects and as a result of the form of the project organization. In this, several of the so-called principles of management, such as 'authority must equal responsibility' and 'a subordinate must have only one superior', must be disregarded, with consequential problems in human relations.

There is a particular need for the project manager to be skilled in the following areas:

1. Leadership to achieve the project's objectives.
2. Achieving power in a fluid situation, i.e. politics.
3. The motivation of individuals and groups.
4. Developing teams and teamwork.
5. Managing conflict.

These skills may be considered the normal human relations skill requirements for any manager. While this is true, in general and in operational management, these requirements tend to exist in the background in a muted ongoing manner. In project management, every project is a new challenge in man-management to the project manager, and these requirements have a very high profile. The project manager, specifically for each project, in a very complex and difficult situation as outlined, has to motivate the people involved, build teams and exercise leadership to achieve the project's objectives as very definite and discrete activities. In addition, because of many factors, conflict is an ever-present reality in project management and the project manager must be expert in the management of conflict. Many projects fail simply due to conflict.

Project culture

In many ways it is organization culture which differentiates project management from many other branches of management. Project managers need to be concerned with all the contributions and contributors to their project. They cannot think parochially of only their own department or company's contribution, but need to think in global terms about all the departments and companies working on the project and accept responsibility for all their work. This is a significant change of culture for many people.

Everybody involved in the project must learn to think in terms of the project's global organization, that is, considering client, consultants, design organization, manufacturing, construction, subcontractors, suppliers, etc., as a single organization or team. The project manager must learn to manage across organizational boundaries, and to think of and integrate the people involved from all the companies and departments as part of a single project organization.

The project manager and everyone involved in the project should have a total commitment and loyalty to the 'project'. The project can become almost a living entity which unites people to achieve its satisfactory completion on time and to budget. They should develop loyalties to the project and its team, as well, or instead of their parent organizations. This includes adopting a project attitude of mind which involves subordinating their own and their parent organization's interests to that of the project.

People in a project must become goal-oriented, rather than operations-oriented. Not only must they be oriented to achieving the project's goals, but these goals must be broken down into individual and group goals that they are committed to achieving. They must be totally results-oriented with a highly developed time and cost consciousness. These attitudes often involve a significant change in culture and outlook for someone who is only used to day-to-day operations.

The project manager and the people involved must also accept change as a way of life. Nothing is ever static in project work and the project personnel live in a world filled with uncertainty and complexity where nothing exists in a permanent state and they must be flexible in everything they undertake.

Project management is the management of change, and there is no such thing as the status quo. This is quite disruptive to some people. Not only is the project manager concerned with implementing change, but the project is itself a dynamic ever-changing entity. The project personnel must adapt to living in a world where nothing is the same from one day to the next, neither the work nor the human interrelationships involved in carrying out the work. The managers involved must learn to manage in a complex, flexible, dynamic and often uncertain organization structure.

The project manager has to manage without clear-cut superior–subordinate authority over all those involved. The project manager's authority is often uncertain, usually inadequate to match the responsibilities and partly based on contractual arrangements. The project manager must learn to achieve power to manage the project through any means available, rather than through the usual positional authority.

In project work accountability and responsibility for parts of the project are delegated to all the managers involved. Thus there must be an acceptance of both accountabilty and responsibilty for the project results by everyone, not simply the project manager. This involves the attitude that 'the buck stops here; there are no excuses, only success or failure', being adopted by all the managers in a project.

All those involved in a project must also have a philosophy of management which includes a commitment to planning and control as a way of managing. This involves looking at a plan not as something cast in concrete, but as a tool to help make decisions, allocate resources and manage the project. This planning commitment applies not only at the start of the project but throughout its life. The project personnel must also be committed to controlling the project, that is, constantly to monitor progress and performance, and take action to control deviations and resolve problems. They must be committed to teamwork, or working cooperatively.

A project normally involves many people, groups and companies. These organizational entities interact and are interdependent, and project performance is always enhanced if teamwork can be achieved, for teamwork involves the following:

- Mutual support.
- Open communication.
- Trust.
- Respect.

In addition, in crossing organizational boundaries with inadequate authority, the project manager must manage in a participative manner with the other managers involved. The prime example of this is when both the client and the principal contractor have a project manager for the same project. They are bound together by contractual lines of power and a joint commitment to the project, and they must work in a participative manner for full effectiveness.

At the same time as the project manager has a commitment to teamwork and participation, he or she must also exert leadership and drive to achieve the project's objectives. Teamwork and participation can sometimes lead to a happy, satisfied project group, but not necessarily the highest performance of which they are capable. Project managers must be strong leaders, and drive themselves and sometimes others, when necessary, to achieve results; it is results that count. Teamwork, participation, drive and leadership are not incompatible, and the best results are obtained when they are combined.

Finally, the project manager must have a strong imagination to take a project from nothing but an idea or vague proposal to a completed project, which may involve billions of pounds of expenditure. All this necessitates a culture which is very different from the ongoing management of operations and it is not surprising that many people find it difficult to adjust to project management.

Integrated and structured project management

The three critical functions or systems of project management – organization, planning and control, and human systems – are not separate compartmentalized areas of management. They interact and are interdependent, and therefore they must be treated as an integrated whole. Each system influences the other two systems and cannot be considered in isolation. For example:

- The project organization structure is one determinant of the design of the project's management information systems, which includes planning and control.
- In turn the effectiveness of the project management information system will strongly influence the effectiveness of the project organization structure.
- The form of organization structure used can strongly influence human behaviour, including such factors as the motivation of individuals and groups, the development of teamwork and the extent of conflict. The size of the groups, the effectiveness of integration, the patterns of authority, the 'tallness' of the organization hierarchy, and the tendency for organic or bureaucratic working are factors largely determined by the organization structure which influence man-management.
- The planning and control system can influence teamwork and the motivation of individuals and groups. Achievement motivation, goal theory and feedback on performance are intimately involved with the planning and control system, which can be one of the most powerful motivational tools available to the project manager.
- A suitably designed planning and control system can facilitate the use of different organization structures, e.g. the federal organization.
- Finally, the needs of the human behaviour system or man-management, can influence the design and effectiveness of both the organization used and the project information systems design.

In order to manage a project successfully, it is necessary not only to integrate the project management information systems, but also to take a 'total' integrated approach to the management of projects. Thus the organization structure, the project management information systems, including the planning and control system, and the human system must be viewed as one integrated system. This integration is achieved by combining the organization structure and the structure of the project to provide a framework for integration. This is the essence of the advanced approach to project management implied by structured project management.

By tackling these systems as a totally integrated system through structuring, each contributes to the other and synergy is obtained, that is the sum of these systems when integrated is greater than their individual worth. In other words, the project organization used is designed to facilitate effective planning and control, to minimize the potential for conflict, to contribute to the motivation of individuals and groups involved and to encourage teamwork. In turn, the management information systems are designed to give the members of the organization the necessary information for them to manage the project effectively, and to motivate all those involved.

Notes

1. B.N. Baker, D.C. Murphy and D. Fisher (1983) 'Factors affecting project success', in D.I. Cleland and W.R. King, *Project Management Handbook*, Van Nostrand Reinhold.
2. P.J. Duffy and R.D. Thomas (1988) *Project Performance Auditing*, Proceedings of the 9th World Congress on Project Management.
3. Department of Energy, Peat Marwick Mitchell & Co., and Atkins Planning (1976) *North Sea Costs Escalation Study*, HMSO.
4. H. Kerzner (1984) *Project Management*, Van Nostrand Reinhold.
5. F.L. Harrison (1985) *Advanced Project Management*, 2nd edn, Gower Publishing Co. Ltd.

Chapter 2

INTRODUCTION TO THE PROJECT ORGANIZATION

A project will always involve a number of people to carry out the work required. This number will vary from a handful to literally thousands, depending on the size of the project. These people will inevitably belong to a number of different functions, professions or specialisms, and their work will be highly interrelated and interdependent. As well as being part of the project organization, they may belong to a number of other organizations, external to the project. These 'parent' organizations may be functional departments or divisions, and/or different companies.

The importance of the project organization structure

In order for the people involved to work efficiently and effectively to achieve the project's objectives, they will have to be 'organized', that is, a project organization structure must be created, otherwise there will be chaos. This organization structure involves the dividing and grouping of tasks and people based on the project requirements and the division of labour by functional specialization, with the establishment of the lines of authority and coordination which integrate these divisions and groups.

The design of this structure, for example, the size of groups, both small and large, their composition, the number of levels of management, the degree of centralization, is of crucial importance to the performance of the people and companies involved, and to the success of the project. Overall project performance depends not only on how individuals perform, but more importantly on how well individuals work together in groups, and how these groups, larger organizational units and companies work together in the overall project organization to achieve the project's objectives.

There can be significant differences in the performance of the same people and companies in different forms of project organization structure. Not only does the form of organization structure influence how efficiently the work is carried out as a system, but it also strongly influences the motivation of individuals and groups, and the extent of teamwork, conflict and politics.

The basic elements of the design of the organization structure

In a small project, with only a handful of people involved, the organization structure is relatively simple. The project manager directly manages all the people in one, usually mixed group. However, there are limitations on how many people one manager can directly manage, that is, how large a span of control does the manager have?

Management in the project setting, as in any other, involves the following functions:

- Organization
- Planning
- Directing
- Controlling
- Decision-making
- Integration
- Coordination

- Leadership
- Motivation
- Team-building
- Conflict management
- Welfare
- Administration
- Communication

In a large project with many people involved, no one manager can directly carry out all these functions for everyone involved. Thus as soon as the size of the project, and consequently the number of people involved increases beyond that within which a manager can reasonably exercise these functions of management, then the people will need to be divided into groups, each with their own manager to carry out all, or some of these functions. Authority and responsibility for management functions must then be delegated from the senior or project manager to the managers of these groups.

As the size of the project increases and more people are involved, so does the number of groups increase. Again there are limitations on the number of groups one manager can manage and the same process must be repeated, possibly several times. Thus in the first instance, people are formed into groups and then these groups are consolidated into larger units. The basis of this grouping can be in either of two ways:

1. People, or groups of the same function, profession or specialism may be grouped together, e.g. functional departments.

2. People and groups of different functions, professions or specialisms who work together on the task or division of the project and who interact and are interdependent, are grouped together. These groupings tend to be semi-independent, self-contained, mixed 'organizational units'.

Thus the people from the companies involved in carrying out the work on a project are formed into groups, functional departments and organizational units. One of the first steps in the design of the project organization is to break down the work required into divisions and sub-divisions that are of such a size that they can be allocated to these individuals, groups, departments, organizational units and companies. Thereafter as the work of the various groups requires a large amount of interaction between groups and they are interdependent, the work and the people carrying it out need to be integrated, that is, the structure of the authority, coordination and communication relationships between groups, departments, organizational units and companies must be established.

In the larger project, these larger groupings are consolidated into the overall project organization with a managerial hierarchy, or organizational superstructure. The number of managerial levels of this hierarchy depends not only on the number of people involved, but also on the mode of operation or managerial philosophy.

A large number of levels, that is, a 'tall' superstructure, is generally associated with centralized decision making and close control or supervision of the people involved. A small number of levels, that is, a 'flat' superstructure, is generally associated with decentralized decision-making, with a greater degree of delegation of accountability and less supervision by the centre. In the latter case, a larger span of control is possible than in the first case.

The complexity of this project organization structure involving groups, functional departments, organizational units and an organizational superstructure is compounded by the fact that many of the people and groups may also belong to other organizations that are external to the actual project organization, that is, 'parent' functional departments and/or companies. This often means that individuals in a project group may also belong to different external organizations; similarily, groups in a project organizational unit, and even whole organizational units may also belong to different external organizations. Thus not only must the internal project organization structure be designed, but also the form of the relationships with these external organizations must be determined.

Thus the design of the project organization structure involves decisions on the following factors:

1. How the work involved in the project is broken down into divisions and sub-divisions that are of such a size that they can be allocated to the individuals, groups, functional departments, organizational units and companies involved in the project.
2. How the people involved, principally managers, professionals and technical

staff, who may be from several external organizations and companies, are grouped together at the lower, middle and higher levels, i.e.

- How individuals are grouped together to form the 'basic' working groups.
- How these groups are consolidated into larger groups, such as functional departments and organizational units.
- How these groups, departments and organizational units, are linked together into an overall project organization with a managerial hierarchy or superstructure.

3. What the relationships are between these components of the structure and the external organizations they may belong to, e.g. the functional departments or divisions of the companies involved, i.e. the 'global' project organization.
4. What the basis of this grouping is at the various levels of the organization, e.g. are the groups made up of people of the same function or expertise, or are they made up of people of different functions, i.e. a mixed group.
5. How the work of the people is integrated, which includes coordination, communication, reporting and information systems, team-building and conflict management.
6. How authority, decision-making and responsibility are delegated, which includes decisions about the degree of centralization or decentralization, and whether the organizational superstructure is tall or flat.

The basic building blocks of the organization structure

Whenever a manager starts to set up an organization, that is thinks about organization design, the first action is to sketch out an organization chart, or 'organigram'. Traditionally this would take the form of a functionally organized, hierarchical pyramid structure, as shown in Figure 2.1, and this does represent the organization structure of many companies and public bodies. Despite the fact that this organigram is sometimes considered to be an unsatisfactory and inadequate way of representing an organization, it does in fact define the main elements, or building blocks of the organization's design:

- How people, mainly managers, professionals and other staff are grouped to form the basic 'foundation block' groups of the organization structure.
- How these groups are consolidated into larger organizational groups, both:
      large single function groups or 'departments'; and
      mixed function 'organizational units'.
- How these groups, large functional departments and organizational units are consolidated into the total organization, either company or project, i.e. it defines the organizational hierarchy or superstructure.

At the same time it also defines the following:

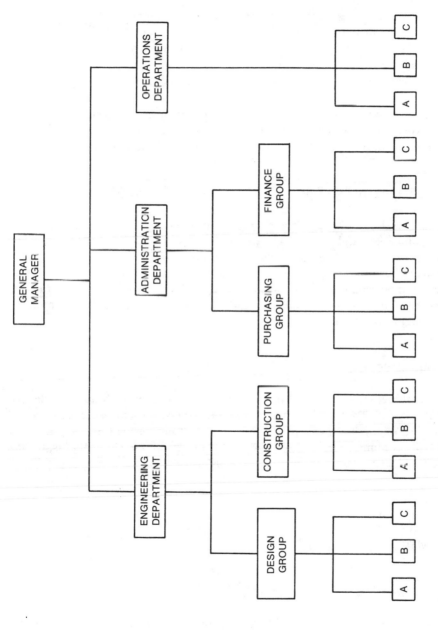

Figure 2.1   Functionally organized, hierarchical pyramid organization

- The division of labour in terms of specialization of functions, generally termed functionalization, in project work, e.g. finance, production or marketing, etc.
- How the work of these groups, functional departments and organizational units are 'integrated'.
- The levels of authority of those shown on the chart and the superior–subordinate relationships.
- The span of control of the managers involved.

Thus before describing the specialized forms of project organization structures, it is worthwhile examining these basic building blocks of any organization structure, and the importance of functional specialization and integration.

Basic managerial groups

Groups exist at all levels in the management hierarchy, but the basic managerial, professional and staff groups are the foundation blocks of the hierarchical organization chart. The subordinate members of this basic group may be foremen, but are more generally the first level managers, or specialists such as accountants, engineers or software analysts. The managers, or superiors of these basic management groups are individuals who have made it up onto the first rung of the hierarchical tree.

Group structure

In this three-tiered organization structure of basic groups, functional departments/organizational units, and organizational superstructure, the organization structure of the basic groups will take one of four forms, three of which are formally recognized in the organigram and one of which is not, that is, it is an informal group. These group structures are as follows:

1. Functional.
2. Horizontal (informal).
3. Mixed.
4. Matrix.

Functional groups

These groups are made up of individuals of the same functional, technical or professional specialism, for example, production, marketing or finance; or on a different scale, design, construction, planning, software engineering, electrical, etc. This specialization by function leads to an efficient division of labour and utilization of resources. Figure 2.1 is an example of this form of organization structure.

Horizontal groups

It is generally necessary for individuals in functional groups to work with people from other functional groups. Where there is interaction and interdependence between functional and other groups, both small and large, the organization chart does not show these necessary and usual working relationships which exist between peers and near-peers in the different functional groups.

These relationships define a secondary group, that is a horizontal group, which exists as a ghost organization group, or collateral organization. This group is generally ill-defined with no clear superior or superior–subordinate relationships. In many ways it is similar to a weak form of matrix group with no integrating superior and no group entity. For example, if the individuals noted as A in the functional groups shown in Figure 2.1 have to work together on a project, they form a horizontal group, with the only common integrating superior being the General Manager. Integration is through mutual adjustment or the planning systems and there is no single manager who is totally responsible for the project. Thus, as noted in Chapter 1, this conventional form of organization structure does not handle projects effectively.

Mixed groups

Mixed groups as implied by the name, are made up of individuals from different functional, technical or professional backgrounds. This form of group is used for the smaller organizational unit, which may in this case consist of only one mixed group. Examples of mixed group structure include task forces, product and geographical groups. These groups tend to contain all the resources and skills necessary to complete their assigned task. Mixed groups do facilitate teamwork in the organizational unit and lead to less conflict and politics, but do not use resources as efficiently as functional groups.

Matrix Groups

The matrix group is a form of organization which attempts to combine the efficient use of people, associated with the functional organization, and the effectiveness or goal achievement and teamwork potential associated with the mixed form of organization. A typical organigram of a matrix group is shown in Figure 2.2.

A matrix group is a secondary form of organization which formally integrates people from different functional groups into a mixed group under a separate matrix group manager. Figure 2.2 shows the addition of a matrix group, or

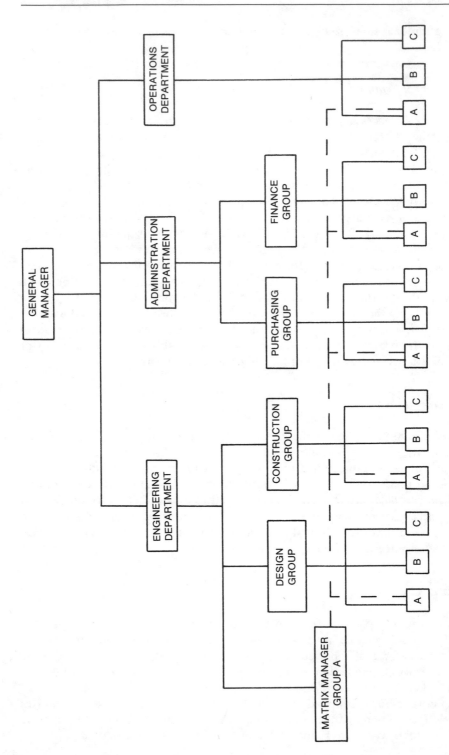

Figure 2.2   The matrix organization

project manager to the conventional pyramid structure. Its function is to manage and integrate the individuals noted as A on the project in which they are involved. The functional or parent groups are maintained intact and the matrix group members thus belong to two groups and report to two superiors, that is, there is dual subordination.

Larger groups

Whenever there is more than a handful of groups in an organization it becomes necessary to consolidate them into discrete larger groups, each with their own manager. These larger groups may take two forms:

1. Functional departments.
2. Organizational units.

Functional departments

Functional departments consist of two or more basic groups of the same or similar expertise. They are grouped together for reasons which will be outlined later, under one manager, who normally has the same technical background. Most companies have one or more such functional departments, such as production, marketing, finance, personnel, design or construction. Functional departments do not by themselves form a complete organizational entity, in that they must interact and are interdependent with other functional departments to carry out the organization's mission.

Organizational unit

The term organizational unit is often used loosely, but in fact it has a very different meaning to that of the total company organization. An organizational unit is defined as the total collection of individuals and/or groups, who have the following characteristics:

1. They interact and are interdependent.
2. They work towards common goals.
3. They have relationships determined according to a certain structure, either formal or informal, or both.

However, the senior manager of such an organizational unit, if one exists, will normally also belong to a senior management group, that is, the organization superstructure or corporate group.

An organizational unit can thus carry out its assigned task without requiring support from outside functional departments or other groups. It contains within it all the expertise and resources required to achieve its objectives. In military terms it is a self-contained combat group; in management terms, it is similar to a division of the company, a subsidiary company, a factory, or a dedicated project group.

A small project may have only one such organizational unit, the project itself, whilst a large project will have many such units, some or all of which may cross company boundaries. The crucial factor is that, except for the senior manager of the unit, individuals and groups in such an organizational unit, interact and are interdependent only, or in practice nearly only, with individuals and groups within that organizational unit, and not with others in the company. It is thus almost a self-contained entity, independent as far as conflict, power, politics and teamwork are concerned, and a project may be made up of one, several or many organizational units.

Size and structure of the organizational unit

Organizational unit size can vary from the very small to the very large:

1. Small
    Composed of individuals who form a single basic group.
2. Medium
    A single, large group organizational unit, made up of two or more basic groups.
3. Large
    Comprises two or more large groups, each made up of two or more basic groups. This can range upwards in size to a multi-company organizational unit made up of small, medium and large groups from different companies.

The organizational unit structure of the small unit is that of the group making up the unit, that is, functional, mixed or matrix. The structure of the medium and large unit can be as follows:

1. Single function
    All the groups in the unit are made up of people of the same similar function. Typically this single function organization unit tends to be in a professional organization, e.g. accountants, architects or quantity surveyors.
2. Functionally organized
    Each group in the medium-sized organization unit, or large group in the large unit, is a single function group.
3. Matrix based
    Single function groups, drawn from their parent large groups or departments are organized into one unit, under a matrix group manager, as shown in Figure 2.2.
4. Mixed organization

Each group in the organization unit is a mixed, all function group. In such situations, interactions and interdependencies tend to be of a pooled or sequential nature, as described later (p.38).

Organization Superstructure

The medium to large project organization is made up of a number of organization units, and thus in most organizations there exists an organizational superstructure, or management hierarchy. In very large organizations there may be multiple layers of such groups. This superstructure is deemed necessary to manage, control, coordinate or integrate the organizational units. The subordinate members of this superstructure are thus generally the senior managers responsible for the organizational units.

There will typically be a management hierarchy in each functional department and each organizational unit, and in a large project that has a number of organizational units, there will be a senior management hierarchy or superstructure to manage, control, coordinate and integrate the units. Thus the organization structure of a large project will have a number of levels of management. In some projects the number of levels of management hierarchy has approached or exceeded double figures.

Functionalization

Functionalization, or the specialization of managerial and professional labour, is the grouping of people of the same function, or expertise into both large and small groups, and could be termed the conventional, or classical organization design. Despite its widespread use, the degree or extent of functionalization used in an organization can be a strong indicator of the likelihood of conflict in that organization. Despite this, functionalization in management and professional groups is in widespread use and has many advantages.

The principal reasons for the widespread use of functionalization in organizational design are as follows:

1. It facilitates the efficient use of resouces.
2. It allows the development of functional expertise.
3. It permits the management of specialists by specialists.
4. It allows the coordination of the functional policies and systems.
5. It provides a home base and a career path for the functional specialist.
6. It exists and has power to survive.

In a mixed group or divisional organizational unit, the workload for a function may vary and at times the mixed group may be undermanned for that function, while at other times it may be overmanned. A functional group permits the number of people from that function assigned to any one organizational task or unit to be varied as the workload varies, and thus permits a more efficient use of these functional resources.

This is particularly marked in projects, where the specific requirements of functional expertise vary considerably over the life span of a project. A functional organization can resource a stream or portfolio of such projects more efficiently than a divisional or mixed group organization.

Functionalization is also essential to the continuing development of that specialism and the functional skills of those involved. An isolated specialist divorced from contact and interaction with professional colleagues, becomes easily obsolete. The interaction and support that exists between each specialist leads to them keeping up to date, exchanging ideas, and to more effective training and personal development. An additional advantage is that it also allows there to be specialization within a function.

The superior within a functional group will normally come from the same professional background as the group members and so will understand the group members and their problems, will be able to give support from their greater experience and/or expertise when required, and will be able more effectively to control work output and technical standards. Thus there will be more effective management of the function than would be the case with a generalist managing a mixed group.

The functional group also provides a home base for the professional specialist in a stable environment with a clear superior–subordinate relationship with someone of the same professional background. In addition, one of the most important functions of a large functional group, at least to its members, is that it gives the functional specialist a career path, and this does not generally exist in a mixed group.

Finally, in most organizations, the existing historical organization structure will probably involve some measure of functionalization. Thus functionalism is the established norm, the heads of the functional departments will wield considerable power, and they will probably resist any change that is seen likely to reduce that power.

Thus functionalization is the most common form of specialization in an organization. Unfortunately, specialization by function is also one of the principal contributors to the accentuation of politics and conflict in an organization, both directly and indirectly. This is principally because functionalization leads to the following:

1.   A functional orientation.
2.   Problems relating to the different cultures formed.
3.   Problems with the integration of these functional groups.

Functional orientation

The grouping of people into functional groups leads them to be oriented to that function's goals and not to the project's goals. They tend to think in terms of their specialization rather than in more holistic terms. For example, people in production, design, construction, finance, etc. are oriented to these functions rather than to the combined working of their organizational unit or the complete project. They thus tend to be introverted and their loyalty is given to their function rather than to the project. All this inhibits teamwork between different functional groups and the project manager, and encourages conflict.

Problems related to the different cultures formed

Each individual group, both small and large, company and organization unit is as distinctive and unique as the people in it. Each has its own personality, character, core values, norms, attitudes and sometimes language that influence how people conduct themselves, work together and even think. This uniqueness is termed 'culture', it evolves over time and is not easily changed. It reflects the deeply held beliefs, even the subconscious feelings, of the people in the group.

Functionalization draws into one group, people of the same background, skills and outlook, and thus such groups tend to have a highly developed and specialized culture. This culture is particular to the function involved, such that groups of architects, design engineers, programmers, construction managers, accountants and project managers from different companies will have a culture with more in common than those individual groups have with other groups in their own companies.

Differences in culture between groups can lead to conflict in many different ways. Different cultures tend to lead to incompatible objectives in functional or professional groups. For example, a design group will instinctively want a design that is sure to work, is of the highest technical standards and is a monument to their expertise and perhaps their egos. The operations group will want a production plant that is easy to operate, has many installed spares, has capacity for expansion and a high standard of amenities. The project group will want to balance time, cost and technical standards. When these groups work together there will always be the tendency to conflict over these incompatible objectives.

Even given goodwill between groups with varying cultures, they may draw different conclusions, make different decisions and take different courses of action, based on the same information, simply because of their different cultures. Differences in culture go far deeper than merely factors such as core values, and lead to people being, thinking and feeling differently. All too often these differences lead to dysfunctional conflict without any obvious intent or self-interests involved. Thus functionalization tends to lead to the development of strong, specialized professional cultures, and differences between cultures can lead to conflict between professional groups.

Integration

Hand in hand with the division of labour implicit in the functional form of organization, must go the integration of that labour. This includes coordination, communication, reporting relationships and information systems. When individuals and groups are interdependent and must interact to achieve the organization's objectives an important factor in the organization's performance is how well they are integrated.

Lawrence and Lorsch identified that with increasing complexity and size of organizations, there is an increasing necessity for both greater differentiation and tighter integration.[1] The greater the size of the project and the specialization therein, the more critical is the need for this integration, the more difficult it is and the more likely it is to be ineffective.

Integration involves more than just the coordination of work to achieve the organization's goals, in that it must also have a large man- and group-management emphasis. Integration has thus two roles in the design of the organization:

1. An operational management role to integrate the individual's and the group's work or contribution to the organization's effort.
2. A man- and group-management role in:

    • Managing and resolving conflict and reducing the amount of political activity taking place; and
    • Developing a team, or at the very least establishing a cooperative working relationship between individuals, groups and companies working on the project.

The need for integration varies with the degree of interdependency. J.D. Thompson[2] identified three types of interdependency:

1. Pooled interdependency, essentially 'A + B', i.e. the interdependency is similar to two excavators digging a hole.
2. Sequential dependency, essentially 'A → B', i.e. the excavator digging a trench is followed by a machine laying a pipeline.
3. Reciprocal interdependency, essentially 'A ⇄ B'.

The problems with integration are much less with pooled resources and sequential interdependencies. Unfortunately project work usually involves reciprocal interdependencies, and thus integration tends to be a problem. There is thus the critical necessity in the project setting to integrate individuals, groups of various kinds, functional departments, organizational units and companies to achieve the project's objectives. The following outline describes the methods of integration available to the traditional functionally organized firm, and then looks at the development of the project organization structures to achieve integration:

1. Key integrating superiors.
2. Management systems.
3. Mutual adjustment.
4. Coordinating committees.
5. Liaison positions.
6. Task forces, special teams or working groups, i.e. project groups.
7. Matrix groups

Key integrating superiors

The primary integrator in any group, department, organizational unit, project or company should be the senior manager in charge of it. This manager is the common superior to everyone involved, and it is his or her managerial function to see that their work is integrated, that coordination and communication exist, to build teamwork and to manage any conflict that arises between the subordinates. The senior manager's actions and leadership, together with the 'tightness' of the organization structure and authority, are critical to achieving this integration, to developing teamwork and limiting conflict.

However, in project work in a functionally organized company with a departmental structure, the common key integrating superior is often ineffective as he or she is normally a senior general manager who has many responsibilities and is remote from the scene of the 'action'. The further away in hierarchical terms the common superior is, the more ineffective they will be in carrying out the integration function. If conflict occurs between individuals or groups on the project, they will not be fully aware of it until too late. They may have to deal with it through one or more levels of intermediate functional subordinate managers, who may or may not be involved, or who may not be averse to it occurring. This is where the mixed group structure is better in that the common superior is near the scene of the action and can quickly deal with it directly. Thus projects carried out using the functional organization cannot rely on the normal key integrationist superior to integrate the work and the people, and other methods of integration must be used.

Management systems

One method of achieving integration of the work on a project is through the use of its management systems, particularly the planning and control systems. The actual organization of the work and the people assigned to a project is carried out in the planning phase, where the integration of the work of the various groups, departments, organizational units and the complete project is explicitly detailed. Planning techniques or methodologies such as work and organization breakdown structures ensure the integration of organization, work and plan. Control systems emphasize communication channels and links to maintain the integration of the work as it progresses. Thus the trend today for the integration of organization with planning and control, can be used to integrate effectively the work on a project.

However, these systems do not by themselves meet the man- and group-management needs of integration, in terms of developing teamwork and managing conflict. In addition, unless the organization has well-developed project-oriented systems, and they are backed up by a key integrationist superior, they will also tend to be less than effective in integrating the work.

Mutual adjustment

The need for integration is often not formally recognized, or not spelled out explicitly, and individuals and groups are implicitly expected to work together to achieve results. They often do so, in spite of the organization or lack of it, particularly on the smaller project. In a non conflict situation this can work.

This method of integration is implicitly assumed in horizontal groups in a functional organization. Horizontal groups are expected to work together by the 'system', with no defined close common integrating superior. Often this works satisfactorily and an organic group or team is formed, sometimes uniting against their own vertical group superiors. This mutual adjustment involves individuals at both lower and higher levels in the organization achieving integration by the process of informal communication, give and take, or mutual adjustment. If this did not work in practice, all organizations would soon grind to halt, but in no way does it handle a conflict situation.

However, often no group identity is established, loyalty can remain totally with the parent functional groups and the cooperation that does exist tends to be neutral or coldly formal. There is no recognized accepted key integrationist superior who can lead the group to teamwork and manage differences before they reach a conflict situation. In such situations, unless an organic team forms naturally, it is worthwhile to have one person defined as the group leader, or coordinator.

Coordination committees

Often when such a functionally organized firm is handling projects, special coordination committees are formed, consisting of a group of senior managers, to act as the common integrating superior. Although this type of committee can perform to limited extent a general liaison and supervisory function for the project, it is usually totally ineffective on the human side of project management, and can do nothing to build teamwork or manage conflict.

These coordination committees are made up of what may be termed political players, with their own vested interests, and they may themselves be arenas for conflict and politics. Such a senior manager group is generally totally ineffective in managing conflict and the subordinates reporting to such a group often have little option but to employ politics in working with this group of superiors. The individuals or factions in the superior group have to be influenced by political actions, and such a group is unlikely to knock heads together, or to take other actions to manage conflict or minimize politics.

Liaison positions

When there is a certain amount of interaction between groups, one individual may be nominated to a liaison position, to facilitate communication and coordination, that is, integration. This individual is essentially a weak coordinator, with little or no formal authority. Any power they do have is based on their centrality, the ear of senior management and the information channels they control.

An extension of this liaison position is where the individual concerned may have some authority over the decision-making process, but not over the people from the different groups and departments involved in the project. They therefore have to influence, persuade and be a supplicant to the people over whom they have no formal authority; they cannot give direct instructions. Thus in a conflict or political situation, this manager is in a very difficult situation.

Task forces, working groups, special teams or project groups

Task forces provide a single, short-term mission, mixed group to perform a particular task. Special mixed teams are similar, but deal wirh regularly recurring problems. The fullest extension of this concept is the formal project group, where the individuals and groups involved in a particular undertaking or project, are formed into a separate mixed organizational unit, with a project manager appointed as the group's key integrationist superior with partial or full line authority over the people involved.

These integrationist arrangements, designed to solve the differentiation and integration problem are usually temporary, albeit temporary may be a period of years in the project manager relationship. However, they do involve an actual change in the organization structure from a functionally structured organization to some type of mixed organizational unit.

Matrix organization

The matrix organization attempts to combine the advantages of the functional organization and the mixed group organization by creating a dual reporting responsibility. It can give both work and people integration, but it also creates many problems of its own.

This form of organization structure does provide an integrationist superior and therefore can increase the potential for teamwork. However, the functional group manager may resent this invasion of his or her territory and therefore the matrix structure can also increase the potential for conflict between the functional manager and the project manager. Nevertheless in the matrix organization there is a defined group entity and key integrationist superior and leader, although their authority is limited and there are problems with dual subordination.

Summing up

The most effective method of integration is that carried out by a close key integrating superior supported by effective management systems, but this can rarely be achieved on projects in functionally organized firms. Reliance on informal or weak methods of integration may go some limited way to integrating the work on a project, but do little for the human side of integration. Liaison positions, task forces, project teams and the matrix organization actually involve a restructuring of the organization to varying extents, into a project-oriented organization. Thus, the need to integrate multi-disciplinary work has tended to be one of the main reasons for the adoption of project management and project organization structures.

Notes

1. P.R. Lawrence and J.W. Lorsch (1967) *Organization and Environment: Managing Differentiation and Integration*, Irwin.
2. J.D. Thompson (1967) *Organizations in Action*, McGraw-Hill.

Chapter 3

THE BASIC FORMS OF PROJECT ORGANIZATION STRUCTURE

'External

The forms   on two levels:

1. The e
    This   als and groups
    invol   nents and com-
    panie
2. The i
    This   uals and groups
    invol   endently of the
    exter   ith their parent
    orga   project.

Thus th   hin the external
structure   structure will be
describe   ion to the larger
project.

    The f   g:

1. Bas

- • Dedicated project teams
- • The matrix organization
    The functional matrix
    The balanced matrix
    The project matrix
    The contract matrix
- • The hybrid structure
- • Modular network structures.
2. The larger project organization and the internal structure
- • Internal functionalization
- • Divisionalized
- • The internal matrix structure
- • The 'federal' organization
- • Centralized/decentralized forms of the larger project organization.

The project team form of organization

The task force, working group, special team or, in project terms, the dedicated project team or division is much the preferred form of organization from the one-sided project manager's point of view. People and groups are allocated completely to the project organization for the life of the project and the project manager has full line management authority over them. This is in effect setting up a separate goal-oriented division of the company, with its own functional departments. The project manager still has the problem of managing and integrating the other companies contributing to the project, but is the complete master of his or her own company's organization. However, this does mean that in multi-company projects the dedicated project team organization can exist only in individual companies, and thus it forms only part of the overall project organization.

This goal-oriented organization makes the management of projects, and their planning and control much easier than with other forms of organization. There is much better integration of those involved, communication both formal and informal is more frequent, and there is more commitment to the project's objectives. Teamwork is much easier to achieve and conflict managed. It thus tends to maximize the probability of achieving the project's objectives, that is, completion on time, to budget and to specification.

Unfortunately it tends to use the scarce resources of a company less efficiently. It is necessary in this form of project organization to duplicate the specialists in each project, and to allocate them in total to each project, more or less for the life of the project. It is also very difficult to have a division of labour within a specialism, and a divisionally organized project may have to make do with a generalist in a function rather than individual specialists. Therefore, though the separate divisional form of project organization enables projects to be managed more effectively than the functional organization, and it avoids some of the problems of the more complex forms of project organization, it can generally be used only on larger projects. For example, when a company is handling a single important project, or where one project is so very much more important than others, that it justifies setting up a completely separate company division. The size of the project and the volume of work has to provide full-time activity for each of the functional specialists or groups assigned to the project organization.

It cannot generally be used where a company is handling several projects on a continuous basis, as it splinters up the the functional specialist departments. This splintering reduces the number of projects that a company can handle, and it inhibits the transfer of personnel from one project to another as required. There are good reasons for maintaining these specialist or functional departments intact, as outlined previously.

In one study resource sharing between projects achieved savings ranging from 11 per cent to 50 per cent in labour depending on the size of the project, in this case $20m to $3m in 1989.[1] Scarce resources can be utilized more effectively by spreading key individuals over several projects. The supply and demand balance for trained and experienced designers, software engineers and programmers, etc. is very tight and resource sharing helps to increase the number of projects that can be executed with limited resources.

Thus the functional form of organization is more efficient in the use of resources, but less effective in achieving a project's objectives, whereas the dedicated project team or division is more effective in achieving a project's objectives, but less efficient in the use of resources. What is required in project work is an organization which is both efficient in the use of resources and effective in achieving the project's objectives. This is what the following form of project organization, the matrix organization, attempts to do, although at the expense of organizational complexity.

The matrix form of project organization

The matrix form of organization is an organization design which became fashionable in the 1970s and 1980s. Although it became prominent first in the organization of project work, it has become more widely used in more general management because of its flexibility and ability to cope with complex organizational requirements.

In fact, the complexity implicit in the matrix organization of lines of authority, different from the simple superior–subordinate relationship and involving dual subordination, exists in most organizations. Whenever there is a horizontal group, there is an embryonic matrix relationship outside the conventional vertical line of command. In addition, whenever there are strong central functional groups, such as finance, claiming some form of authority over their functional members in the company's divisions or operating groups, then there is in fact an implicit matrix relationship.

In project work, the matrix form of project organization has tended to predominate in the in-company project organization, and it is used almost totally in the global project organization where different companies work together on a project. A matrix or project manager is appointed to manage and integrate the work and people on a project, but the functional groups are retained intact. Lines of authority and responsibility, communication and coordination exist horizontally and diagonally as well as in the conventional pyramid form. Personnel working on the project are responsible to two managers, their parent group functional manager and the project manager. Thus in the matrix form of project organization, personnel working on the project have in addition to their responsibility to their own functional manager, and/or separate company, a responsibility and a loyalty to the project and the project manager. There may be several such groups on any one project, for example, for the client or owner, consultant, management contractor, contractor, subcontractor and main suppliers.

In this matrix form of project management, authority over the project contributors is shared by the project manager and the functional managers. The project manager is not the complete master of decisions affecting the project, but operates in a decision-making matrix. The project manager's authority or influence cuts across the traditional vertical lines of command and leads to a matrix or network of authority relationships.

A typical organization chart for a matrix project organization is shown in Figure 3.1. It is a supplementary form of organization which integrates people from the primary functional departments for the purpose of achieving the project's objectives. The project manager in the matrix organization acts as a junior general manager, and the in-company work is undertaken by the various functional departments, for example, design, purchasing, finance, production, computing and construction. It maintains these functional departments intact, and permits the transfer of staff between projects. Departmental members can be allocated to a project for its life, or part of its life on a full-time or part-time basis, but still remain part of their parent functional department and under the management of their functional superior. At the same time, the project relationship integrates them on the project dimension, provides a means of communication and coordination, management and leadership, facilitates planning and control, and gains their involvement in the project and their commitment to meeting the project's objectives. By making the individual a member of both a functional and a goal-oriented project organization it attempts to obtain the advantages of both.

The project manager must rely on support and services from these functional departments. The project manager determines, in consultation with the managers, what is required and by when, and the functional managers control how and by whom. The functional line managers can do a better job of allocating their own departmental personnel to the various projects they are working on, than can the project manager, as they know the capabilities of their people and the resources available. The functional managers also have respons-

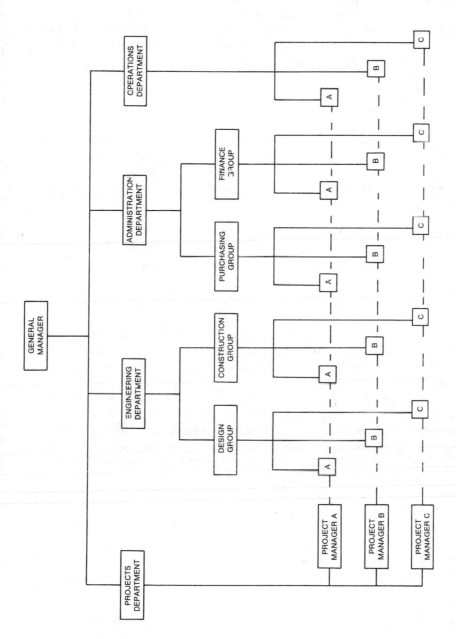

Figure 3.1   A company with a matrix organization

ibility for technical decisions within their area of specialism. The project manager can bring pressure to bear regarding schedules and budgets, and ask for a re-evaluation or re-assessment of alternatives, when there are problems or differences of opinion. Nevertheless, responsibility for specific technical decisions lies with the functional managers, as they know their own area of specialism best, are doing it and are responsible for it.

Forms of the matrix organization

There are three or four recognized forms of the matrix organization, with many shadings of emphasis between them:

1.   Functional matrix.
2.   Balanced matrix.
3.   Project matrix.

In addition, in a multi-company organization there exists a form of matrix organization which could be termed the 'contract' matrix.

Functional matrix

In the functional matrix the project manager with limited authority is designated to coordinate the project across different functional areas and/or groups. The functional managers retain responsibility and authority for their specific segments of the project.

The project manager's role in this form of the matrix approximates to that of the liaison or coordinator form of integrator, whose prime role is that of an integrator, rather than that of a full-blown manager. The emphasis is thus on coordination, communication, planning and control. The project manager acts as a focal point for information on the project, but has very little direct authority. This position has often little status or seniority, and the project tends to be coordinated and administered, but not managed. The project manager can only monitor progress, practice a weak form of coordination, dependent on the goodwill of the functional managers involved, and is in the position of a supplicant to the managers of the functional departments. Project managers cannot bring any great degree of pressure to bear, or exert direct authority to obtain action or change the course of events. They must persuade others from a position of weakness, and normally feel very insecure, frustrated and unsure of their role.

Project managers find it difficult to manage, or exert leadership on such a project, and control tends to be weak. When evidence of an adverse trend is slight or inconclusive, they cannot normally get action. It is only when such adverse trends are patently obvious, that they can implement change and this is often too late. Thus this form of the matrix organization can achieve the integration of the work, but loses many of the advantages of the project management concept. It is only suited to the smaller projects, for handling projects in a non-project-oriented firm, or when functional departments are strong and unassailable.

Balanced matrix

In the balanced matrix, a project manager is assigned to manage the project and shares responsibility and authority for completing the project with the functional managers. Project and functional managers jointly direct many workflow segments and jointly approve many decisions. This is the classical form of the matrix organization, and its operation is as described in the introduction to the matrix organization (p.45).

Project matrix

In the project matrix, a project manager is assigned to manage the project and has primary responsibility and authority for the completion of the project to its objectives. Functional managers assign personnel as needed and provide technical expertise. This form of organization approximates to the dedicated project team or division form of organization. It is the form of matrix organization preferred by project managers and disliked by functional managers. It is generally only applied in project-oriented companies, whose principal business is projects, and who recognize that project managers are their new line managers. In this form of organization the organigram that defines the matrix is rotated, as shown in Figure 3.2, and the functional departments are in essence now service departments to the projects.

The principal difference in these three forms of matrix organization is the relative authority and power of the project manager *vis-à-vis* the functional managers. In the functional or weak matrix the project manager has very little formal authority, and the functional manager is all powerful. In the project matrix, these positions are reversed and the project manager has the greater authority. In the balanced matrix there is a position somewhere between these two extremes.

The 'grade' or position in the hierarchy of the project manager, who he or she report to, whether there is an overall project 'group' manager and what grade the project manager holds, are all topics subject to considerable debate and much power politics in many organizations. If the company handles multiple projects, someone has to 'integrate' the project managers, as there will inevitably be interactions between projects, if only for scarce resources from the functional departments. The grade of the project manager in the matrix organization depends on the size, value, complexity and importance of the project, the form of matrix organization used and the distribution of power in the organiza-

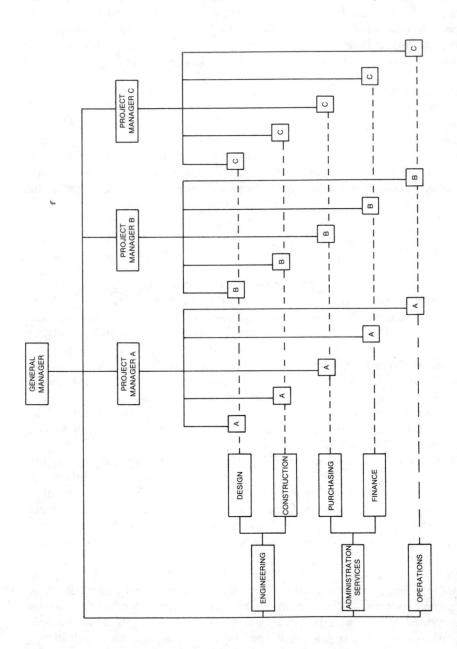

Figure 3.2   The project/rotated matrix

tion. The higher the grade, the more likely the manager is to be effective and vice versa.

Figure 2.2 (p.32) showed the matrix group, or project manager responsible to the engineering department manager, which is a common arrangement. The project manager is also placed in the organigram at a level below the group managers but above their subordinates, which symbolically indicates the position's grade. As such, it is likely to represent a functional matrix organization.

Figure 3.1 (p.47) shows a separate project department, the manager of which reports directly to the general manager, and who is on a par with the functional department managers. By implication the project managers are on the same grade as the functional group managers, in this balanced matrix.

Figure 3.2 shows the project managers as the principal line managers in the project matrix, reporting directly to the general manager. They are thus on a par with, or perhaps are graded above the functional department heads. There are many permutations and combinations of these arrangements, and the seniority of project managers, who they report to and that person's seniority, are significant factors influencing the effectiveness of project management in any company.

Contract matrix and the 'global' project organization

It is necessary in project work to integrate the people and groups from all the different companies involved, into a single organization. The viewpoint that all involved – client, contractor, consultant, architect, production manager, subcontractor, material and equipment supplier – belong to one organization is critical to the success of project work. If the performance or lack of it, of any group or company, no matter how remotely, can influence the success or failure of the project, then the project manager must consider them to belong to the project organization. Thus project management, communication, coordination, planning and control must be extended to embrace all these contributing organizations and to integrate them into a global organization. Global does not imply worldwide, although in some projects the organization might actually be worldwide, but that the organization extends to cover all the companies involved.

The matrix form of organization is the implicit structure used in multi-company projects. For example, there are often at least three principal companies involved in such projects:

- Client/operations.
- Architect/design.
- Construction/manufacturing/programming.

Each of these companies tends to operate as a separate entity whose objectives are to maximize its own best interests. However, if the project is to be completed effectively, the people from these companies must be integrated, and the companies must be considered to be managed as part of a 'global' project organization. The matrix organization is the only way to look at this global organization, as no other organizational concept is applicable, and can tie together all the separate companies.

These separate organizations or companies are linked by lines of authority, or influence, which are sometimes very weak, and often based merely on contractual and purchase order agreements. Thus the form of contract and conditions of purchase are lines of influence which determine how the global organization operates. This global organization structure is therefore of necessity complex, often loose, and full of 'dotted'lines.

The project manager's positional authority over people from the other companies involved is limited to that arising from the form of contract used. This form of the matrix organization can thus be termed as a 'contract matrix' The contract matrix form of organization structure can operate in any of the basic forms of the matrix, dependent on the power of the project manager which arises from the following:

- The strength of the form of contract used.
- The skills and attributes of the project manager.
- The dominance of the project manager's company, e.g. a large oil company project manager will have more power than one from a small company.
- The methodologies and systems used.
- The people.
- The project.

If the project manager is solely reliant on positional and contractual authority, he or she will not be very effective. This is then likely to lead to the situation resembling a functional matrix, and generally results in contractual bickering, conflict and litigation. However, at present, there is no alternative to this matrix concept for the multi-company global project organization.

Hybrid project organization

It is quite common for the organization of a project to have a hybrid structure, that is for it to be a mixture of the above basic forms. This hybrid structure can exist in the individual company and also in the mix of organization structures used in the companies involved in a large project.

In the single company hybrid organization structure, those individuals and groups whose work is totally utilized on the project are allocated full-time as a dedicated project team. Those who cannot efficiently be utilised full-time, or whose skills are too scarce, are retained within the functional departments and allocated part-time in a matrix basis. The project manager's relationships with each functional department may also differ. For example in a chemical company, all the work may be carried out internally. The project manager may be from the engineering department and have under direct line management control the construction personnel involved. The design group may be from a different department and the project manager may have only a balanced matrix relationship with them. The operations department will be the client and it is very likely that the project manager will have only a weak matrix relationship with them, with very limited authority or influence.

In a large project, each company may have a different form of project organization structure, and each company's project manager may have a different authority relationship with their people. The overall project manager may thus have the difficult task of integrating them, with perhaps radically different organization structures in each company involved.

Modular and network structures

Some companies, whose business is primarily project-oriented use modular and network structures to give themselves the ultimate in flexibilty. In this arrangement, individuals, functional groups and complete, small, mixed organizational units operate as discrete entities with loose, flexible networks of relationships within and between them.

These entities can operate on a modular basis, are 'plugged' in and out of the project, as required, and are combined and recombined in varying network structures for different tasks or projects. While in a project, they are full members of the project team, but they are there for only a limited period of time. Consultants and computer software companies often operate on this basis and develop the necessary flexible attitude of mind to operate this form of organization successfully.

Advantages of the matrix concept

The matrix organization concept in its basic form, in its hybrid adaptions or in its global form, underlies most project organizations. Although the dedicated project team is the most effective in achieving results, it tends not to use resources efficiently, except in the larger project. It also cannot extend to cover the multi-company global project organization, where the matrix form of organization is essentially the only alternative.

Although there are many problems with the matrix organization, it does have many advantages:

- It permits the integration of individuals, groups, organizational units and companies across formal organizational boundaries into a single organization.
- It is a very flexible organizational tool that can be used to organize a small

mixed function project group, but is just as appropriately used to link together and integrate hundreds of groups, departments and companies on a large project.

- It establishes a group or organization identity, which is essential to the management of that group, the organization and the project itself. In this respect it makes it possible:

    to have a matrix group leader or project manager who can provide the essential leadership to the achievement of the project's objectives;

    to develop teamwork and manage conflict;

    to establish communication, coordination and management information systems; and

    to motivate the matrix group members and build commitment to the project and its objectives.

- Thus the matrix group can be made a goal-oriented organization that facilitates the achievement of the project's objectives.
- At the same time as creating a project group identity, the matrix organization retains the functional groups, departments or companies intact, and thus it can also have all the advantages of the functional organization. For example, it can create a small mixed function project group or organizational unit from a company organized into functional departments, without disruption to these departments.
- The matrix form of organization thus combines the efficient use of resources with the project orientation essential to the achievement of the project's objectives.

Problems with the matrix organization

Unfortunately, although the matrix organization can achieve results and facilitate teamwork, it also creates many human relations problems. In order effectively to manage a project, the project manager must understand and be able to handle the problems associated with the matrix forms of organization.

The matrix form of project organization conflicts with traditional organization theory in many ways. Inherent in it are dual subordination, division of authority and responsibility, without corresponding authority and a disregard for the so-called hierarchical principles. These basic principles of organization which it contravenes, are no more than generalizations about what has been observed to work in the past. Being derived from experience, they are subject to revision in the light of new experience and circumstances. It is as foolish to be totally bound by past experience as it is to ignore it.

Nevertheless, disregard for these principles does mean that the matrix organization has organizational complexity and an inherent conflict situation. However, in project work where different functional departments and companies have to be integrated across formal organizational boundaries, there is a new set of circumstances. In order to bind these diverse elements into one organization, committed to complete a project to its time, cost and technical performance objectives, and effectively to manage it, a new set of ground rules has had to be evolved.

In fact it is wrong to blame the matrix form of project organization for the problems that arise. The complexities and ambiguities that arise are not really a consequence of the use of the matrix organization, but are the basic reasons for adopting it. The traditional hierarchical pyramid simply cannot handle the number of different groups and the complexities involved in a project of any size, and there is little alternative to the use of some form of the matrix organization, particularly in the multi-company situation.

The principal reasons for the problems that arise in the matrix organization are as follows:

1. It brings into direct confrontation the project manager and the functional departmental or other company managers.
2. Project managers' authority does not match their responsibilty, i.e. there is an 'authority gap'.
3. It creates dual subordination and divided authority, i.e. members of the project organization are responsible to two managers, the project manager and their functional or company manager.
4. The matrix organization structure can be complex, ambiguous and is often uncertain.

Confrontation

The project organization sets the project manager and the functional managers as protagonists in an arena, with often very different points of view. There will often be a total difference in cultures and objectives between these protagonists, yet they will be interdependent and have to interact to achieve results; each party's performance will be strongly influenced by the other's. In addition, the common superior to the project and functional managers is likely to be very remote, if one exists at all. The most natural outcome in such a situation is conflict.

The project manager's authority gap

In theory, in the traditional pyramid organization, formal positional authority flows from the Chief Executive to the next level of manager, and cascades down to the lowest level of management, defining each superior–subordinate relationship and the span of control. The individuals in this organization are split into groups, each with a superior who in turn belongs to a higher level group, which in turn has its superior. The concept extends upwards defining higher level groups until the top management group is reached, of which the chief executive is the superior. Each person knows who their 'boss' is, as does their superior, who has clear-cut authority over subordinates.

Authority patterns in the traditional pyramid structure are thus primarily vertical, with the superior–subordinate relationship being close, unambiguous and more or less permanent. When different groups work together, they theoretically have a common superior somewhere in the organizational hierarchy with a superior–subordinate relationship with the group managers, and thus can integrate them. ·

Whilst this may be the theory, the practice is much more ambiguous. Responsibility, accountability and authority are often unclear or indefinite, and relationships are sometimes ill-defined. Organizations rarely work as shown in their organization charts; in the unlikely event that the chart correctly portrays the relationships and authority patterns, as they were when it was constructed, they are often out of date the next day.

Among the organizational ambiguities that often exist is the fact that authority or power is often dispersed, ill-defined, inadequate or does not match the responsibilities of the manager. When the power stucture is weak or uncertain, or the position holders are weak, power is up for grabs, decisions will be made by political processes, and there is competition for power, which leads to conflict and politics. Individuals and groups will question why they should follow the instructions of the project manager. In a situation of uncertainty, some will act assertively, assuming power which in the eyes of others they do not have. Others will act defensively and be cautious, and resent their assertive colleagues.

This weakness in authority or power is what makes the liaison or coordinator methods of integration ineffective, and leads to many of the problems of the matrix organization with what is termed the project manager's 'authority gap', that is his or her responsibilities exceed their authority.

In the matrix organization, the organization structure is much more complex than in the traditional pyramid. Authority patterns and interpersonal relationships can be vertical, horizontal, diagonal and multi-dimensional. Project managers in the matrix organization must manage across departmental boundaries in their own company, and across company boundaries if other companies are involved, to integrate the parties involved to achieve the project's objectives. Even in the dedicated project team or division form of project organization, no project manager can have direct superior–subordinate authority over all the departmental and company interfaces. What authority they do have will be subject to many constraints and is inevitably limited. Thus the principle of management that the matrix concept most contravenes is that responsibility should always be coupled to corresponding authority, that is, the project manager almost always has an authority gap.

Project managers in the matrix organization are responsible for the success of the project, but generally have limited authority over the personnel from the functional departments in their own company, and only contractual influence with personnel from outside companies. Yet if they are not simply to be administrators, they must have some form of power over these personnel to manage them effectively.

This lack of formal authority makes it difficult for project managers to persuade the personnel involved in the many functional groups to do what they want them to do, when they want them to do it. This in turn leads to the project manager becoming frustrated and using political means to achieve power, which has a great danger of leading to conflict.

Conversely, if the project manager does have the formal authority, or power, the functional managers involved, their superiors and perhaps their subordinates may resent this power. They may consider their authority and position is being undermined, and this in turn may lead to resentment, hostility, withdrawal of support and conflict. Thus there is almost a no-win situation in the matrix organization.

Dual subordination

A related problem to that of the authority gap is that of dual subordination. One of the main characteristics of the matrix organization is the existence of dual subordination, leading to split loyalties and often to conflict. This dual subordination is not unique to the matrix organization, but it is more clearly recognized in it than in the traditional forms of organization. Most managements recognize that the classical unity of command concept, with authority and responsibility packaged in neat boundaries on a conventional organization chart, does not portray the organizational reality. Most managers in any form of organization are subject to several sources of power or influence.

In theory, dual subordination may be a weakness in the matrix organization structure, but in practice it can work . As long as instructions are non-conflicting, a subordinate can receive instructions from two people, the project manager determining what is to be done and by when, and the functional manager concerned with technical factors, and perhaps with who does the work. When differences between these factors occur, one superior must clearly be recognized as the one who must initially be obeyed. The differences then have to be resolved by the two managers, rather than the subordinate, before conflict arises. In practice dual subordination works only if there are good relations between the project and functional managers, and a willingness in both managers to surrender some of their 'rights' over the subordinate. All too often, matrix management fails over this issue and the strongest person wins control over the subordinate.

Dual subordination in the matrix organization is a complex psychological situation and puts stress on all three people involved, just as in a love triangle. Subordinates must abandon their permanent home, old friends and loyalties, for a set of temporary loyalties and relationships, with consequential feelings of insecurity. The project manager will want everyone working on the project to have their loyalties totally committed to the project and its objectives, and to the project group, and will tend to resent the subordinates' loyalty to their functional home and 'interference' from functional managers. The functional manager will tend to resent losing power or complete control over the subordinates and the pressures exerted by the project manager. These factors will press both managers towards conflict.

In order for dual subordination and the matrix organization to work effectively, the functional manager must be willing to abdicate some control over the subordinates, and the project manager must recognize and accept both the subordinates' and the functional manager's old ties. In situations where there is open communication, trust, respect and mutual support, this can occur, but like many factors in teamwork it is a chicken and egg situation. All too often dual subordination is a struggle for power over the subordinate and leads to conflict.

Complex, ambiguous and uncertain structures

If an organization structure is complex, ambiguous and uncertain, not to say also temporary, it means in practice that the authority and responsibility of the individuals concerned are uncertain, integration may be ineffective or non-existent, groups may not be defined and relationships will be indefinite. This situation may occur in any form of organization, particularly with large endeavours, but it is especially marked in project work, and in the matrix form of organization. Typically on a project, at least two or more companies are involved, each with two or more functional groups. In a large matrix organization, the number of groups, departments, organizations and companies can number in the hundreds.

However, in such cases it is unfair to blame the matrix organization for the problems that arise because of the resultant organizational complexity. The complexities that arise are not the consequence of using the matrix organization, but could be considered the basic reason for the adoption of the matrix organization form. The traditional hierarchical pyramid form of organization simply cannot handle the number of groups, the necessity of crossing organizational boundaries and the complexities that are unavoidable in the organization of a large project, or in handling multi-projects. There are few alternatives, if any, to the matrix organization in such situations.

One of the problems is that often senior management does not face up to the problems and the possible conflicts involved in clarifying authority responsibility and reporting relationships. Sometimes it is not aware of the need to do so, more often it ducks the fight that might occur. As a result, organization relationships, authority and responsibilities are often uncertain. More often, they are not understood by the people involved, even if they are defined. Thus an important point is people's awareness of the organization. If people do not understand the structure of which they are a part, then you have the same result ambiguity and uncertainty. This uncertainty itself contributes to many of the interpersonal and intergroup problems, and thus to conflict.

A special problem that exists in project work is that the organization is a temporary one. Projects by their nature are temporary entities with typical 'lives' of from three months to five years. This temporary nature of the project organization and the groups involved, means that members of these groups only work together for a limited period and there is little time for interpersonal relationships and teamwork to develop into a static state, as in line management. There is also not much time to resolve interpersonal and intergroup problems and conflicts. Technical problems in a project can almost always be solved given time and money, but 'people' problems are much more difficult, if not impossible to 'solve' in the short life span of a project. The problem is compounded because the composition of the organization and the groups making it up is usually constantly changing, with new members joining it and the role of some of the older members changing in importance as the project passes through its life cycle. Relationships and interdependencies are thus constantly changing.

Despite the above problems, the matrix organization is effective in giving a goal-oriented form of project organization which facilitates the achievement of the project's objectives. Its use is also unavoidable in many projects, particularly in the multi-company situation or where functional departments are large, strong and well-established.

There are, however, two concepts or techniques which can be used to overcome some of these problems:

- The contractor/consignee principle
- The matrix of responsibilities

The contractor/consignee principle

One method of overcoming the project/functional manager conflict situation, particularly for in-company contributors to a project, is known as the contractor/consignee principle.[2]

One of the realities of project life is that the project manager often has less difficulty with the management of contributors to the project from the other companies involved, than with the functional departments from the manager's own company. The project manager usually has written contractual relationships with these other companies, and these companies want to maintain good-will and reputation to ensure future business. The project manager has a formal basis for authority with these contractors' personnel in the contracts or purchase order agreements. It may not be complete superior–subordinate authority, but it is formal authority, and both parties know the extent and limitations of this contractual relationship. The personnel working for these contractors can, for all intents and purposes, be integrated into one project organization, and can work together as a team in an organizational unit. Conventional contracts have clearly defined deliverables, cost, schedule and technical or quality requirements, and in the event of a dispute there is a legally binding path to resolve them.

In the project manager's own company, the manager's position is usually one of getting the work done without the formal line authority or contractual arrangements to manage or control this in-house work. The in-house work is often not clearly defined or specified, with costs, schedules, resources and objectives loosely set and difficult to control. The project manager thus has great difficulty in bringing pressure to bear for higher performance to achieve the project's objectives with these in-company groups.

On this basis there are benefits to the project manager, the functional managers and to the project as a whole, in the establishment and agreement of internal pseudo-contracts between the project manager and functional managers. This has been called the 'contractor/consignee' principle, and it can eliminate or minimize many of the problems outlined. These pseudo-contracts may be based on work packages, cost accounts, products, deliverables, etc. The jargon name is immaterial; the important point is that a specific element of work has been defined and an informal or formal contract has been agreed between the project and functional managers. This pseudo-contract is a self-contained entity, essentially a small project, with a simple management structure, that is, one functional manager is responsible for it. This internal pseudo- or real contract has the following characteristics:

1. A single person is responsible for it.
2. There is a formal specification of the work involved in it.
3. It has its own workplan with key events or milestones integrated with the overall project plan.
4. It has a manpower/resources plan.
5. It has a time-phase budget.
6. It has a control and information system.
7. Its performance is measured.

When this contractor/consignee principle is combined with the matrix organization, it can resolve some problems, particularly with the functional or balanced matrices, and lead to improved project performance. In addition to providing a basis for the project manager's authority, these pseudo-contracts do increase the motivation of the people working on them.

The matrix of responsibilities

It is difficult to show the matrix organization in the traditional form of an organization chart without a great deal of complexity and the use of many 'dotted lines' Even then, all the relationships can never be displayed. One way of

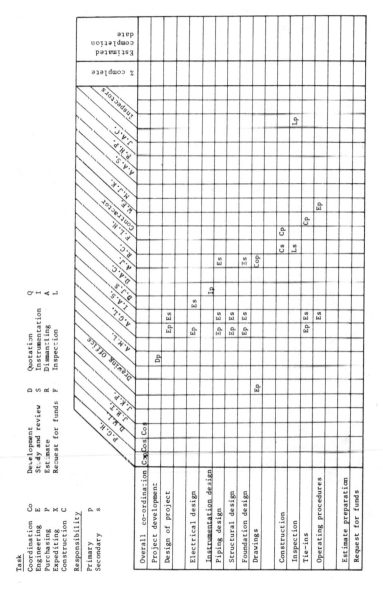

Figure 3.3 Matrix of responsibilities (with initials of those responsible)

clearly defining organizational responsiblities and relationships is to use a matrix of responsibilities, or task/ responsibility chart.

A responsibility matrix is simply a graphical way of indicating who is to do, or be responsible for the various activities and elements of the project and the relationships between the parties involved. Figure 3.3 shows a large-scale quad-ruled chart on which jobs are shown on the ordinate, and people, and or companies on the abscissa. Symbols can be drawn in the coordinates to represent the type of work or responsibility of each person or group, on each job.

The matrix can show who has the responsibility for which aspect of the project, what that responsibility is, and all the jobs which make up the project. It is easy to compile and, permits individuals to check what their responsibilities are, so that nothing is overlooked and job overlapping is avoided. It also shows whom to consult on other aspects of the project and permits everyone to see at a glance who is responsible for what. It is a form of organigram that is more appropriate to the matrix organization than the traditional one, and which can show much more information.

Notes

1. E.C. Brod and B.P. Pohani (1990) 'Integrated Project Management Organization for Multiple Projects', *Managing by Projects*, 10th Internet World Congress.
2. J. Prigl and S. Stoldt (1990), 'Implementing Strategic Project Management at Mercedes-Benz AG', Car Division, *Managing by Projects*, 10th Internet World Congress, 1990.

Chapter 4

ORGANIZING THE
LARGER PROJECT

In the previous chapters the basic forms of the project organization structure have been described, that is functional, dedicated project team, and several forms of matrix structure. In addition, the importance of integration was emphasized, not just to coordinate the work undertaken, but also to integrate the people, by establishing teamwork and managing conflict. In this section the design of the organization structure of the larger project is outlined. This is even more critical to successfull project performance than in the case of the smaller project, and much more complicated.

The importance of the 'internal' project organization structure

The form of project organization used in the larger project has to encompass the global multi-company organization, that is the external organization of the project, and the more complex project 'internal' organization. The internal organization of a project is the structure of the relationships between the individuals and groups working on the project viewed as a separate organizational entity. It ignores the external relationships of the organizational elements with their parent departments or companies.

The concepts outlined previously, have to be enlarged on when considering the larger project. In designing the organization structure of the smaller project, the global project organization may only involve one or two companies, and one or two functional departments in each of the companies. Even with this limited number of building blocks there can be problems with the form of organization used and the definition and allocation of responsibilities for the individual manager and segments of the project. These problems are compounded exponentially with the larger project with often ten, twenty, a hundred or more companies and organizational units involved.

A large project will almost always be a multi-company undertaking, but many of its personnel and groups can be allocated full-time to the project. Therefore most of its external relationships may be based on the dedicated project team or project matrix forms of organization. However, all too often, little thought is given to the form of internal project organization used, and as a result the people involved have a hard fight simply to overcome the negative impact of an unsatisfactory organization structure.

In a large project the internal organization structure of the project has to be designed, as well as the external relationships of the organizational elements with their parent organizations or companies. Therefore in the following description of the organization structure of the larger project, these external relationships will be ignored and only the internal relationships and structures will described.

Most large projects can be organized internally in several different ways, including such factors as the form of the overall project organization structure, the size of the organizational units, the internal organization structure of the organizational units, the degree of centralization or decentralization, which in turn influences the 'tallness' of the organizational unit superstructure or hierarchy. The relatively simple project organization structures of the functional, matrix or dedicated project team have to be extended to include such concepts as internal functionalization, divisionalization, the project headquarters assuming the role of a parent company, the federal project organization and permutations and combinations of organization structures, one within another, for example matrices within matrices within divisions.

In order to demonstrate the problems involved, we must consider the changes necessary to the project organization as the size of the project increases. Although the following analysis is concerned with a relatively simplistic organization, it does demonstrate the alternative organizational forms and some of the problems arising from them.

Small project organization

Figure 4.1 shows a simple, single group project organization comprised of individuals from different functional backgrounds. In this simple example these are design engineering, construction and administration/finance. These functional individuals are shown as members of a small mixed project group, or organizational unit, despite the fact that they may still belong to their functional groups, as described above, that is it may actually be an external matrix organization. This is the internal project structure implicitly assumed when the basic project organizational forms were described.

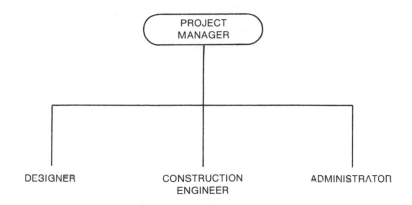

Figure 4.1   Small project organization

This embryonic project group is an organic group, in which the potential for teamwork and individual motivation is high, and the potential for conflict is low. Integration is good, as the project manager integrator is very close to everyone involved. An organic group emphasizes informality, flexibility and adaption between individuals and is recognized as appropriate to the management of change. Thus in this type of project group, conflict tends to be minimal, motivation is high, teamwork tends to prevail and there is a great feeling of vitality and enthusiasm.

Medium-sized project organization

As the project grows in size these individuals from the different functions are replaced by functional groups, each generally with their own supervisor or group manager, as shown in Figure 4.2. Thus the medium sized project organization is already developing functionalization within the internal project organization. This internal project structure is that of the functionally organized, hierarchical pyramid.

Despite internal functionalization, this form of project organization does not suffer all of the problems associated with the use of the functional organization on projects. This is because there does exist an integrating manager who is relatively close to the action, that is the project manager, the organization is still relatively small and mutual adjustment and horizontal groups can be reasonably effective. Nevertheless there is now a two-tiered level of organization, namely a functional organization within an external project organization of some form. The potential for teamwork and individual motivation is still relatively high and the potential for conflict relatively low, but conditions are not quite so favourable as in the small organic group project organization.

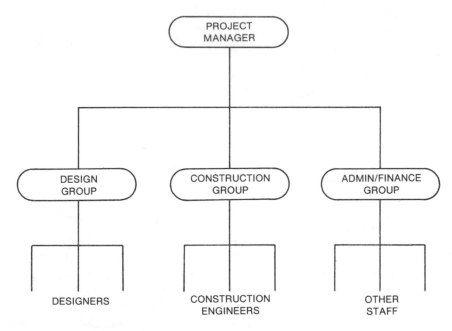

Figure 4.2   Medium-sized project organization

The larger project organization

As the project grows larger still, there can be a tendency to extrapolate the conventional functionally organized, pyramid structure used in the medium-sized project, to the larger project, as shown in Figure 4.3. This creates a single large organizational unit with the only key integrationist superior being the project manager. The functional groups of the medium sized project organization have now become functionally organized large groups or departments in the larger project. These large groups may belong to different companies in any of the conventional external project structures, but internally to the project they are in the traditional hierarchical pyramid structure.

In this single organization unit structure, the organization structure of the larger project may have turned a complete circle in that the internal organization of the project is now totally functional and there exist all of the problems previously described regarding the use of the functional organization in project work. In particular the project manager integrator is now very far away from the 'coal face', with all that implies for the growth of conflict, and integration must depend largely on mutual adjustment and informal horizontal groups within the project organization.

Thus the problems of integration and of the functional organization in project work, mean that as projects get larger, it becomes impossible to continue with a larger and larger single organizational unit. A large project organization

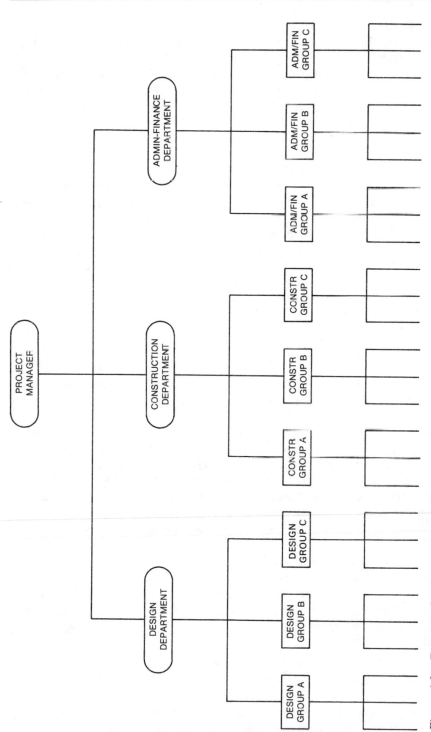

Figure 4.3 Functional organization of a large project

structure has to become divisionalized with dedicated internal project teams, or the functional structure has to be supplemented by a matrix organization. Thus a large project has to develop its own internal organization structure with multiple organization units handling different segments of the project. Each unit may integrate one or more companies, and different companies may be involved in different organizational units. The project itself must now be considered as a parent organization, or company; the organization units are now separate sub-projects or projects, and the project 'headquarters' is now managing multiple interrelated projects.

The basic building blocks of the project organization can be assembled in a number of different ways for any one project, to give a different shape and size to the management hierarchy. Each different organization design will influence overall project performance and human behaviour in different ways, and in particular they can encourage or discourage teamwork and conflict, and the motivation of individuals and groups.

The number of levels of management in this hierarchy and the complexity of the organization structure will be influenced by the following factors:

1.   The number and size of the organizational units.
2.   The form of organizational structure of these units.
3.   The extent of functionalization.
4.   The span of control at each level.
5.   The degree of centralization or decentralization.

These factors tend to interact, both with themselves and the number of levels of management and the complexity of the structure, some as cause and some as effect.

This multi-project, large project organization can be organized in many different ways, based on the project organizational forms previously described. It can maintain its own internal functional departments or divisions intact and adopt any or all of the three forms of the matrix organization. Alternatively, and particularly in the very large project, it may adopt the divisional form of project organization and create dedicated project teams for each organizational unit or sub-project. Then again it may adopt a hybrid organization, part matrix, part divisional.

Figures 4.4–6 show several combinations of the above factors for the organization of a project. Although simplistic in outline, they demonstrate the variations that can exist, which can be multiplied several times over in a large project. The same nine basic working groups used in the single organizational unit structure shown in Figure 4.3 are organized in several different ways as discussed below.

Matrix organization

In this structure, shown in Figure 4.4, a matrix relationship is superimposed on the above functional structure in order to improve integration at basic group

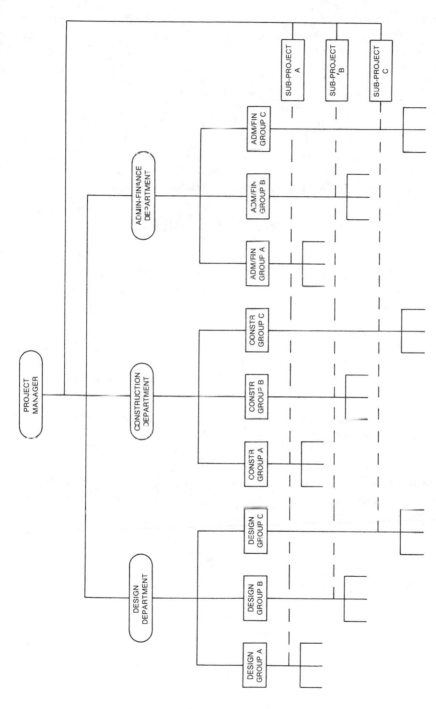

Figure 4.4   Matrix organization of a large project

level. Three matrix organizational units are formed, and the project engineers or sub-project managers integrate the contributors to their segment of the project from the various functional groups and departments.

Divisional/dedicated project team organization

In this organization structure, shown in Figure 4.5, the project is divided into three separate organizational units or sub-projects, and each leg of the same structure is now a mixed function dedicated project group. This involves a measure of decentralization, but this is often decreased by retaining a strong central administration, planning, control and financial functions at the centre.

Small unit organization – The federal organization

In this structure, shown in Figure 4.6, each of the nine basic groups forms a small mixed function organization unit, splitting the project into nine segments. In its unmodified form it creates a decentralized flat organization structure; the federal organization. However, it can be varied in the following ways:

- Made more centralized by retaining strong central staff groups.
- Made 'taller' by introducing another level of management between the units and the project centre. Each 'middle' manager then manages, controls, coordinates and integrates three of the small dedicated project teams.

All these variations can be used whilst retaining the same number of basic groups actually to carry out the work, and to form the foundation of the hierarchy. The complexity and height of the organizational hierarchy can increase in the larger project, where all of the above may form only one of many divisions. In the very large project, there can be permutations and combinations of these basic project organization structures, or multi-layering of structures as illustrated in the example below:

1. In the divisional form, separate divisions in the project may have:
   - a functional medium-sized project structure;
   - functional departments and a matrix structure; and
   - dedicated project teams, i.e. a further divisional breakdown of the organizational unit, or sub-project.
2. Alternatively, within one matrix organization, there may be another matrix structure, and within that yet another...!

Centralization versus decentralization

There will typically be a management hierarchy in each functional department and each organizational unit, and in a large project with a number of organiza-

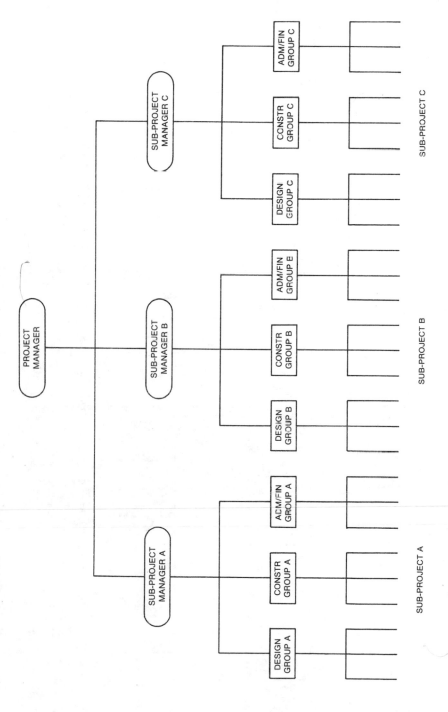

Figure 4.5 Divisional organization of a large project

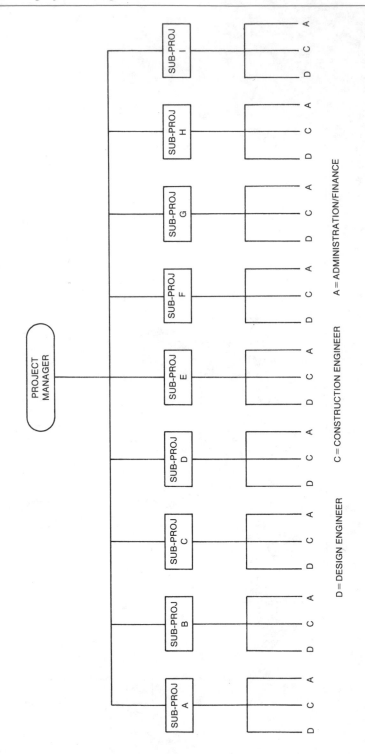

Figure 4.6 Federal organiization of a large project

tional units, there will be a senior management hierarchy or superstructure to manage, control, coordinate and integrate the units. Thus the organization structure of a large project will have a number of levels of management. In some projects the number of levels of management hierarchy has approached or exceeded double figures, creating a 'tall' superstructure or management hierarchy. In addition to the influence of the general shape of the structure, two factors particularly interact with it to influence performance and human behaviour: centralization and bureaucratization.

An important problem or decision to be made in such organizations is what degree of centralization or decentralization should be used. There are two, possibly three conflicting needs:

1. Although it is possible to divide a large project into discrete segments which can be handled almost as independent separate projects, there is also a need for the integration of segments. This need for integration between segments will vary from project to project, and with the stage of the project. Integration needs will tend to be high at the beginning and end of the project, that is, the initial design stages and commissioning, but lower in the middle of a project, in the construction, manufacturing or programming stages.
2. There is a need for control and performance measurement, formalization of procedures and standardization across the project.
3. There is a need for individual project units to be as autonomous as possible to increase internal teamwork and motivation.

These needs require to be balanced for the individual project, as the degree of centralization and control used can greatly influence overall performance and human behaviour.

Centrally controlled project organization

The conventional approach is that the project manager has to plan and control all of the activities required to complete the project. This view is reinforced by the power of modern computer software packages for project planning and control. In addition, in order to plan and control such a large project effectively, there tends to be the growth of central staff support functions for the project manager. In turn this leads to the growth of a project headquarters with strong staff groups at the centre, that is, the generation of line and staff situations with all their implications for conflict and politics.

Tall hierarchical structures with small spans of control, generally emphasize close control of subordinates at all levels, often combined with strong centralized staff departments to assist in this control. They are normally combined with a centralization of decision-making, have a structured hierarchy of graded authority and control, together with formalization and standardization of procedures, organizational rules and regulations. They thus tend to produce a disciplined and rigid organization.

This does enable senior management to be 'in control', and superiors are readily available to subordinates for consultation and back-up. However, this describes a mechanistic and over-bureaucratic organization in which central-decision making tends to slow down decision-making, leading to organizational arthritis, reduction in initiative and little autonomy at lower or even middle levels. This reduces teamwork and motivation. In addition, political manoeuvring and conflict in the tall hierarchy is commonplace, and information tends to be censored or distorted as it flows up the hierarchy.

There is a great danger that if centralized control is emphasized it will result in the creation of a tall hierarchical, centrally controlled, complex organization structure, which will inevitably become over-bureaucratic and lead to the following problems:

- Integration of the work and the people become more difficult as the project increases in size.
- The complexity of the large project organization leads to uncertain authority and responsibility, which in turn increases the likelihood of conflict and politics.
- Large project organizations tend to develop internal functionalization, which leads to functional orientation, clashes of cultures and groups with incompatible objectives.
- The centralization of the large project organization tends to lead to problems with the following:
    An information overload at the centre.
    Large central staff groups in an attempt to deal with this information overload.
    A tall management hierarchy, i.e. many levels of supervisory managers.
    The slowing down of decision making.
- The organization tends to become formalized and bureaucratic.
- Motivation and teamwork are reduced.

Although divisionalization, leading to a measure of decentralization tends to reduce these problems, there is general tendency to implement only pseudo-decentralization. Many so-called decentralized organizations are in fact decentralized in name only, as important factors controlled by the centre totally negate the effects of this decentralization. One way to overcome this is to move towards a decentralized organization, the extreme example of which is the 'federal' organization of a project.

The federal organization[1]

The opposite extreme to the centrally controlled project organization is the flat and flexible decentralized federal organization structure. A flat organization generally emphasizes decentralized decision-making, small central staff groups and an organic style of operation. The federal organization form is a relatively new form of large project organization which came about because of problems with the centralized structure as described above and also as a result of the following factors:

- Experience in larger projects.
- Developments in project systems.
- Developments in organization theory.

Experience on larger projects

Experience on large projects has led to a move to reduce the number of levels of management and increase the degree of decentralization, for example:

> The Trans Alaskan Pipeline (TAPS) remains one of the largest and most ambitious of recent superprojects. ... Senior management was required to concentrate on a series of strategic issues of startling variation..., [including] the development of a highly decentralized matrix organization once construction began....
>
> Nowhere was the organizational concern more clearly evident than in the change about 15% of the way through construction from a 9 tiered centralized functional organization to a 4 tiered, decentralized matrix organization. The result was a highly flexible construction organization relying like Apollo on a small cadre of senior managers. Emphasis was on leadership, horizontal and informal communication, simple structures and tight reporting relationships – and getting the job done.[2]

Developments in project systems

Modern project systems and their computing back-up are not only concerned with the management of time, resources and cost, but also can be integrated with the project organization structure through the concepts of the work and organization breakdown structures. They can also be used to motivate individuals and groups by giving them targets and feedback on their performance. They can thus facilitate the decentralized management of projects and the use of federal types of organization structures.

Organization theory and the federal organization

Organization theory is beginning to emphasize the federal organization as a solution to many of the problems of organizing the larger company.[3,4,5] This form of organization involves the following:

- Replacement of pyramidal, functionally structured organizations by more decentralized, federalist organizational forms; this yields distinct units with clear-cut responsibilities of their own, including profit.
- At the same time, restriction of hierarchical interference and control, in particular by the introduction of horizontal exchange and comparison.[4]

In the project federal structure, the project organization is structured into semi-independent organizational units, each dealing with a distinct segment of the project and having their own time, cost and performance responsibilties. These organizational units can be defined by the use of the work and organization breakdown structures, as described later (p.123). However, in the federal organization these units become the 'prime' organizational element, with all the other elements, such as functional departments, acting in a purely supportive or service role. Thus in the federal organization, the larger project is broken down into a portfolio of smaller projects, or mixed organizational units.

Although this appears little different to the divisional form of project organization, there is a difference in one vital factor: accountability as well as responsibility is delegated to the units. The use of the federal organization involves not just decentralization, where the centre delegates certain tasks to the units and retains overall control, but a situation where the smaller organizational units have a great deal of autonomy. Not only are they responsible for their segment of the project but they are also accountable for it. Normally it is only responsibility that is delegated, with accountability being retained by the centre. This distinction between responsibility and accountability is important, as it is the delegation of accountability to federal unit managers that distinguishes the federal organization from other forms of project organization. These factors are defined as follows:

- Responsibility is the obligation incurred by individuals in their roles in the formal organization in order effectively to perform assignments.
- Accountability is the state of being totally answerable for the satisfactory completion of a specific assignment.[6]

Each federal organizational unit has an individual identified as its relatively autonomous manager, who is both responsible and accountable for the unit's end product and its performance. The project headquarters or centre then tends to control along general lines, setting the project strategy and mediating between units. Control is based on outputs and performance indices, and if targets and milestones are achieved there is little interference from the centre. The span of control of the project or senior managers is increased and a very flat organizational unit superstructure is used. Important decisions are no longer the sole prerogative of the project manager, if they ever were, and decision-making is shared with the managers of the organizational units.

Whichever form of large project organization is adopted, over-bureaucratization and tall management hierarchies, particularly above the level of discrete organizational units, should always be avoided as they badly affect performance and human behaviour. One of the most fashionable and effective steps taken today in any organizational restructuring is to eliminate one or more levels of the management hierarchy. Although the federal organization is an extreme and may be too decentralized for integration purposes in some stages of the project life cycle and in some projects, it is a pointer to the advantages of decentralization and the use of a flatter organization structure. It can handle the control requirements, and it does increase motivation and teamwork, and reduce conflict. However, many of the benefits of the federal organization can be achieved by the delegation of accountability and responsibilty using the modern approach to the organization of projects.

Delegation of accountability and responsibility

The modern approach to the project organization emphasizes the delegation of personal accountability to every manager, right down the line to individual work element and group managers. There must be discrete responsibility for individual project tasks, not only for the efficient completion of these tasks, but also to motivate individuals and encourage teamwork. Each manager and group should know what is expected of them and the group, and know what they have to do to achieve high performance.

This concept should extend to the internal company contractor/consignee assignments and to the various cross boundary groups that exist in a multi-company project. This includes the formal, matrix and informal horizontal groups of managers and others who must interact, are interdependent and share responsibility for discrete segments of the project. For example, the client's, consultant's, and contractor's electrical design engineers, with possibly a project engineer, are responsible for the electrical design of a project. Such groups must be defined and recognized, particularly by those in the group, as a discrete organizational group with shared objectives and mutual self-interests. There must also be someone whose responsibilties are the leadership, management and integration, of the group, that is, someone who acts as a key integrationist superior, no matter what is their positional authority.

The individual manager, group, contractor/consignee and organizational unit responsibilities are then discrete entities with their own deliverables, clear objectives, performance and output criteria, and which act as cost, performance and profit centres in their own right, and have a high degree of autonomy with responsibility and accountability for results. This delegation enables the organization structure to have wider spans of control, and thus a flatter and less hierarchical structure, with fewer levels of management.

The psychological impact of adopting this approach cannot be overrated. The consequences include the following:

- Individuals and groups can identify themselves with the smaller unit and internal solidarity and unit loyalty are increased.
- Team development and teamwork are facilitated.
- It creates shared values, common clear-cut objectives and aligns self-interests.
- Individual, group and unit motivation are increased.
- Integration is improved.
- Hierarchical steering and control are minimized, and replaced by self-control within the overall agreed plans and budgets.
- Dysfunctional conflict and politics are reduced.

The adoption of this approach necessitates the following changes in many organizations:

- A significant change in attitudes and culture in many firms, e.g.
    The delegation of accountability as well as responsibility.
    A reduction in supervision and control by the centre.
    The allowing of junior managers to operate in a largely autonomous manner.
    The sharing of power by the senior managers; the project is now being managed by a group of managers, in the same manner as in the federal organization.
- The establishment of a management information and performance criteria system to facilitate the loose/tight form of control consistent with the delegation of accountability and responsibility.
- The implementation of a revised reward system.
- The establishment of a career progression structure in the absence of a tall hierarchy.

In practice there has to be balance between formalization and central control on the one hand, and decentralization and an organic style of management on the other. Some factors need to be centrally controlled, but as much as possible should be decentralized and the organizational units made as autonomous as is consistent with the requirements for integration and control. These are very 'woolly' guidelines as 'as much as possible', like 'as soon as possible' can mean very different things to different people, but the actual balance must be contingent on the givens of each unique situation.

This approach improves performance in many ways. Objectives and responsibilities are clearly defined, and motivation and teamwork are increased. It facilitates the combination of the organization of the project, the modern structured methodology of project planning and control and the application of human behaviour strategies to increase the performance of all those involved in the project and in the achievement of the project's objectives.

The project organization and the project life cycle

Projects by their very nature have a characteristic life cycle, and thus the organization of a project tends to be subject to change as it passes through this cycle. The following phases or stages in the cycle are common to all types of projects in every branch of industry, commerce or government, in one way or another.

1. Conception (childhood)
2. Definition (teens)
3. Design (young adulthood)
4. Procurement (adulthood)
4. Execution (mature adulthood)
5. Commissioning (old age)

In addition there are often contracting processes which may occur both after the definition stage and the design stage, or at many stages in the life cycle of a project.

A project is 'born' in the conception stage as an idea, a need or a problem that needs solving, and this stage normally involves the development of the project's objectives, preliminary estimates of cost, resources, time to completion, what is involved, feasibility and pay-off. Very many projects do not progress further than this stage and are not accepted as a viable project by the company's management, that is, there is a 'go, no go' decision point at the end of the conception, and also at the end of the definition stage.

If the project proposal is accepted as a viable project at the end of the conception stage, it moves on to the project definition stage. In this stage, the project proposal is developed into a full-scale definition of a project, sufficient to enable design to proceed and contracts to be placed. This definition stage involves an increase in the number of people and functions involved in the project, and of expenditure. In some industries it often involves the employment of consultants to assist the project owner company to develop the project proposal and to carry out the contracting process: the preparation of tender documents; the drawing up of a tender list; obtaining and evaluating bids; pre-contract negotiations and award of contracts for the design, or design and execution stages.

At the end of this definition stage, there will be a complete definition of the project, more developed estimates of the project cost, resources required and time to completion and pay-off. If the decision is taken to go ahead with the project it then moves into the detailed design stage. In the design stage the project is now a full-blown 'adult' project, with many more people, functions and generally companies involved in developing a detailed design.

If the contracts placed are not design and execution, the contracting process is repeated towards the end of the design phase, and contracts are then placed for the execution of the work required to complete the project. This may involve construction, fabrication, manufacturing or programming, etc., dependent on the nature of the project. Typically there are many more people, functions and companies involved in the project execution phase.

The commissioning phase is often neglected, but it is of extreme importance. For example, in the off-shore oil industry, commissioning is actually an additional execution phase, but in any project commissioning is a complex stage and involves a project interface or hand-over to the operating organization and project wind-up.

Although each stage of the project can be considered a distinct entity, they cannot be considered in isolation, particularly in the design, execution and commissioning stages. Decisions taken in the design stage materially effect the later stages of the project, and important factors in the execution and commissioning stages should be taken into account in the earlier stages. Integration is required across stages as much as everywhere else in a project.

In addition there are two variations of overlap between design and execution stages. The time to completion is a critical factor in the success of projects, and for the company as a whole, both from a financial and marketing point of view, i.e. the time taken to get a new product to the market. Thus there is a trend to overlap stages, particularly the design and execution stages, but also the other stages including commissioning, for example fast track construction when construction starts before the design is finished, or simultaneous engineering when design and production work together in the design stage to ensure production of the project components starts quickly and that producibility is taken into account in the design stage.

However, even in the conventional approach, the initial work in the execution stage will almost always start before the design work is complete, and similarly for the commissioning phase. Conversely design involvement does not end with the start of the execution phase, and may even extend into the commissioning phase, for example changes will almost always be required. Similarly, execution work will continue into the commissioning phase, if only to complete 'snags', 'but-lists', incomplete work, debugging, etc. Thus these three stages will almost always overlap.

In the design phase, the various companies carrying out the design may form one or more functional organization units, with a limited almost consultancy input from the execution group. With the exception of this relationship, these organizational units will contain almost all the interactions and interdependencies, and the design function will be the lead function. This situation can continue for some time on a large project. However, when the project enters, say, a construction phase, these same organizational units will expand in size to be mixed design, procurement and construction organizational units, with perhaps construction as the lead function.

Thus it is obvious that the organization both of the organizational units and the organization structure of the project as a whole will change with each stage of the project life cycle. It will always tend to grow in size and complexity until it reaches the commissioning phase. Therefore the project organization structure cannot be considered as a static entity; it is dynamic and can change form markedly with each stage of the project life cycle.

In the conception stage it will probably be a one-company project with a relatively simple organization structure, perhaps a small dedicated project team. In the definition stage, there will probably be several functional departments involved, with the external company involvement limited to perhaps consultants. At this stage, although the organization may become a balanced matrix, there will essentially be only one or a few organizational units. However, when the project enters the design phase, it will tend to become a multi-company project and enter the global sphere. At this stage, its organization structure expands considerably. There will probably be many organizational units, and their number will increase as the project moves on to the execution stage. The project structure may have now become a divisional form with perhaps a matrix structure within the divisions.

Whereas the organization may have been centralized in the earlier stages, during design and execution, it may have become decentralized. In the commissioning stage, it may then revert back to a more centralized mode of operation. Thus the organization structure of both the organizational units and the complete project, particularly in the larger project, is dynamic and constantly changing. Nothing is ever static or steady state in a project.

Management contracting

There are several common variations of the global project organization, some of which involve contracting out one or more of the management roles in a project. This is management contracting. In any project there are normally several discrete management roles that can involve the use of management contractors:

1. An overall project management role that manages and integrates all those involved including the client, design and execution construction contractors.
2. Client management roles (which may involve contractors or consultants acting as their agents):

   a) Pre-contract management, organization, planning and control of:
      - conception;
      - definition;
      - the contracting process.
   b) Post-contract:
      - decisions, approvals, liaison, direction.
      - administration, supervision, technical monitoring and quality control of:
         design (and procurement)

execution/construction.
3.   Design management role.
4.   Execution/construction management role.

Each of these roles requires different skills, cultures and experience, and each of these role players can have different objectives. They also require the resources necessary to carry out these roles, that is, experienced people. If the project sponsor or owner has these skills, cultures and resources, it can carry out all of these functions in-house, and the organizational problems are much diminished. However, in many industries this is the exception rather than the norm. For example in the building and construction industries, consultants, architects and construction contractors are traditionally employed by the project owner or client, and increasingly, specialist management contractors are also used.

Two, three or more principal players/partners share these roles, involving the contracting and/or combining of these management roles in several ways, as in the following examples:

- The dual management of a project, often involving a mirror image form of organization structure.
- The tri-partite management of a project, as in the traditional building and construction industries.
- Management contracting:
    construction management;
    design, manage and construct, i.e. design and build.
    project management contracting.

Dual management of projects

In several industries, such as the computing, oil, chemical and defence industries, there are often only two principal companies, namely the client and the contractor. Although there may be many other companies involved, they have a secondary role to these principal players, who share the management roles between them. Both of these players are likely to have their own project managers, and there tends to be dual management of the project. In very large projects, there may be several principal contractors, each of whom forms a dual management team with the client. This concept of dual management is thus extended to cover the client and each principal contractor as if there were multiple projects.

Dual management can take several forms:

- The client's project manager and his team take the prime lead in the project management role, and the contractor the secondary.
- A contractor takes the prime project management role and the client the secondary. In the very large project, the contractor may project manage the other principal contractors, i.e. it has a project management services contract.

- Both project managers manage their respective company's roles, and they form an implicit partnership, which may be effective or may be stormy.
- A principal contractor's project management team and the client's will be combined to form an explicit partnership, and they will jointly manage the project.

These organization structures are implicit in many industries, but are developed most clearly in the oil and associated industries. In these industries, project owner companies usually have many of the skills required, but do not have the necessary resource for the typically large projects handled. Thus these project organizations tend to involve the owner's project management team working closely with the contractor's or contractors' management teams.

These relationships can take any of the above forms and often there is a mirror image organization. For example, the owner can carry out the overall project management, that is carry out the management contracting itself, and its team can be supplemented, or mirrored by the contractors involved. Alternatively a contractor will be employed to carry out the overall management role, and its organization will be mirrored by the owner's project management team.

Thus there is a mirror image organizational structure whereby the owner and the management contractor, or principal contractors involved have almost duplicate organizations. Often the owner's duplicate project structure will merely be a skeleton image of the contractor's structure. These projects are usually large and divisionalized, with different contractors involved in the divisions or sub-projects.

Overall accountability and responsibility, and thus active project management and integration may be vested in the owners project team, in which case the owner is said to be doing its own management contracting; in a specialist management contractor; or it may be shared between the principal contractor and the owner's project managers. Thus project management in this case is a dual responsibility, and teamwork between the two project managers is essential. Similarly, each party's functional groups, or groups working together in an organizational unit, must work as a team, or performance suffers. Each party will have both common and differing objectives, but at least they will probably have common cultures.

In recent years there has been a move away from the full mirror image form of supervising contractors in these industries, due to the large amount of resources required, the inefficient use of these resources, their cost and the adverse human reactions to having someone constantly looking over your shoulder. This has resulted in three other forms of this type of global organization:

- A large reduction in the owner's supervisory staff, varying from a very skeleton mirror image with only a few supervisory people involved to almost complete abdication and reliance on the contractor.
- A merger of the owner's and contractor's staff into one team, or partnership, with the work being shared, on an individual contract.

- A longer term 'partnership' arrangement between the owner and the contractor covering many projects over a period of years.[7]

These 'modern' organizational forms are based on trust and teamwork between owner and contractor. They are simply larger examples of the practice of many smaller companies in the past, when after a successful experience with a contractor they have tended to negotiate further projects with it. The projects are discussed in the pre-contract stage, with the contractor assisting the client in the project conception, definition and design, and then carrying out the work. Where there is trust, mutual support, respect and open communication these arrangements can work well.

This partnership arrangement has advantages for both client and contractor. The contractor has a long-term workload and less interference by the client's personnel. There is less staff required in both the client's and contractor's groups, time is saved over the project life cycle and the owner has a resource pool of skilled manpower and know-how on which to call to complete its projects.

There is also a move away from the 'adversary' roles which typify much of contract work. Much effort in the adversary situation is put into the design and legalistic interpretations of contracts, and the climate that exists in many industries is biased by this culture. Integration and cooperation between the parties involved can produce better results than the legalistic interpretations of contracts, continual bickering and concentration on exploiting the contract.

Tri-partite management of projects

In the UK building and civil engineering industries, the project owner or client does not usually have the skills, culture and resources to carry out all the management roles. Large scale public and private sector clients may have some of the skills but are unlikely to have the necessary resources. Thus in these projects, the use of consultants, architects and quantity surveyors to carry out these roles is the conventional approach, with specialist project and construction management contractors increasingly being involved.

Traditionally the management roles in such projects were shared between three parties, each of whom may have had their own project manager, though sometimes they were not given that title:

1. Client.
2. Consultant or architect, who basically carried out the same role in the construction and building industries respectively.
3. Construction contractor.

In this situation, the client's representative, or project manager often performs a weak role in the overall project. This generally involves the client's representative or project manager being the contact person in the owner's company for the project, who thus obtains decisions when required, monitors progress and keeps management informed on the progress and any problems that occur, and authorizes payments to the contractors on the advice of the consultant or architect.

The consultant or architect's traditional role is to advise and assist the client in carrying out the project definition and the contracting process, as well as with the management and execution of design, and the administration, supervision and quality control of the construction contracts. In the building industry, this administration of the construction contract is normally shared with a quantity surveyor. The consultant or architect carries out the lead role in the project, but traditionally this falls somewhat short of overall project management and integration. They are not usually accountable and responsible for all aspects of the project, including the construction phase.

In the past when construction and building projects were perhaps a little more straightforward than today, and were often carried out by a single main contractor, with several smaller subcontractors, the management and integration of construction work was also rather easier. However, the construction or building work on such projects is becoming more complex and involves a large number of specialist skills or contractors, for example mechanical, heating and ventilating, electrical, electronic and computer installation. Therefore several different specialist contractors are often required in addition to the basic construction or building contractors. This may be due to technical reasons, because the client believes it can obtain better prices, or simply because it wishes to support local firms. Whatever the reasons, these contractors need to be managed and their work integrated, leading to a requirement for an overall construction management role.

Contract procurement method

Increasingly, this traditional tri-partite management of projects is becoming less popular because of the following factors:

- The lack of single point accountability and responsibility for the overall project.
- A lack of overall integration between client, designer and construction contractor. In particular the need for integration:
    between designer and construction contractor;
    of multiple construction contractors.
- The adversary bias of this form of organization.

If the consultant or architect carries out this role in addition to their other conventional roles, there is the danger of role conflict unless they differentiate them. In such projects in the past, there have been problems in that the traditional culture of the consultant or architect has been more attuned to the initial consultancy, design and construction administration roles, than to the project and construction 'management' roles. There is a significant difference in skills, cultures and experience between these two groups of roles, and it is difficult to combine them. If one organization carries out more than one of these roles, it must differentiate them internally. There is thus an increasing trend to move away from the traditional tri-partite management of these projects towards other types of contract procurement methods, such as Constuction Management, Design and Build, and Project Management Contracting, which combine several management roles.

Construction management contracting

As an alternative to the use of a principal contractor to integrate all the construction contractors involved in the construction and building work, there is a move towards using management contractors to manage and integrate them, through one of the following arrangements:

- A construction management agent for the client.
- A construction management contract, or management contractor.

In both these forms of organization, the contractor integrates the construction or building contractors used. In the construction management contracting agency arrangement the construction contracts are let directly by the client and the construction management contractor acts as the client's agent. In the management contracting situation, the contractor lets the construction contracts directly, after approval by the client. The management contractor may also have widely varying responsibility for managing and integrating both design and construction. Whichever arrangement is adopted it does lead to the necessary improvement in integration and management of the multiple contractor construction phase.

Design, manage and construct – design and build

In this form of organization structure, one contractor is employed to design, manage and construct the project. As in construction management contracting, the contractor's role may take a variety of forms:

- As principal contractor who carries out all the design and construction, with only minor sub-contracts.
- As the client's agent, managing the consultants and contractors who carry out the actual work of design and construction.
- As management contractor who is responsible for and manages these consultants and contractors.
- A combination of principal contractor for design or construction and management contractor for the other function.

These forms of organization thus also improve the integration and management of design and construction.

Project management contracting

There is still a need for an overall project management and integration role with any of these forms of organization, even with the design, management and construct form of organization. All three principal parties need to be managed and integrated, that is the client, designer and constructor, in the management of the project as a whole. In addition, the client's pre-contract and post-contract responsibilities need to be executed, managed and integrated with the other stages of the project. Thus there is still the need for the other three management roles, which are the responsibility of the client, either directly, or through its consultants and project management contractors:

- Pre-contract.
- Post-contract.
- Overall project management.

It is the client's responsibility to see that the work and the people of all the parties involved are managed and integrated, as it is 'its' project. If the client does not have the skills, experience and resources, it can hire management contractors or consultants to carry out these roles in its name. However, their function is not to advise or consult, but to perform an executive managerial role.

It must be emphasized that the project management role is critical in the pre-contract stages of the project. All too often, there is ineffective management of the project in the conception, definition and contracting stages, which 'sets' the stage for project failure and which is solely the responsibility of the client. If the client does not have the project management expertise to manage these stages effectively, then management contractors must be appointed at the earliest possible moment, and certainly no later than towards the end of the conception stage. Unfortunately the need for project management expertise early in the project is sometimes not recognized until too late.

The client's management role in the post-contract stage is also important and is often carried out by the other parties involved. Nevertheless, this role is still important and needs to be managed, both in itself and as part of the overall project management. To achieve the best results the client must either carry out the overall project management role itself, but only if it has the suitable managers, or it must employ a project management contractor to carry it out either on its own, or in conjunction with the client. This contractor must be on the 'side' of the client, and be able to balance impartially the conflicting needs of all the parties involved in the project.

Conclusion

Any organization is made up of individuals, groups, departments, companies, complete organizational units and an organizational superstructure or management hierarchy, with a network of relationships tying these component parts together.

Designing a project organization structure involves the following:

1. Dividing up the work.
2. Dividing up the people.
3. Determining the external relationships of the component parts to their 'parent' organizations.
4. Determining the internal relationships.
5. Deciding the basis of the grouping of individuals.
6. Establishing the methods of integration.
7. Determining the authority allocation and degree of decentralization.

All forms of organization structure are a balance or compromise between the need for specialization of labour and the need to integrate that labour. In project management, one of the prime functions, if not *the* prime function, of the project manager and the project organization structure is this integration, both of the work done and the people, in terms of developing teamwork and managing conflict.

The traditional form of company organization is functional, either at company or divisional level, and this form of organization does not handle the integration requirement of projects effectively; it is simply not designed to do this. Thus in order to handle projects, such companies need to introduce a form of project organization, either in addition to, as part of, or in place of its existing organization form.

A unique characteristic of project organization is that its structure exists in two dimensions: an internal organization structure linking the component parts which work on the project; and an external organization structure which links these component parts to their external 'parent' organizations, that is, functional departments or divisions, and/or different companies. This external organization relationship can exist within a single company to integrate the contributors to the project from different company functional departments, or it can be used to integrate the contributors from several companies, or both.

The internal project organization for the small to medium sized project is relatively straightforward, and often takes the form of a single mixed group, or a conventional functionally organized single organization unit. However, the external organization structure is more complex and can take several forms. The basic project organizational forms are as follows:

1. Dedicated project team.
2. Functional matrix.

3. Balanced matrix.
4. Project matrix.
5. Contract matrix
6. Hybrid organizations.
7. Modular networks.

The dedicated project team external organization structure is the most effective for goal achievement in the individual project. However, every member of the team must be fully employed, if there is to be an efficient use of resources. This only occurs in the larger project, and even then this rarely occurs for the life of the project. Thus although the dedicated project team form of project organization is the most effective in terms of goal achievement, it tends to be inefficient in terms of the use of resources, particularly where a firm is handling multiple projects. The sharing of functional resources between projects can result in significant manpower savings in the multi-project situation. Furthermore, the dedicated project team structure can only apply to the project organization of the individual company and it cannot embrace a multi-company organization.

Another important factor is that the major functional centres tend to carry out the principal functions of the business, and although they are involved and contribute to projects, it would be illogical to divide and splinter them up to handle multiple projects, as it would adversely affect their main function. In addition, if they do carry out the main functions of the business, they will have the political power to ensure that this splintering does not occur.

Thus for both practical and political reasons, the matrix organization, which retains these functional departments intact, is widely used in project work. This is not only because of the above reasons, but also because it is one of the few forms of organization structure that can integrate several interrelated and interacting separate companies into one undertaking.

The functional matrix is used explicitly to integrate strong functional departments, and is the least project-oriented form of the matrix. It is widely used implicitly, whenever project integration is carried out by liaison individuals or managers, or project coordinators.

The balanced matrix attempts to combine the project and functional managers as more or less equal partners. It is the classical form of the matrix and is widely used as it can effectively combine both project and functional interests. It can work efficiently, but both 'partners' need to give and take organizationally and there is a great danger of conflict if this does not occur.

The project matrix, in contrast, is used when a company recognizes that the project axis of the matrix is carrying out the main functions of the business, and that the functional departments are service departments to the projects. In this matrix the power relationships are the reverse of the functional matrix in that the project manager is now the more powerful individual.

In the multi-company project organization, the matrix structure is the only practical structure to integrate the individual companies into a single project organization. In this situation, the authority of the project manager is based on contract conditions and thus this can be termed the 'contract' matrix structure.

Whichever form of the matrix organization is used, but particularly in the functional and balanced forms, the contractor/consignee principle should be implemented to eliminate some of the problems associated with it.

The hybrid form of project organization, in which some individuals and groups are totally dedicated to the project and some work in a matrix relationship with their external parents, is used to overcome the problem of achieving an efficient use of resources in dedicated project teams. Where people can be fully employed on the project, they are allocated to the dedicated group; where they cannot, they work in one form of the matrix. This does not resolve the splintering problem or the continuity of functional expertise development, supervision or career advantages of the functional organization.

The ultimate in organizational flexiblity is represented by the modular network project structure, in which individuals and groups can be plugged in and out of the project as required and there is a network of relationships between them.

The larger project

The external structure of the organization of the larger project, which involves several companies or large company divisions, is normally a mix of the basic forms outlined above, with each company perhaps having its own different form of external project structure for its contributors to the project. If their contribution to the project is significant, it is likely that the principal companies involved will use dedicated project teams or the project matrix, but this is not always the case. As the project grows in size, the internal organization structure of the project becomes of greater importance, and is more complex.

The extension of the single organization unit functional organization of the medium-sized project is impractical because of the problems associated with functionalization in general, and integration in particular. Internal functionalization in a large project has the same problems as a functionally organized company in dealing with project work. Thus a large project will have to be organized on the basis of several organizational units similar to a divisionally organized company. Each organizational unit is a sub-project, and is equivalant to a medium-sized project, or in a mega-project, a large project in its own right. The main project itself is now in the position of a project oriented 'parent' company handling multiple interrelated projects. It may have its own functional departments, or even divisions, and use any or all of the three forms of matrix organization, or it may use a dedicated project group for each of its 'projects', or a hybrid of them all.

Each of these organizational units, sub-projects or projects will have an external structural relationship with the parent project, perhaps with its external company, and an internal organization structure. In the very large project, the internal organization structure of the organizational units may replicate that of the overall project, and there may be combinations and permutations of the basic project organizational forms and multiple layers or levels of them, that is, organization structures within organization structures within..., to as many as seven, eight or nine levels.

The size of sub-projects, the span of control at each level in the organizational superstructure or hierarchy, the number of levels or height of this, and the degree of decentralization or centralization all strongly influence the amount of teamwork and conflict, the motivation of the people involved and the performance of the project organization. Tall, centrally controlled organizational hierarchies tend to lead to bureaucratic and arthritic organizations, which reduce performance in the project setting. Therefore great care must be taken in the design of the organization structure of the larger project and its hierarchical superstructure to balance the conflicting needs of integration and central control, with those of flexibility and autonomy for the organizational units. The emphasis today is on the delegation of both accountability and responsibility to individual managers, groups and organizational units in flatter, more decentralized and flexible organization structures, of which the federal organization is the extreme.

Organization design

The reasons why a company's project organization is organized as it is may be lost in the distant past, a result of chance, natural evolution, incompetence, the whim of the chief executive, subtle political manoeuvring or power struggles, or it may actually be a logical and sensible choice or balance based on the technical and human factors which should be taken into account, such as the following:

1. The requirements of the individual project.
2. The requirements of the the total portfolio of company projects.
3. Knowledge of organization theory and the options available.
4. Knowledge of human relation factors which influence teamwork, conflict and motivation.
5. The requirements of the other operations of the company.
6. Power and politics.

The project organization used must be contingent on all these factors, and often a structure has to be adopted which may be less than ideal for the project, but does take into account the needs of the overall company operations and/or the reality of the existing power structure. However when projects are becoming more widely used, and more important to the company's overall mission, this contingency approach should be applied within a conscious longer term strategy of moving the organization structure to one that leads to higher project performance. In some cases under dynamic, rapidly changing market conditions, this change has to be implemented rapidly.

It is the responsibility of the chief executive or senior general managers of the company, or division, to set up the company's project organization structure, and it is important that they specify it and do not leave it uncertain or muddled. It should be a conscious decision based on a balance of the above factors, and it must emphasize the integration role of the project manager and the organization structure used. They must establish it in both dimensions, that is the external or company project organization structure, and the internal organization structure of the project. In the latter, the individual project manager will have more influence in setting up the project's internal organization. They must recognize that the form of structure used will not necessarily remain unchanged through the life of the project, and they must be ready and willing to change it as the number of people and companies involved increases during the project's life cycle.

In general, the organization structure should be as simple as possible, consistent with the organizational requirements or functions, and tall hierarchies should be avoided. The trend today is towards flat and flexible network structures, such as one, two or three level divisional or federal type structures, with smaller organizational units and wider spans of control. 'Small' is again beautiful, and if integration and control needs can be satisfied, small can lead to higher motivation, teamwork and performance.

Notes

1. F.L. Harrison (1990) 'Is the Federal Organization Set to Replace the Matrix Organization as THE Project Organization of the 90s?', *Management by Projects*, 10th Internet World Congress.
2. P.W.G. Morris (1983) 'Managing Project Interfaces – Key Points for Project Success' in D.I. Cleland and W.R. King, *Project Management Handbook*, Van Nostrand Reinhold.
3. C. Handy (1989) *The Age of Unreason*, Hutchinson.
4. W.F.G. Mastenbroek (1987) *Conflict Management and Organizational Design*, Wiley.
5. A. Jay (1988) *Management and Machiavelli*, Hutchinson.
6. H. Kerzner (1984) *Project Management, A Systems Approach to Planning, Scheduling and Controlling*, Van Nostrand Reinhold.
7. E.C. Brod and B.P. Pohani (1990) 'Integrated Project Management Organization for Multiple Projects', *Management by Projects*, 10th Internet World Congress.

PART TWO

Chapter 5

AN INTRODUCTION TO PROJECT PLANNING AND CONTROL

The main emphasis in project management literature, training and education has tended to be on the techniques of project planning and control, and in particular those concerned with scheduling the work. This is unfortunate in that there is much more to project planning and control than the use of these techniques. Planning and control carry out many more functions than simply the scheduling of the work, and are often inadequately executed because of the difficulties involved, not the least of which are the human factors.

The biggest change in planning and control in the 1980s has been the increasing adoption of several methodologies of project planning and control, backed up by integrated management information systems. These methodologies emphasize total integration across all systems, including the human system; a structured approach; and hierarchical, two dimensional planning and control. Control of the project is given greater emphasis with the adoption of performance analysis and earned value approaches, explicit change control and a modern control cycle. The following chapters will deal with these planning and control topics:

- The many functions of project planning and control.
- The difficulties involved.
- The systematic methodologies.
- Total integration.
- The structured approach.
- Hierarchical, two dimensional planning and control.
- Change control.

- Performance analysis using earned value.
- Integrated project management information systems.
- The modern control cycle.

Functions of project planning and control

The amount of information available to project managers will vary according to the stage of the project life cycle in which they become involved, but in general their role will be to create order out of a vague and chaotic situation. At the very start of a project, the only information available to the project manager may be an outline project proposal and much uncertainty.

Among the project manager's first tasks will be to determine what the project is, to establish or crystallize its objectives, and to determine how the project is to be carried out – that is the project strategy. If contractors are to be involved, this will also include the determination of the contracting strategy. The work required to achieve these objectives will then have to be defined, and the people to carry out this work will have to be assembled or recruited from within or without the parent organization. This may involve contracts being let and other companies being involved, as well as contributions from many different groups and departments within the parent company.

Responsibility for elements of the project work will have to be assigned and a project organization established. These organizational elements will have to be coordinated, and relationships and communication links established, that is, these people will have to be integrated. Particular care will need to be taken to achieve effective integration, coordination and communication if several different companies are involved in any one project.

The work required to complete the project will then have to be sequenced and scheduled in such a way that it can be carried out in a logical and efficient manner. The resources required to complete the project will have to be determined, both in total and over time. The cost of the project will also have to be estimated, and a time-phased budget and cash flow constructed. These schedule, resource and cost plans must be treated as a single integrated entity, and related to the project organizational elements involved in carrying out the work.

In all, many decisions will have to be taken and resources allocated to start up, or launch a project and carry it out efficiently to achieve its time, cost and technical objectives. The mechanism to enable the project manager to take these decisions, allocate these resources and carry out the above actions, is the project planning process, the end result of which is the project plan or plans. Planning can be used to provide the mechanism to integrate the many diverse elements and companies and to provide the necessary information and communication links so that they can be managed as one 'global' organization, instead of several separate entities. Every project has to be planned more or less uniquely, and effective project planning is critical to the success of a project.

However, rarely, if ever, does everything go to plan or budget. Just as in the military field, where a plan only lasts until the enemy is engaged, so in the project field, as soon as work starts, deviations from plan and unexpected events will occur, productivity and performance will differ from that assumed in the plan, errors and omissions will become apparent and many changes will be made to the original project. Nevertheless, project plans are still required, not only to enable project management to take these initial decisions and resource allocations logically and efficiently, but also to enable it to take the many decisions and resource re-allocations that are necessary throughout the life of the project. Project plans are not cast in concrete, but are merely management tools to enable the project manager to manage the project effectively to achieve its objectives.

In order to do this, in addition to the initial planning requirement, the project manager must be able to determine quickly and with the minimum of effort, how all parts of the project are progressing, and how the people and the organizations involved are performing. The manager must be able to highlight the problem areas and deviations from plan and budgets, and be able to take action to maintain efficiency and achieve his objectives. This is achieved through the collection and analysis of information and comparison of actual progress and performance with the baselines of schedule, cost and resources established in the project plan. Reports on progress and performance should be prepared and the project manager can then take action to deal with the problems identified, that is, troubleshoot. In other words, the project manager must be able to 'control' the project.

Although the importance of planning is well recognized, control is just as important. Planning launches a project and effective planning is critical to the success of a project, but launch planning is the dominant function of project management for perhaps only 20 per cent of the life cycle. As soon as a project is launched, control becomes the dominant function for the remaining 80 per cent of the project life cycle. Indeed after the launch phase, planning and control merge through the 'control cycle' into one integrated managerial function. Once a project is launched, control *is* project management, and without effective control the project manager has little influence over the project. It will meander to completion, but it will inevitably take longer and cost more than would have been the case if there had been effective control. Control is but another name for the ongoing management of the project. Thus the control function of project management is of equal importance to the planning function. It is certainly operational for a longer period of time, takes more effort and is highly dependent on effective information systems.

In project work, planning and control are not separate and discrete functions; they interact with each other and are interdependent. The trend today is therefore to refer to project planning and control as the 'management of cost, resources and time', or more simply 'project control'. This project control extends far beyond the planning and control of the project schedule. All the activities and organizational units involved are brought under the umbrella of project control. This includes such activities as cost management, materials management, design information, quality, safety and changes to the project, etc.

In addition to these 'management science' aspects, there are many 'human relations' aspects to project control, as it interacts in many ways with the people side of project management. Planning, if undertaken correctly, should always increase the involvement and participation of the key groups and managers contributing to a project. This is essential to obtain their commitment to the project's objectives and to the execution of the project plans.

There are also problems in establishing the authority or power of the project manager, both with people drawn from other departments in the project manager's parent company, and with people drawn from the other companies involved. Project planning and control can be used to enhance the power of the project manager with these organizational elements. Commitments agreed to in the planning process, effectively give power to the project manager to enforce them. In addition, the project manager's centrality in the project control information system, his ability to make reports to senior management and the implied power to exercise control action, also enhance the manager's power, if used correctly.

Planning can also be used to develop cooperative working relationships and even teamwork, by making explicit the interrelationships and interdependencies of the people and groups involved, and the integration requirements. The planning process is also an ideal 'team development problem-solving workshop', which is one of the most effective organizational development tools in building teamwork.

The control function influences motivation in several other ways. The traditional accounting view of control is that without an effective control system to monitor and measure performance, an organization and the people in it will inevitably become slack and inefficient. Therefore the time and cost to completion of a project will always be greater if there is no real objective measurement of performance and control. Thus it is assumed that the implied threat of control will motivate people to a higher level of performance.

This traditional view is only one of the motivating functions of control. There is another motivational function of control which can have a much greater influence on performance. In project work, planning and control can be combined to give a strong motivator to achieve higher performance by giving people targets or goals that they must achieve to perform well and giving them feedback on how they are performing. Thus planning and control should be used to promote time and cost consciousness, in that everyone should know and thus be motivated to achieve their own personal targets within the overall project plan.

Finally, project control also enables a post-audit, some would say a post-mortem, to be carried out, and this has two important functions. First, it can be used to resolve, if necessary in the courts, the claims and counter claims that often arise in a project. The information available in the original plans and budgets, the control information relating to actual performance and in particular the changes made during the life of the project, are essential evidence both for the defence and the prosecution. The absence of this information is telling evidence in itself.

Second, it is important to gain from the experience of the successes and failures in any project, and all too often this experience is lost without a post-audit of the way the project was completed. The project planning and control information provides the basis for this.

Effective project planning and control is thus critical to the success of a project, and in summary is a means to achieve the following tasks:

1. Define the objectives of the project, the project strategy and the contracting strategies.
2. Define the work to be done to complete the project.
3. Organize the individual project, i.e.
   - decide who does what; and
   - allocate and define authority, accountability and responsibility.
4. Integrate the work, and also the people if used effectively.
5. Establish communication and coordination channels.
6. Establish a 'global' organization, which links all the groups and companies involved in the project.
7. Sequence the work to be performed so that it can be carried out logically and efficiently.
8. Determine and allocate the resources required, e.g. the manpower budget.
9. Determine and allocate the time-phased planned expenditure budget.
10. Integrate cost, resources and schedule.
11. Integrate the project management activities and systems.
12. Make the many initial decisions and resource allocations necessary to launch a project.
13. Establish the baselines for control of the project.
14. Provide information to management, to enable the project manager actually to manage the project, rather than simply to administer it, i.e. to be in control of it.
15. Make the many decisions and resource re-allocations necessary throughout the life of a project.
16. Increase involvement, participation and commitment.
17. Enhance the power of the project manager.
18. Develop a cooperative working relationship and teamwork.
19. Motivate the people involved to achieve higher performance, both through the monitoring of performance and goal setting.
20. Create a sense of urgency and cost-consciousness.
21. Provide information to support:
    - a post-audit of the project and the performance of its organization; and
    - the resolution of disputes in the legal or arbitration arenas.
22. Above all, improve project performance and achieve the objectives of the project, in terms of time, cost and performance targets.

The difficulties of project planning and control

Project planning and control is difficult, and many projects fail because of problems with both the scientific and human elements of these functions of project management. The principal problems in project planning and control arise in the following areas:

1. The uniqueness of every individual project and its organization.
2. Human factors related to people's abilities, training, philosophies and cultures.
3. The complexity and dimensionality of the typical project, involving a large number of activities, people, groups and companies.
4. The large amount of uncertainty and change associated with any large project.
5. Knowledge of, and skills in the specialist techniques and advanced methodologies of project planning and control, and the design of project management information systems.

Uniqueness of the individual project

Each project is unique and therefore its planning and control is also unique, and is not the repetition of a standard system such as in production planning. Although some projects are perhaps similar to others that a firm has carried out previously, they are never identical in their planning and control. Different people, groups and companies will be involved, information systems will have to be designed and introduced for that particular project, and the problems encountered, which will be unique to that project, will take this so-called similar project down a totally different path to any previous project.

Before a project can be planned, it must be defined; many management problems are caused by a poor or inadequate definition of the project's objectives, its scope and its definition. Even more are created by a lack of these definitions for individual segments of the project and for the responsibilties of the individuals, groups and organizations involved in the larger project. The larger the project the more activities and organizations involved, the more difficult this definition is and the more critical it is to the project's success.

Difficulties due to human factors

Planning and control are difficult functions for some people to carry out and there is sometimes resistance to their implementation. Formal project planning is very difficult and requires the following:

- Systematic analysis.
- The ability to look ahead.

- An understanding of all the activities involved in completing a project *and* their relationships.
- A knowledge of, and the ability to use modern computer based planning systems and techniques.
- Imagination, creative ability and the ability to think about intangibles and uncertainty.

Some people find these activities difficult to perform, and others have to change their work methods or, indeed, their philosophy of management. Planning is a philosophy, not so much in the literal sense of the word, but as an attitude or way of life. Planning necessitates a determination to look ahead constantly and systematically as an integral part of the management process, and to take decisions and allocate resources based on an integrated plan of action that has been thought through. Thus effective planning is difficult to carry out and puts much more emphasis on a manager's conceptual skills, than does the traditional management of operations.

Resistance to formal planning often occurs because many managers have little experience of such planning, and find it difficult to think through and anticipate events. They are far more at home managing routine operations than in thinking systematically about a future which is full of uncertainty. Some are also reluctant to be involved in planning, as they dislike having to commit themselves and display their plans or lack of them to senior management. They prefer to work 'by the seat of their pants', in a *laissez-faire* situation, and not to be subject to control action or post-mortem analysis of their planned work.

As a result of this, and a lack of experience with formal planning, and the time, effort and knowledge of the techniques and systems required for it, many firms employ planning specialists, or set up separate planning departments to carry out project planning. Unfortunately this in itself is insufficient to achieve effective planning. Although in themselves they may be effective, it is not possible merely to graft on formal planning to an organization. The managers of the various parts of the project and of the groups involved must want to, be able to, and actually plan their contribution to the project. In some cases there has to be a change of attitude, the adoption of a different philosophy of management and the learning of new techniques and methodologies.

However, merely to adopt planning as a way of managing, attitude or philosophy is not enough. For many people, to be 'in control of' their project, or their contribution to it, also implies a further change in management philosophy. This involves the project manager actively working to be aware of what is happening on all parts of the project at all times. It includes a constant comparison of progress and performance against the baselines set by planning, a search for trouble spots, and a commitment to do something about deviations from plan or planned performance. This involves the use of the formal project management information systems, informal networks of communication and management by 'walking about', that is control by involvement: you are where the action is, you are involved in it or talk directly to the people who are involved in it; you know what is happening, when it is happening. Control makes the essential difference between delegation and abdication, decentralization and fragmentation.

This control is not the sole prerogative of the project manager; every manager and individual involved must accept thet they are responsible for the control of their contribution to the project. They must also have a managerial philosophy which includes a commitment to controlling their own progress and performance. This concept of real time control, that is being aware of how you are performing as you are actually carrying out the work, is the fastest and by far the most effective method of control. Thus one of the difficulties sometimes involved in project planning is persuading the functional and group managers to accept that planning and control are an integral part of their jobs, and to persuade them to do the planning for their areas of responsibilities.

The complexity and dimensionality of projects

Many problems in project planning and control are caused by the sheer complexity and dimensionality of projects. This includes the following factors:

- The large number of activities that must be planned and controlled.
- The large number of individuals, groups and companies, whose work must be integrated, planned and controlled.

The complexity and dimensionality problems of the larger project are much more common than many managers are aware. It must be appreciated that where a firm, or a project manager is handling a number of small or medium sized projects, which although independent in every other way, use at least one common resource, then they must be treated collectively as one larger project. In the case of the portfolio of smaller projects, the plans for the individual project may be relatively simple and easily comprehensible. However, the interaction between projects due to common resource requirements are usually complex, difficult to understand and consequently often ignored, at great cost to the individual projects and the company as a whole.

Thus many firms and managers are involved in managing a larger project without being aware of it, and without the experienced project managers and planning and control systems appropriate to the larger project. Therefore difficulties due to problems with project complexity and dimensionality apply to both the individual larger project and to the portfolio of smaller projects.

The management, planning and control of the larger project, or portfolio of smaller projects, is a very different 'ball-game' from the handling of the individual smaller project, and is a very professional and specialized area of management and systems. The impact of poor management and systems is much more expensive for the firm because of the large amounts of money and resources involved, and this puts a premium on effective project management and effective project systems. The basic project planning and control techniques are perfectly adequate for the smaller project, but are merely sub-systems of the methodology necessary to cope with the problems inherent in the dimensionality of the planning and control of the larger project.

Defining and specifying the work involved in a large project is an important task with hundreds, thousands and perhaps tens of thousands of activities required to plan and control it adequately. The ad hoc breaking down of the project, as used in the early days of project planning cannot handle the dimensionality of the problem and more systematic methods are required to do this successfully for the larger project. Another dimension has to be added to the conventional planning and control methodology in advanced project management.

Unless planning is very coarsely done, with a consequent loss of control, the amount of detail required to represent the large number of activities involved in such projects results in very large plans. Many large projects involve thousands of activities and computer packages often proudly advertise their ability to handle 35,000 or more activities. The concept of having a single plan with 35,000 activities is horrendous and would lead to an impossible managerial task. Such a plan cannot be used effectively to organize, plan or control a large project and other means must be found. Such large monolithic plans are very difficult to understand and to use. The span of comprehension of the human brain varies from person to person, but in most people it can be overwhelmed by the dimensionality involved in very large project plans. It is easy to become confused and lost in such plans; it is difficult to grasp in one's mind the model of the project, which is all that a plan is, and actually to manage the project.

Uncertainty and change

The dimensionality problem is compounded by the large amount of uncertainty which often exists in the larger project. A general characteristic of such projects is for there to be insufficient information fully to plan the project at the start and for change to be endemic throughout the life of the project.

There is never enough information available at the start of a project to plan it in the detail required for efficient working and effective control, due to the characteristic flow of information during the evolutionary life cycle of such projects. It is more likely with the larger project than the smaller project that the information required to plan the later stages only becomes available as work on the earlier stages is completed. Despite this it is essential to integrate the planning of all stages of the project into one integrated but flexible whole.

Project plans are used to organize the work, allocate responsibility, enable decisions to be made sensibly, allocate resources efficiently and to provide baselines for control of time, resources and cost, or in other words the ongoing management of the project. Thus despite the lack of information, the project must be planned and controlled from the very start.

In addition to lack of information, no project plan is ever a static entity due to the many changes that always occur throughout the project life cycle. Therefore these baselines are useless unless they are kept up to date with actual progress and performance, and the consequences of the many changes that happen to all projects. These changes must be integrated into a dynamic concept of these baselines, which retains the original baselines for comparisons.

Finally it can take considerable time to plan a large project and thus there is the danger of producing 'paralysis through analysis'. Not only must there be a means of planning the project speedily but the methods used must take into account the fact that it is likely that the later parts of the project cannot be fully planned in detail until work on earlier parts is completed.

Control

The problems of controlling a project, as previously described have a much greater impact on the control of the larger project; it is much more difficult to be 'in control' of a project of 3,000 or 30,000 activities, than one of 30 or 300 activities. Whereas control 'by involvement' overcomes many of the faults of an organization's control systems in the smaller project, this is more difficult to achieve with the larger project. More emphasis and importance has to be given to the formal project control and information system. Project control is highly dependent on the use of effective project management information systems, which have to designed or at least tailored for each individual project.

In the larger project, in which considerable amounts of money and resources are involved, management cannot afford a control system which is slow, historic, backward looking, insensitive to trends, and which uses inadequate evaluation methods such as variance analysis, does not incorporate changes adequately and is subjective. The amount of data and information involved in the larger project means that there is a danger that management will be completely buried by mountains of reports, due to the sheer dimensionality of the larger project. Thus the design of the reporting system is also critical as there is the danger that the manager will not be able to control, in other words manage, the project because of this factor and personal accountability will be lost.

However, one of the significant factors leading to ineffective planning and control of projects is the lack of integration of all management systems involved in managing a project. It would appear to be simply common sense for all the management information sub-systems on a project to be integrated using the same information centres and the same structure of centres. Unfortunately, in the past this did not always happen, or perhaps rarely happened. In fact this integration is not as easy or as simple as it appears.

Techniques, methodology and systems

The planning and control of the larger project, or portfolio of smaller projects employs specialized and sophisticated techniques, methodology and systems.

The techniques such as precedence diagrams or Gantt charts are merely subsystems of the methodology required to handle the problems in planning and control of the larger project. In turn this methodology has to be backed up by effective project management information systems, in order to cope with the problems inherent in the dimensionality of the planning and control of the larger project.

Therefore the planning and control of a large project, in modern terms the management of cost, resources and schedule, is a difficult and specialist area of management. An elementary knowledge of project planning techniques and concepts is only an introduction to the advanced methodology required to be proficient in this area of project management.

Introduction to the methodology of project planning and control

The techniques and basic concepts of planning and control are necessary but not sufficient for the effective planning and control, and indeed the management of projects. The methodology used is actually much more important than which technique is used. Methodology is defined as 'the system of methods and principles used in a particular discipline' and methodical is defined as 'characterized by method and orderliness: systematic'. Both are required in the planning and control of projects, and they are independent of the techniques used. Methodology is concerned with how you go about planning and controlling a project in a systematic manner, that is, the process rather than the ingredients.

Methodology deals with such factors as the following:

1. How the planning process is carried out, including such essentials as:
    a)   What plans to make, i.e. planning the planning.
    b)   How to plan effectively large projects.
    c)   How to deal with the lack of information to plan in the early stages of a project.
    d)   How to handle the level of detail of planning which is required by different people.
    e)   How to 'personalize' planning and control information.
2. How to integrate the planning and control of schedule, resources and cost, and all the other project systems, its organization and people.
3. The design of the project management information systems.
4. How to analyse and report project and organizational performance effectively.

Project planning and control methodology is also highly interrelated with how you organize the project, the work and the people.

Established methodologies

There are several established methodologies or ways to plan a project. The following discussion outlines these briefly before describing the common characteristics of the modern structured methodology approach to project management, planning and control. They include the following:

- The traditional approach.
- Outlining.
- Multi-stage, multi-level, hierarchical planning.
- Cost, time and resources methodology (CTR).
- Cost/schedule control system (C/SCS) or (C.Spec.).
- Projects in controlled environments (PRINCE).

Traditional planning methodology

The traditional, oldest method was to specify all the activities required, and to detail the project plan on paper first, and then if a computer was used, a mass of data was fed into the machine, and 'hey presto' a plan was produced, or more realistically, after a number of attempts, a plan was produced. This methodology is hopefully used today only on small projects, and is now superseded by more modern methodologies.

Outlining

The advent of computer packages on interactive systems, particularly the personal computer, led to the adoption of the process of 'outlining' the project on the terminal screen. The plan was built on the computer screen, rather than on paper first. This is fast and very flexible, particularly when used with graphical user interfaces. It gives an idea processor which allows you to write down a list of headings, activities or ideas, according to their importance and shuffle them around until you are happy with the results. A list of tasks and sub-tasks can be input, arranged in blocks, and the computer techniques enable you to build, change and re-arrange the plans using bar charts, linked bar charts, arrow or precedence diagrams, easily and quickly.

This outlining also involves the 'indenting'of activities. This allows the planner to establish summary activities, which consolidate several activities. Indenting simply means that the names of the subsidiary activities are offset, or indented to the right by a single space in the list of activities input to the computer. The software package then recognizes that these activities should be consolidated into the summary activity positioned just above them in the list of activities. This process can be applied to several levels of summarization, and thus can generate hierarchical, multi-level plans.

However, this process is generally unsystematic and is not formally structured for integration. Thus this methodology, although very useful, is only appropriate for the smaller project or for individual planning modules within a more comprehensive planning methodology for larger projects.

Structured project planning packages

Most modern computer packages enable you to structure the plan, for example into sub-projects, phases, activities and tasks. Some packages have gone further to adopt a highly structured top down planning process, breaking the project down into its sub-projects and smaller elements. This is in the right direction but does not take the concept far enough. Structuring is portrayed as an option to be used rather than a central and essential element of the planning and control methodology.

Oil and petro-chemical contractors

The large international contractors who developd their methodology in the oil and petrochemical industries, but who have extended its use to many other applications have developed sophisticated multi-stage, multi-level hierarchical planning and control systems. Such systems can involve a four stage planning process, which is implemented as the project evolves and more information becomes available.[1]

The first stage would include a proposal schedule, or initial plan, and a first cost estimate. These would be expanded into a front end schedule following contract award, which would identify activities for the first twelve to eighteen months. Thereafter as more information became available, the plans would be developed further until in the final stage, the project plans would be structured in a hierarchical and sequential manner, to include the following:

1. A milestone summary schedule with around 50 lines of project milestones.
2. Project summary schedules covering engineering, procurement, construction and start-up.
3. Intermediate schedules.
4. Short-term rolling schedules detailing the work to be done.

Cost, time and resources methodology (CTR)

Cost, time and resources (CTR) methodology[2] was adopted by many of the operators on North Sea oil projects as the basis of their planning and control systems. These projects were planned using networks prepared in conjunction with a cost, time and resources catalogue. The CTR catalogue defined the scope of work of each activity or node on the network, along with its estimated cost, resources required and the time allowed for its completion.

Contractors were required to develop sub-networks for their work, as well as the CTR catalogue to go with them. What this meant is that for each activity in its contract, the contractor was at the outset required to provide details of the costs, time and resources involved in completing that activity. This then became the basis for measuring progress, valuing the work done, cost reporting and forecasting and thus the overall control of the project.

The networks were developd only to the level of detail necessary for the person or organization using them. Everyone working on the project was involved, as well as every contractor, and each had a sub-network describing their work. They knew what they had to do, by when it had to be done and what other activities related to theirs. The CTR methodology thus imposed a discipline for planning and control uniformly across all parties involved on a large project, and therefore simplified the interfaces between the organizations involved.

Cost/schedule control systems (C.Spec.)

Developed along different lines was the US Department of Defense so-called C.Spec. methodology. In this the Department of Defense standardized the planning and control methodology to be used for major defence projects, by issuing an instruction entitled 'Performance Measurement for Selected Acquisitions', which contained the 'Cost/ Schedule Control Systems Criteria (C/SCSC)'. This was followed by the C/SCSC Joint Implementation Guide covering projects carried out by the Departments of the Air Force, the Army, the Navy and the Defense Supply Agency.[3]

These criteria covered the requirements of contractor's cost/schedule control systems for the project in terms of the following:

1. Organization.
2. Planning and budgeting.
3. Accounting.
4. Performance analysis.

Contractors bidding for projects above a minimum threshold size, usually excluding firm fixed price contracts, were subject to a systems audit to ensure their systems met the criteria listed in the Guide. The methodology implied the use of contract work breakdown structures (WBS), the integration of work breakdown structures with the functional organization structures, the integration of cost and schedule in planning and control, and the use of a performance analysis system based on earned value concepts.

The full implementation of a C/SCSC methodology based on the US Department of Defense system tends to involve a severe discipline and a large amount of paperwork. In the past the application of this methodology thus tended to be limited to these defence contracts and other US government agencies' contracts. This was unfortunate as the principles contained in this methodology are applicable to any project and can be implemented to advantage in a modified form by any organization. Irrespective of any contractual requirement, any company in the public or private sector engaged in managing projects, as they are defined in this book, can apply the basic concepts of the C/SCSC methodology to their internal project organization, planning and control systems.

PRINCE

Projects in controlled environments (PRINCE) is a complete structured methodology for the organization, planning and control of information technology (IT) projects. It is the UK government's standard for its computer-based information systems (IT) projects, but it is also a publicly available methodology.[4]

PRINCE defines the following elements:

1. The organization structure, covering:
   - the project board – combining senior management, user and technical representives;
   - project management – including the project manager and individual 'stage' managers; and
   - the project assurance team – again combining all parties.
2. Structured planning and control
   - The project is structured into 'products', using a product breakdown structure (PBS), i.e. a WBS, and 'stages'. The first level product breakdown is into management, technical and quality 'products'.
   - A control system is established covering all stages of the project from initiation to closure, with a formal change control system.
3. Configuration management
   - Standards are included for managing the configuration of the end products. It is recognized that when a software tool is used in a project, it will be necessary to use the configuration method imposed by the tool. Neverthless, PRINCE does provide a suggested approach covering:

   - organization;
   - configuration management planning;
   - configuration identification;
   - configuration systems account;
   - configuration control; and
   - configuration auditing.
4. Quality
   Quality assurance is emphasized throughout the project, and includes the detailed planning of the quality procedures, and the reviews which will operate during the life of the project.

Modern planning and control methodologies

All these methodologies, excluding the traditional one, display common characteristics and if considered together, create what could be called an integrated structured approach to project management, planning and control. The principal characteristics of this modern project control methodolology are as follows:

- The concept of 'total integration', with an emphasis on personal acountability and responsibility.
- The concept of 'structuring' the project in one, two or more dimensions.
- The use of hierarchical, multi-level, two-dimensional, rolling wave, distributed, but integrated project planning and control.
- The use of 'performance analysis' based on 'earned value 'concepts.
- The use of modern project control computer software packages, integrated with 'data base management' systems, to give an integrated project management information system.

Total integration

One of the principal, if not the principal means of integration in project work is the planning and control system. Yet planning and control systems, in addition to being a means of integrating the organization, the people and the work must also themselves be integrated to be fully effective, not only within themselves, but also with the project organization and the people involved. This 'total integration' will involve the following:

- The integration of schedule, resources and cost.
- The integration of planning and control.
- Integration with the organization.
- The integration of all the project systems.
- Integration of the above with the human system, to give 'total' integration.

Integration of cost, resources and schedule

In the early days of project planning, planning the work, that is, scheduling, tended to be carried out separately from manpower planning and expenditure budgeting. The original computer-based planning systems were just that – planning systems, which produced an outline work schedule. Although manpower, or resource planning options were available they tended to be cumbersome and require large amounts of computer time, and thus were rarely used. In addition, although PERT/COST, the linking of costs to the Project Evaluation and Review Technique was an early development it never became popular, and budgets and costs were generally handled separately by the firm's accountants and accounting systems.

Yet the work schedule, the resources required and available, and the expenditure, both budgeted and actual, all interact and are interdependent and must be planned and controlled together. Very few project work schedules or plans are not resource limited; continuity of work is important for the efficient use of resources and the resources used and time taken are important determinants of cost.

Effective project management and control does not only require planned baselines for schedule and resources, it also requires expenditure budgets, that is, cost plans. Many projects in the past, and possibly some today, did not establish baseline time phased cost budgets, on a disaggregated basis. They may have forecast an overall cash flow, but did not establish planned expenditure for labour, materials, services, sub-contracts and overheads for activities or segments of the project. Yet without these cost baselines, control of expenditure and of the project is difficult, if not impossible.

Therefore the planning and control of the work that is the schedule, the manpower or resources, and the cost, that is the budget, must be integrated for effective project management and this integration is a basic necessity in the planning and control of projects. Project 'plans' are really an integrated 'set' of three plans, namely a work schedule, a manpower budget and an expenditure budget.

Integration of planning and control

Planning and control are often regarded as separate functions, and most textbooks have separate chapters on each. Yet the functions of planning and control interact and are interdependent, and thus they need to be treated as an integrated whole. For example, planning does not stop with the initial or launch planning of the project. Control of a project will inevitably require keeping the plan up to date and replanning the project to enable ongoing decisions and resource re-allocations to be made as change, unexpected events and deviations from planned performance occur. Planning thus becomes an integrated part of the control function as the project progresses.

In addition, the effectiveness of the control function will depend greatly on how planning is carried out. Schedules, manpower budgets and expenditure budgets establish the three integrated baselines for the critical, analysis function of control and quality plans, which are of increasing importance. Without these baselines you cannot control the project, the individual parts of it, and the various organizational entities working on the project.

The size of the activities, or level of detail used, will both be influenced by, and influence planning and control implications. If planning is coarse, deviations from schedule, performance and budget may not be identified until too late to do anything about them. If it is done in too great a detail, it may necessitate a large and complex information gathering and processing effort, which increases the cost, the amount of paperwork produced and the accuracy of the data and information. In this last factor, the smaller the activity monitored and the larger the amount of data required to be collected, the more likely that the data and information produced at the point of work will be inaccurate.

Thus not only must cost, resources and schedule be integrated, but also their planning and their control. In practice, this integration is simply the 'management of cost, resource and schedule', and the term 'project control' is used to cover both project planning and control.

Integration of organization with project control

It is not sufficient to manage the planning and control of cost, resource and schedule as an integrated whole. They have also to be integrated with the organization of the project.

The work required to complete a project will typically be planned by dividing and sub-dividing the project into elements, each of which will form part of the overall project plan and be allocated and carried out by parts of the organization. In addition the work, manpower and expenditure of the groups, departments, divisions and/or companies must also be planned and controlled. In order for the project work to be carried out effectively and for it to be controlled, each organizational entity and project element will require its own plans and control system for cost, resources, schedule and quality, among other factors. In a multi-project matrix organization, any one or all of these organizational entities may be working on two or more projects at the same time. In that situation, they must have plans and control systems for all three factors for all of their commitments to projects, and these have to be at least partially integrated.

In large projects, there is always the danger that each organizational entity, project element or even project will produce plans that are isolated or do not recognize the interdependencies that exist with other plans. In other words, the various parts of the project plan will not be integrated. The interrelationships and interactions between these plans for all three factors, and the consequent control functions will tend to be ignored with disasterous consequences for the project. Planning and control of the work, resources and cost must be integrated both along the project dimension and the organizational dimension. In the multi-project situation, this integration must extend into a third dimension, when organizational plans must be multi-project. This two dimensional integration of organizational structure and planning and control was often recognized in the past by the use of 'sorted' output, when plans for a particular resource category, discipline or responsibility were produced. However, this integration was generally implicit, ad hoc and unsystematic.

Integration of the project management information systems

As previously mentioned, a significant factor in the ineffective planning and control of projects is the lack of integration of all the management systems involved in managing a project. As a start, the work plan and the organization have to be integrated. The requirement is not just 'who does what', but 'who does what, when'. Thus it is important to be able to integrate the project organization structure with the project plan. In the smaller project this can often be achieved intuitively and it is simple enough to define. In the larger project, this integration is more critical but much more difficult, and therefore systematic methods are required.

However, the integration of the project systems is a much greater problem than simply the integration of the project organization and plans. All project information systems, including the following, need to be integrated to achieve effective management, planning and control:

1. The project scope of work and specification.
2. The project estimate.
3. The change control system.
4. The organization of the project.
5. Planning.
6. Resourcing.
7. Budgeting.
8. Data collection.
9. Performance analysis.
10. Materials management.
11. Drawings.
12. Correspondence.
13. Quality assurance/control.

The integration of these project sub-systems into one system in a common project structure with common cost, information or management centres is of tremendous value. The lack of such integration has been one of the reasons for the ineffective planning and control of projects in the past. In order to illustrate this necessity for the integration of all the project systems, consider the following description of how many firms used to control projects, and perhaps of how some still do today.

1.   Project specification and estimate

All projects are specified in one way or another, for example a bill of quantities and a set of drawings. An estimate is then made based on the structure of this specification.

2.   Project plan and resource requirements

The project is then planned and resourced, that is, the manpower requirements are determined. Often this is based on the planner's or project manager's judgement of how the work is going to be carried out, based on the breakdown of activities appropriate to the physical completion of the work. This creates another structure of the work, which is often unrelated to the structure of the estimate. It is then sometimes difficult without considerable work to relate the planner's structure of activities and resources to the structure of the specification and estimate.

Organization structure

The project organization structure allocates responsibilities to the individuals, groups and companies involved. Often these responsibilities cannot be related to the project estimate or sometimes to the project plans and resource requirements.

4.   Control of the project

Physical progress and the resources used are measured in some way and compared to that planned. Costs are also collected, but because of the structure of the firm's accounting systems, costs may be collected on an entirely different structure of cost centres that were used neither in the estimate nor in planning.

5.   Change control system

As soon as or even before a project starts, changes occur which should be reflected in the project estimate and plans. If they are not, then the baselines for comparing progress and cost against that planned and budgeted becomes out of date very quickly, and control of the project breaks down.

   Thus to summarize, it was often not possible to relate the plan to the original estimate; to relate the costs to the plan or estimate; and because of changes it was not possible to keep the estimate or plan up to date, so that they could be used as baselines for control. In addition much of the above could not be related to an individual's responsibilities and personal accountability was lost and motivation diminished.

Total integration with the human system

There is one last extension of integration, which is vitally important and that is the integration of the project organization, the cost, resource, schedule and other project systems with the 'human' system. Teamwork, conflict and the motivation of individuals, groups, and departments can all be influenced in positive and negative ways by all of these systems and factors.

The modern methodology of project control, and of project management, emphasizes the personal accountability of every manager, right down the line to individual work element and group managers. There must be discrete responsibility for individual project tasks, not only for the efficient completion of these tasks, but also to motivate individuals and encourage teamwork.

Thus the emphasis of personal accountability and responsibility of individual managers, groups and organizational units is extended and supported by the total integration of the project and its systems. In order to know what is expected of them and what they have to do to achieve high performance, people must be involved and participate in this project planning and control. This establishes their objectives, scope of work, their own set of plans and performance criteria. This must be backed up by the personalized feedback of information, analysis and reports to each and every manager for their own area of responsibility. Control therefore starts with individual managers planning and controlling their own area of responsibility. Structuring a project and integrating its organization, systems and the human element results in this personal accountability and responsibility for every manager and group involved in a project and can provide important benefits for the management of a project.

Thus the total integration of planning and control is critical to the effectiveness of these systems, and to project performance. In summary, total integration involves the following:

1. Schedule, resources and cost
   The work schedule, the resources and cost need to be integrated as they interact and are interdependent. Cost, resources and schedule are simply different expressions of the work required to complete the project. Project management is concerned with the management, planning and control of cost, resources and schedule as an integrated whole.
2. Planning and control
   The functions of planning and control must be integrated as they interact and are interdependent.
3. Organization
   Planning and control must also be integrated with the organization structure, so that people, groups, departments and companies know what is required of them and when it is required, and will receive feedback on their performance.
4. Project systems
   All project management systems require to be integrated to be fully effective. This includes such systems as work definition, estimating, change control, materials, accounting, drawings and documentation, etc.
5. The human system
   The human system also needs to be integrated with all of the above into a 'total' systems approach, as they interact and are interdependent. The

organization structure and the project systems strongly influence motivation, teamwork and conflict, and support the delegation of responsibility and accountability.

Notes

1. F.A. Hollenbach (1983) 'Project Control in Bechtel Power Corporation', *Project Management Handbook*, Van Nostrand Reinhold.
2. B.A. Lavers (1985) 'The Management of Large Projects: A View from the Oil Industry', 'Oracle 85' Symposium.
3. C.M. Slemaker (1985) *The Principles and Practice of Cost Schedule Control Systems*, Petrocelli Books.
4. *The Complete Five Volume Guide to PRINCE*, The National Computing Centre, Blackwell.

Chapter 6

THE STRUCTURED
APPROACH TO
PROJECT PLANNING
AND CONTROL

The principal methodology for achieving integration is 'structuring', both the structuring of the project and the structuring of the organization. This structuring not only provides a framework for integration but is also of assistance in the organization of the project, designing its management systems, planning and control, and man-management. In fact modern methods of management of projects depend largely on this structuring.

Structuring in project work can involve both structuring the project organization and structuring the project itself, and the merging of these two structures to provide a framework for integration. People are familiar with the concept of an organizational structure, but less familiar with the equally essential structuring of the project, in which the project itself is formally and systematically divided into its logical divisions and sub-divisions.

Structuring of a project and its organization are not innovations. Organizations have always been structured to varying extents, and so has planning and control. The process of planning generally involved an instinctive, ad hoc structuring of a project, requiring the division of the larger project into smaller elements for planning. Project planning software packages in widespread use in the 1980s encouraged some form of structured planning, even if it were only into sub-projects and phases, or the use of outlining methods.

Planners have for many years also used 'sorted output', on an ad hoc basis, to produce plans for individual organizational elements, or resource categories.

This is a first step towards planning based on the organizational structure. Accounting systems also structured the project, and sometimes its organization, using a code of accounts that was the basis of the financial control of the project.

Nevertheless, this structuring tended to be ad hoc, unsystematic and was not used for total integration. Yet there is a vital need for a formal, systematic method for structuring any project and for facilitating this integration. Structuring is both central and critical to effective project management and is the basis of a modern 'structured approach' to the management of projects.

The functions of structuring

Structuring carries out functions in the following areas:

- Organization of the project.
- Design of the project management systems.
- Man-management.

Structuring in the organization of a project

Structuring carries out the first step in the design of the individual project organization, as outlined in Chapter 2 (p.27) and described below:

1. How the work involved in the project is broken down into divisions and sub-divisions that are of such a size that they can be allocated to the individuals, groups, functional departments, organizational units and companies involved in the project.

Structuring also carries out the second step in the design of the organization for the individual project:

2. How the people involved, principally managers, professionals and technical staff, who may be from several external organizations and companies are grouped together at the lower, middle and higher levels.

The merging or intersection of these two structures thus identifies or defines the following:

- The work required to complete the project and its component parts, and how these component parts fit together to make up the overall project.
- The workload of all the contributing organizational elements, both at the level of the basic working group and for every larger organizational element up to the total company or companies.

It thus helps to ensure that all the work required to complete the project is identified, defined and integrated, and that no work or cost is missed out. The two structures and their intersection also indentify the responsibilities of all the managers concerned, both project and functional, the organizational elements and the companies involved in the project. This clarifies and communicates to all participants, including clients and contractors, the accountability and responsibilty of the managers, organizations and companies involved.

In addition, this structuring provides a means of disaggregating the project's objectives and goals, both for the main elements of the project itself and for the organizational elements. It thus identifies the individual objectives and goals for everyone involved. The structures not only communicate the authority and responsibility of the managers involved, but also provide a common basis, language and dictionary for information consolidation and communication. They establish a common language to describe the project and its component parts and the organizational entities involved, which forms a basis for communication.

Structure and the design of the project management systems

These structures and the coding system based on them, are used to integrate the project management systems, and these project management systems with the work to be done and the project organization. All the systems outlined previously can be integrated and related to each work responsibility or assignment, and the higher level organizational and project elements, using these structures and their coding system.

The project structures provide the basis for coding each work assignment in both the project and organizational structures. This uniquely identifies all the work involved and how it is integrated. For example, the coding system will identify the work involved in major or minor elements of the project, and the groups, departments and companies responsible for this work. Conversely it will also identify all the project elements with which each group, department or company is involved.

The coding system also provides a basis for designing and integrating the project's management systems. All the systems can be related to each work element, work assignment and higher level of consolidation of work and assignments using this structure. Consider for example the planning and control systems. Each group work assignment in a project sub-division needs to be planned, in order for it to be carried out effectively and for it to be controlled. This planning includes work scheduling, manpower or resource planning and financial budgeting, that is, an integrated 'set' of three plans. These plans require consolidation or integration into higher level sets of plans for the following:

1. Each division and sub-division of the project, and the project itself, i.e a hierarchy of plans.

2. Plans for the total commitment of each basic group on each sub-division of the project, and for each department, division and company involved.
3. In a multi-project matrix situation, where these groups, departments and companies are working on several projects using common resource pools, the plans for these organizational entities must also be consolidated across their commitments on all of the projects.

The project structure and coding system identifies what plans are required and provides the basis for their integration in both the project and organizational dimensions.

Project structuring also identifies what has to be controlled and is a basis for the design of the project management information and reporting system. It identifies the basic group work assignments for which information must be collected, analysed and reported. It further identifies the elements of the project and the managers of these elements for which information must be consolidated, analysed and reported in order to ensure effective management of the project. Again, the coding system is used for this consolidation. In a similar manner, all the other project systems, such as work definition, estimating, materials, quality, drawings and documentation will use the structures and their coding to give a common framework for integration.

Structure and man-management

The project structures identify work assignments for groups, departments, organizational units and companies, which can be established as pseudo- or real contracts to enable the contractor/consignee principle to be used. The managers of each of these organizational entities can have their own 'contracts'. Everyone involved has their individual accountability and responsibility defined.

The structuring of the project and the establishment of these pseudo-contracts contributes greatly to the motivation of those involved. Each manager and organizational element has its own unique goals, objectives, and plan baselines of schedule, resources and cost, the setting of which it has contributed to or participated in. Each receives its own reports on progress and performance against these baselines. Everyone thus knows their performance is being monitored and if it is unsatisfactory, it will be brought to the attention of senior management and their careers may suffer.

A far more positive and effective motivational influence is the fact that they have participated in setting their own goals and plans, they know what they have to do to achieve high performance and they get feedback on their actual performance. As discussed later, achievement and goal theories are practical and effective motivating influences, which can contribute significantly to increasing motivation and performance. In addition clear-cut peer performance comparisons can be made and this further motivates management and group performance. Systematic and effective structuring enables individual achievement to become reality for every manager and group, and this contributes to higher project performance. However, structuring can also be used to encourage teamwork, in that interrelationships and group identities are defined.

Summary

The structuring of the project and its organization in an integrated and systematic manner thus has the following functions:
1.   . It is an aid to the organization of the project, in that it :
   - carries out the basic steps of creating a project organization.
   - identifies the work to be done;
   - identifies the responsibilities for this work;
   - disaggregates the project's objectives; and
   - facilitates communication.
2.   It is the basis of the design of the project management systems.
   - It provides a framework for total integration.
   - The structure and the coding system based on them are used to integrate:
      the work to be done;
      the project organization; and
      the project management systems.
   - It establishes the hierarchy of plans and control reports in two dimensions, i.e. the project and its organization, and the basic foundation blocks of these systems, i.e.
      The intersection of the project structure and the organization structure identifies these basic foundation blocks for planning and control.
      This is the work of one organizational element on one sub-division of the project.
      Thereafter the project and the organization structures identify the hierarchy, or levels of planning, control and reporting for the project and its organizational elements.
3.   It is an aid to the man-management of the project
   - Each individual project and organizational element manager and group has its own unique goals, objectives, and planned baselines of schedule, cost and resources.
   - They each receive their own control information and reports on progress and performance.
   - They have participated in the setting of these goals and baseline plans.
   - They know what they have to do to achieve good performance and they get feedback on their own and their colleagues' performance.
   - Thus structuring facilitates the motivation of the people and groups involved in a project and can be used to encourage teamwork.

This enables even the largest and most complex projects to be effectively managed, planned and controlled, and can contribute to higher project performance in many ways. Structuring should be applied to all projects, as previously defined, at the earliest possible stage of the project life cycle.

The methodology of structuring

The basic methodology of a systematic means to structure and integrate the project, its organization and systems was established as far back as the late 1960s. This was the the work breakdown structure (WBS) approach of the US Department of Defense's cost/schedule control system criteria (C/CSC) or 'C.Spec'. Unfortunately, perhaps because of its close association with the relatively complex C.Spec. total system, acceptance of the WBS methodology as a standard method of structuring and integrating the management of a project was limited in the 1970s and 80s. Its use was generally confined to contractors working for the US Department of Defense, Aerospace, large similar contracts in other countries, and a slowly growing band of professional project managers in private industry. Despite this slow acceptance, the methodology of the WBS approach is the most effective way of structuring and integrating a project, its organization and systems. It provides a basis for the modern and advanced approach to structured project management.

In the 1990s, this situation is changing rapidly, and the WBS methodology is gaining more widespread adoption and acceptance in private industry. In this it is considerably assisted by many of the modern software packages incorporating the WBS approach as integral to their use. These packages are inexpensive, can run on any computer, ranging from the lowly PC upwards, yet they are powerful, easy to use and have automated facilities for the use of the WBS methodology.

The use of the WBS methodology does not necessitate the full adoption of all the complexities of C.Spec., and it can now be applied to any project with considerable benefits. In practice, structuring following the basic concepts of the WBS approach can be applied in several ways. Nevertheless there are basically two approaches to structuring in common use:

- A single dimension approach using only the WBS.
- A two dimensional approach using the WBS and the organizational breakdown structure (OBS), that is the classical C.Spec. approach.

In addition, other structures can be used in several ways, or dimensions with both of these basic approaches, including the following:

- Cost breakdown structures/equipment breakdown structures.
- Multi-tiered structured approaches for large multi-company, and/or multi-nation projects.

The work breakdown structure

The term 'work breakdown structure' is simply a name for an end-item oriented family tree like sub-division of the project, products, deliverables, or items to be built, work tasks and services required to complete the project. It defines the project, the work to be done and graphically displays them. It is very similar to a bill of materials used in production planning. Essentially it is a methodology of project organization, planning and control based on 'deliverables', rather than simply on tasks or activities.

The WBS is constructed by exploding, or dividing the project into its main identifiable elements, component parts and services in a logical and non-arbitrary manner. These elements are then subdivided into their elements, and this process is repeated until the lowest level work breakdown structure element can be divided into work assignments for individual groups. Although primarily oriented towards discrete end products, that is, deliverables, software, services and functional tasks may also be included, provided each element is a meaningful product of a management oriented sub-division of a higher level work element. Figure 6.1 shows a partial breakdown of a commercial project into its 'deliverables'.

In order to illustrate how the process of creating a project work breakdown structure is carried out, consider the simple example, whose network is shown in Figure 6.2. Each time the project and its component elements are divided, it creates what is termed a Level. In this example, as shown in Figure 6.3(a), the project is Level 1, and Level 2 is the first division or breakdown of the project into its major 'elements', that is, Level 2 WBS elements. In this example, the first breakdown of the project divides it into the following elements:

- Basic design.
- Mechanical sub-assembly.
- Electrical sub-assembly.
- Final assembly.
- Administration etc.
- Project management

In the example, the mechanical and electrical sub-assemblies are considered to be the major project elements, and management of the project considers it necessary to integrate, plan and control the work, resources and cost on these two major elements. As explained later, the other elements are also necessary to complete the structure. If a further level of breakdown is desired, the most complicated major element, the electrical sub-assembly can be further subdivided into its logical elements as shown in Figure 6.3(b):

- Electrical.
- Instrument.
- Assembly.

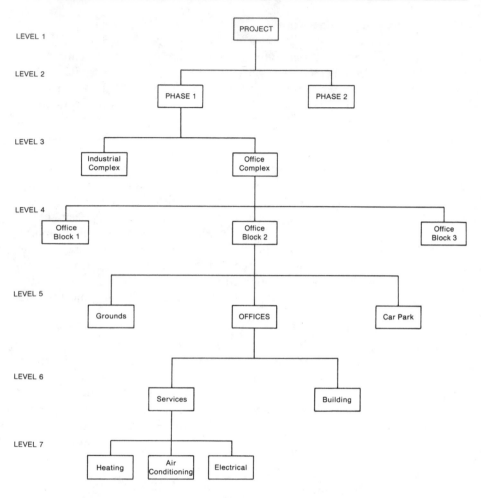

Figure 6.1   Partial (WBS) breakdown of a commercial project

It is often possible to construct a WBS for a project in several different ways, just as with a bill of materials for a product, with a different number of levels of breakdown and number of elements in each level. It is thus useful for a firm to specify a standard format for the characteristic type of projects it handles. One example of this, is the 'Military Standard, Work Breakdown Structures for Defense Material Items' used by the US Department of Defense. This covers the first three levels of breakdown for commonly procured items and leaves the contractor to define the further breakdown of the project. Figure 6.4 shows part of the WBS for a ship system based on this standard.

In most cases, Level 1 is the total project. However, if the project is part of a larger multi-project programme, then the total programme would be Level 1 and the individual projects would be Level 2 WBS Elements. This first level of

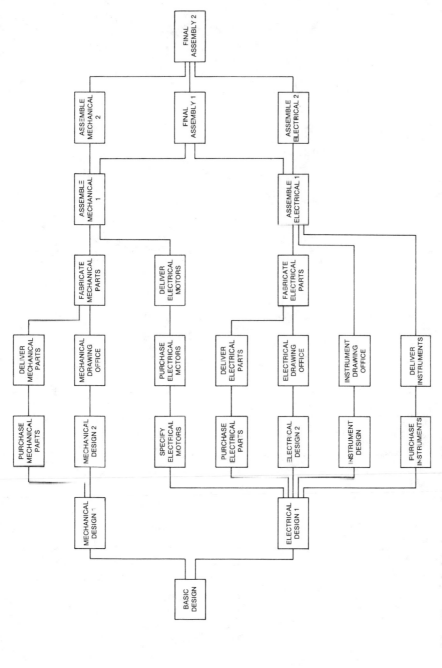

Figure 6.2 Network for the simple example

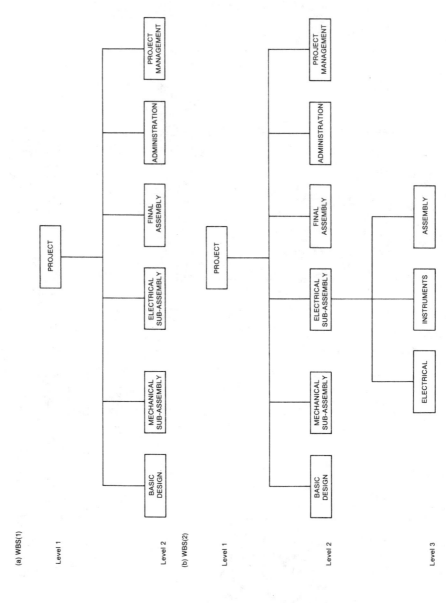

Figure 6.3   Work breakdown structures for the simple example

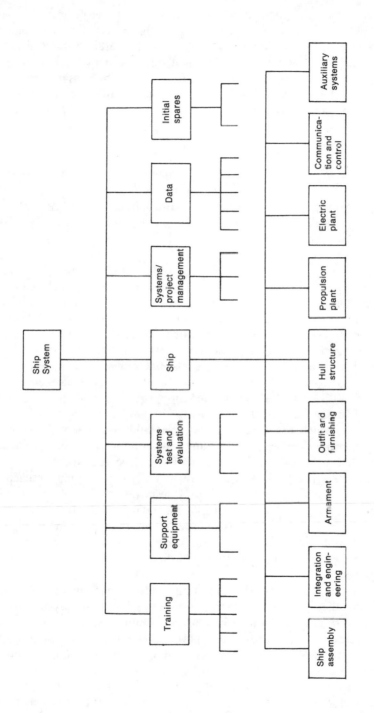

Figure 6.4   WBS for ship system

breakdown can also be made in two ways. In a large project, all the major project physical elements may be represented by one Level 2 WBS element, with the other elements on Level 2 being commercial or other non-physical parts of the project, which are not directly part of the project's main deliverable, as in the ship WBS. However, on smaller projects this is not necessary and these other elements can be included with the major physical elements on Level 2 as shown in the simple example (Figure 6.3).

The general guidelines for applying the WBS are as follows:

1. Each WBS element is a sub-division of the project for which management believes it is worthwhile to integrate management, planning and control. It is thus a discrete part of the project, totally with its own deliverables, in which it is of benefit to have plans, control information and analysis which integrates all the contributors, to enable the measurement of progress and performance in terms of cost, resources and schedule.

2. The project is broken down through several levels of division, until the lowest level considered necessary is obtained. The lowest level WBS element is thus the smallest discrete part of the project which requires planning and control as an integrated whole. This lowest level WBS element can then be divided into meaningful work assignments for individual groups, each of which can be planned and controlled as a separate entity.

3. There is no necessity to divide and subdivide each major element of the project to the same number of levels. Each major element should only be divided to a level which serves some useful purpose. In each case the lowest level WBS element is then divided into group work assignments, as above.

4. Each higher level WBS element is similarly an identifiable part of the project which requires to be planned and controlled as an integrated whole. This involves consolidating the planning and control of lower level 'children' elements into their 'parent' higher level elements.

5. In breaking down the project plans in a hierarchical manner, each level of the WBS structure is a logical and desirable level of planning, and each element in these levels is justified in having its set of integrated plans. Similarly, each level in the structure is a level at which the management of the project desires to have control information collected and analysed, and each element in these levels is justified in having its own performance analysis and reports.

6. In practice the project should not be divided and subdivided over and over again, thereby creating a large number of levels, simply for the sake of structuring. Each level of breakdown should be significant, logical and necessary for the management, planning and control of the project. Each level provides for the integrated management, planning and control of smaller and smaller parts of the project, and there are limits to how far down this breakdown is useful to the management of the project. Each level provides information on an integrated part of the project, possibly to different people on different levels of the management hierarchy, and this

information should be considered necessary for the effective management of the project. Each additional level of breakdown considerably increases the amount of information collection, paperwork and reporting required and reduces the size of the work assignments to functional groups.

7. Four to six levels are usually adequate for most projects.

8. In the simple example, two levels of breakdown would be sufficient, and there would only be a further breakdown to a Level 3, as shown in Figure 6.3(b) if this served some useful purpose. This could occur on a large project, where each element at Level 3 was of such a significant size or importance that the project management believed that it was necessary or desirable to have integrated planning and control for these lower level project elements.

9. On large projects involving separate contractors for major project elements, and/or divisional or organizational unit type organizations, there may be two sets or tiers of work breakdown structures; one for the project as a whole, and one or more for the individual contracts (contract breakdown structure), divisions or organizational units.

10. Integrative work which is common to more than one WBS element at any one level of breakdown is shown as a separate WBS element; similarly with any item which it is pointless to try to allocate accurately, such as perhaps crane use spread among several WBS elements. In the simple example, basic design and final assembly are common integrative elements to the two sub-assemblies and are thus shown as separate WBS elements at Level 2. However, integrative work which is unique to one element is included within that element, for example the assembly of the electrical sub-assembly is included within that Level 2 element.

11. All cost generating items should be included in the structure, either within the individual elements, where this can be identified and sensibly allocated, or as separate WBS elements. In the simple example, project management and administration are included as separate WBS Level 2 elements, each with its own budget.

The use of the WBS in a single dimension approach

Many firms other than the US government agencies, are now using, or beginning to use the single dimension WBS approach to structuring, managing, planning and controlling their projects. They are not formally adopting the classical C.Spec. approach, which combines the WBS and an organizational breakdown structure, but are basing their systems on the work breakdown structuring of the project, to provide the common framework. Thus some methodologies, firms and software planning packages apply formal structuring only to the project dimension, that is, they use only the WBS. Examples of this are some of the North Sea oil and gas projects and the PRINCE methodology.

North Sea Projects

In a typical North Sea project for a single module or link up, structuring may give the following levels:

- Project.
- Stage (Level 1 plan).
- System.
- Work package.
- Element (Level 2 plan).
- Item (Level 3 plan).
- Job-card (Level 4 plan).

This breaks the project down to a lower size of entity at the bottom of the structure. Plans and control systems are produced, using selected or sorted output for different disciplines for the bottom three levels, but this is not usually the hierarchical organization structure as detailed in the OBS system. Planning and control emphasis is still essentially single dimensional. In this system, the term 'work package' sometimes has a different meaning to that used in the classical C.Spec. two dimensional system. It is defined as:

> Listings of work organised by multi-discipline single system order. It is design oriented in that it will contain all elements required for the functioning of a single component or sub-system. Often the initial definition of the listing is prepared by Client engineers and material requirements are defined as Material Take Off proceeds during the preparatory stage.[1]

PRINCE

The PRINCE methodology calls the WBS the product breakdown structure (PBS), and breaks the project down into products and stages. The initial first level breakdown divides the project into three products:

- Technical.
- Managerial.
- Quality.

The first level technical product element is then exploded, as in the WBS, with, for example, individual products being technical progress reports, technical documentation such as user manuals, and programme products such as programme source listings. Management products are exploded in the same way and cover such products as plans, job descriptions and management reports. Quality products establish the required quality of the project's products and quality assurance actions.

The project is then structured into stages, with milestones at the end of each to represent key decision or crux points in the project. Often 'go, no-go' decisions are made at the end of a stage, which typically coincides with the completion of one or more products. As each stage has an identified stage manager, there is to a certain extent a second organization dimension. Nevertheless planning and control of schedule and resources is single dimensional following the product breakdown structure and stages.

These single dimensional WBS approaches do give many of the advantages of structuring and are possibly more readily accepted by industrial users. However, more and more software packages are incorporating the clssical structuring approach, and it is starting to be more widely applied in industry. This uses the OBS, as well as the WBS, and integrates them to provide a two dimensional framework for the project's systems.

The classical two-dimensional approach to project structuring

The classical approach to project structuring invoves the following components:

- The work breakdown structure (WBS).
- The organization breakdown structure (OBS).
- Cost accounts.
- Work packages/activities.
- A coding system based on the above.
- The use of a WBS dictionary/CTR Catalogue/Database/spreadsheet to hold the data.
- The cost breakdown structure (CBS).

Organization breakdown structure (OBS)

The Organization Breakdown Structure (OBS) of the project is concerned with its internal organization and not the relationships of the organizational elements with their parent organizations, matrix or otherwise. It is the 'internal' organization chart of the project, and is constructed in a similar way to the WBS.

In the OBS, Level 1 represents the total organization of the project as one element. Level 2 then represents the first division, or breakdown of the project organization into its main organizational elements. This process is repeated until the lowest level OBS elements are identified, which are normally the basic working groups, disciplines or on small projects even individuals, who are carrying out the work. These groups may be mixed, but are more often single functional groups.

The work of these lowest level organizational elements can then be divided into meaningful work assignments on individual lowest level WBS elements, each of which can be planned and controlled as a separate entity. The same general rules for structuring the WBS apply to the structuring of the OBS.

Table 6.1   Levels of organization breakdown

Level	Smallere organization	Medium organization	Larger organization	Multi-project organization
1	Total organization	Total organization	Total organization	Multi-project organization
2	Depts	Divisions	Companies	Ind. project organization
3	Groups	Depts	Divisions	Companies
4	–	Groups	Depts	Divisions
5	–	–	Groups	Depts
6	–	–	–	Groups

However, the number of levels used depends on the size of the project, its organization and the number of people involved. For example, in a multiple company project, the Level 2 elements would represent the individual companies involved. Thus the various levels of breakdown for different sizes of projects could vary as shown in Table 6.1.

In the simple example, Level 1 is the overall project organization, or company, and the Level 2 elements are the main departments or disciplines involved in carrying out the work, as shown in Figure 6.5(a):

- Design.
- Procurement.
- Works.

In a small project this level of breakdown may be sufficient. However, in a larger project, or if any of the functional groups have resource limitations or work on other projects at the same time, then it will be necessary to have a further level of breakdown to the individual functional groups, as shown in Figure 6.5(b):

- Design
    electrical design
    mechanical design
    instrument design
    drawing office
- Procurement
    purchasing
    expediting
- Works
    fabrication
    assembly

This enables the work of these groups to be integrated, planned and controlled, with progress and performance reports produced for each group, department and the organization as a whole.

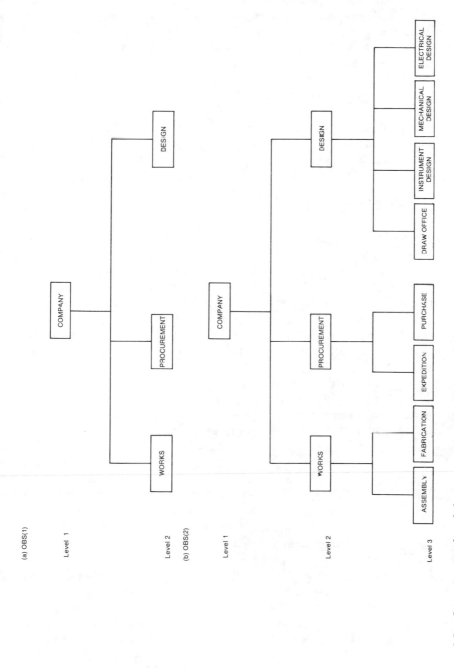

Figure 6.5 Organization breakdown structures for the simple example

The lower level OBS elements will thus be the functional groups carrying out the work. The integrative plans produced for these elements, and the information, analysis and reporting, will represent the integration of all the work carried out by each group on all of the lowest level of WBS elements in which it is involved. Similarly the integrative plans and control information for higher level OBS elements will consolidate the lower level OBS elements for which it is responsible and which it manages. Each manager in this hierarchy has their own sets of plans and control reports for all their areas of responsibility. The OBS thus represents one axis or dimension of the project control and information system for the functional managers concerned in the project. In the same way the WBS represents the other dimension of these systems for the project management structure of the matrix.

Cost accounts

The WBS breaks the project down into its elements until the lowest level elements are identified, and they in turn are divided into work assignments for individual groups. The OBS breaks the organization of the project down until the individual functional or other groups are identified. The contribution of each of these groups to the project is then made up of work assignments on the individual lowest level WBS elements. Thus the work assignments of individual groups on the lowest level WBS elements are common to both the work and organization breakdown structures and are the foundation blocks of both structures.

Thus if conceptually the WBS of the project is viewed as being the vertical axis and the OBS the horizontal axis, the integration of the WBS and OBS identifies the work assignments and organizational responsibilties for groups on the lowest level WBS elements, as shown in Figure 6.6. The C. Spec. name for this work assignment is 'cost account', which in no way describes the full importance or role of this entity. The term 'cost account' has not found great acceptance outside of US government projects, and often other names are used for this intersection of WBS and OBS. One of the commonest is 'work package'. Although this does provide the gist of the meaning better than cost account, the formal US government systems use work package to define something akin to a project activity or task as used in planning techniques.

In practice, the term 'work package' is commonly used very loosely to describe any self-contained 'package of work', and is often applied to the work involved in a WBS or OBS element, Cost account or its formal C.Spec. meaning of a project 'activity'. In view of the fact that modern software packages are increasingly adopting C.Spec. conventions and jargon, the term 'cost account' will be retained in this text. Nevertheless, the principles outlined apply to these work assignments, whichever jargon name is applied to them. The actual name used is immaterial, the important point is that what is referred to is a complete and discrete project task or work assignment of a single organizational entity

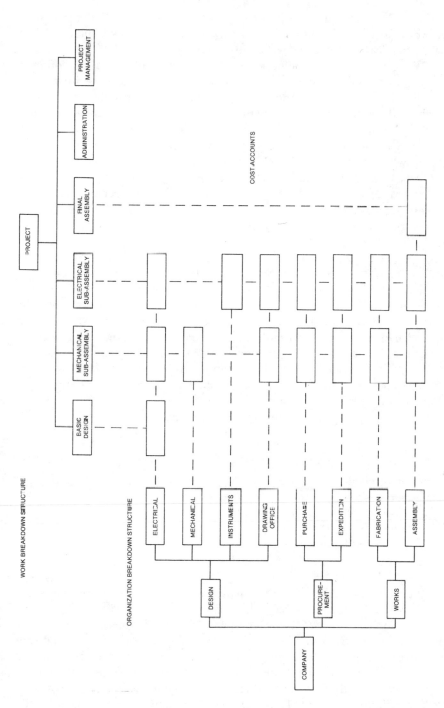

Figure 6.6   Cost accounts – the integration of the WBS and the OBS

on a single WBS element. It is of manageable size, relatively independent of other work assignments, at least internally, and is the responsibility of one manager, who can be called a cost account manager.

The WBS, the OBS and the cost accounts together establish the common framework of the project management systems. This integrates the work to be performed, the organization structure and individual responsibility for work at all levels, with the sub-systems for planning, control, work definition, estimating, change control, resources, expenditure, quality, materials, information, analysis and reporting. The cost account is a natural and logical management centre on which to integrate these factors. The assignment of work on these lowest level WBS elements to individual group managers provides a key automatic integration point for these systems and for the management, organization, planning and control of the project.

The work involved in each cost account has to be specified, planned, resourced and budgeted, and these sets of plans are the foundation blocks, or lowest level of complete plans in the hierarchical, two dimensional planning and control system. This permits distributed, but integrated planning and control of the project. Each of these plans will include one or more work packages, or activities, describing how the cost account manager intends to carry out the work on the cost account. These in turn have resources and budgets assigned to them, and may have simple variance analysis carried out as work progresses. However the cost account is the principal centre where information is collected, analysed, performance is measured and reports are produced. These are then the basic foundation blocks of the total project information and reporting systems for progress and performance.

Each cost account has the following characteristics:

1.   A single person responsible for it.
2.   A formal specification of the work involved.
3.   Its own estimates.
4.   Its own plans for :-
      • work schedule;
      • resources; and
      • expenditure budget.
5.   Its own analysis and reports.

Just as these factors are defined for the project as a whole, so they are defined for the individual cost accounts. The work, resources and expenditure required to complete a lowest level WBS element are identified by the sum of its cost accounts in the vertical axis. Similarly, all the work resources and expenditure of one functional group are identified by the sum of its cost accounts in the horizontal axis. In turn, each of these factors is defined for each of the parent higher level work and organizational elements at all levels by the sum of their lower level children elements. Thus each WBS and OBS element has all of the above factors defined, just as for the individual cost account.

Each cost account is therefore a 'plug-in module' or mini-project in both the planning and control functions. They are common to all the structures used. These structures consolidate and integrate these modules in different ways to produce higher level plans and control reports. Each of the project work and organizational elements, and the individual cost accounts are identified as the accountability and responsibility of one manager. Thus accountability and responsibility are clearly defined, as are the work to be done, the objectives, and performance requirements in terms of schedule, resources and cost. Thus planning and control is personalized.

Work packages

The C.Spec. work package is simply a discrete task, activity, job or material item. In the majority of cases it is represented by the usual task or activitiy used in planning. A work package typically has a start and a finish, an end product of some form, is of short duration, and is the responsibility of a single organizational entity. It will also have estimated cost and resource requirements. Cost accounts are typically made up of several work packages and the cost account schedule, resource and cost budgets are the sum of those of its work packages.

The coding system

The key to integration through structuring of the project, its organization and the project management systems, is the use of a systematic and 'significant' coding system. Although it is useful to describe the cost account as the integration of the vertical work breakdown structure and the horizontal organizational breakdown structure, this gives only a diagramatic or conceptual picture of the structures. In practical use, it is the project coding system which is used to structure the project, identify the cost accounts, WBS and OBS elements and establish their relationships.

Although a code of accounts has long been used by accountants, in a structured approach to project management, the project coding system is used for all the project systems to identify and to integrate everything. Thus the organization, the work definition, the planning and control of work, resources and money, the project accounts, the estimating, the materials, the reporting, the change control, etc, will use the same coding system as a common framework to represent the structures used and to aid integration. All data and information input and output will use this coding system. In many organizations, this may cause a problem in that there may already be an established accounting coding system which is difficult to change for either practical or political reasons. Ideally the project coding system and the acounting coding system should be the same. If they are not, and the accounting coding system cannot be changed, then it is essential that there should be a transformation process which changes data and information held in the accounting codes into the project codes. Fortunately, easy to use, widely available database software packages make this transformation relatively simple, if it is at all possible.

Although it may seem inappropriate to discuss coding as a central issue in project management, planning and control, it is central to the use of a structured approach to integration and a vital component of the project management information systems. Coding simply involves using a multi-digit number, or assembly of numbers and letters, each of which, or a combination of which, has a meaning or significance. Each code number uniquely identifies a cost account, WBS or OBS level and element, and their parent-child relationships in both the WBS and OBS dimensions, and other structures if required. It is used numerically to describe both the WBS and OBS and their common cost accounts. Each level of structure is represented by a part of the code. One code or part of the code is used to represent the WBS, and another to represent the OBS. Combining them, identifies the cost accounts common to these structures. To illustrate this, consider the coding of the simple example, as shown in Figure 6.7.

Coding the work breakdown structure

1. Level 1 code
    The project may be represented by the first one or two digits, or it may simply be assumed and left uncoded, particularly in the larger projects. In this example, the first digit of the WBS code i.e. '4', represents the project. All data with a code number starting with 4 belongs to this project.
2. Level 2 code
    The next one or two digits of the WBS code represents the WBS elements on Level 2 of the structure. One digit allows for up to nine elements; one alphanumeric digit allows for up to 35 elements; two numbers allow for up to 99 elements and so on. In this example, one digit is sufficient. The WBS elements are coded as follows:

	WBS code
Basic design	41
Mechanical sub-assembly	42
Electrical sub-assembly	43
Final assembly	44
Administration	45
Project management	46

All plans, budgets, costs, reports, estimates, materials, etc. for these WBS elements are identified by this coding, e.g. every item of data with the WBS code 43 refers to the electrical sub-assembly on the simple example project.

3. Level 3 Code
    If the project structure was extended to a further level, as shown in Figure 6.3(b), the WBS code would be extended by another digit to represent the

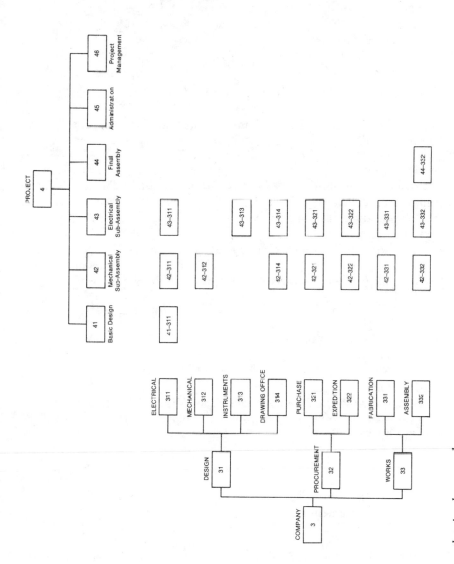

Figure 6.7   Coding the simple example

elements in Level 3 of the WBS. For example, the Level 3 elements making up the Level 2 electrical sub-assembly would be as follows:

	WBS code
Electrical	431
Instrument	432
Assembly	433

Coding the organization breakdown structure

The organization structure is coded in the same way as the project work breakdown structure.

1. Level 1 code
   The overall organization may or may not be given a code. In the simple example, it is coded as '3', i.e. the first digit of the OBS code represents the total organization of project '4'.
2. Level 2 code
   The next digit, or two digits if there are a large number of departments or companies involved, represents the large organizational elements, i.e. the Level 2 OBS elements. In this example this would be as follows:

	OBS code
Design	31
Procurement	32
Works	33

3. Level 3 code
   The next digit in the OBS code represents the Level 3 OBS elements, i.e. the groups. For example, the groups in the design department (31) would be coded as follows:

	OBS code
Electrical design	311
Mechanical design	312
Instrument design	313
Drawing office	314

Thus each digit in the OBS code is significant and identifies an element of the project organization:

- The first digit identifies the project organization.
- The second digit identifies the department.
- The third digit identifies the group.

The code also identifies the 'parent-child' relationships, for example all groups with an OBS code having the same second digit will belong to the same department. Any other structures used, such as a cost breakdown structure would be similarly coded.

Cost accounts

When the two codes are combined, each cost account is uniquely identified and its relationships and position in both the WBS and OBS structures is established, as shown in Figure 6.7. For example, the cost account code 43-311 provides the following information:

1. Identifies the cost account to be the electrical design of the electrical sub-assembly.
2. The first two digits, 43, identify the cost account as being part of the work required to complete WBS element 43, that is the electrical sub-assembly. All other cost accounts with these first two digits also belong the this WBS element.
3. The OBS code 311 identifies this cost account as the work and responsibility of OBS element 311, that is the electrical design group.

Thus this code uniquely identifies the work, the major project element of which it is a part, and who is responsible for it, climbing right up the hierarchical tree.

Activity coding

Generally if an activity identification number is used in planning, for example 912, then it is also used in this coding system, that is 43-311-912. If a one dimensional WBS is used this would then be 43-912, and all activities belonging to the lowest level WBS element would be identified in this manner.

WBS dictionary/CRT catalogue

In conjunction with the WBS/OBS structuring and their coding, there should be a dictionary which defines the elements and cost accounts. This ensures that everyone involved in the project understands the meaning and content of each of these elements. The dictionary can be extended to include the scope of work, and the cost, resources and time requirements, and as such it is similar to the cost, resources and time (CRT) catalogue of the North Sea projects. This can then be extended to the work packages, or activities making up each cost account to complete the CRT catalogue. This systematizes and consolidates work that has always had to be done at some stage in the planning of a project, as for each activity of a project plan the estimated time, resources required and estimated cost must be identified. This is simply the necessary planning and control database for the project.

The sum of the cost and resources of the work packages or activities belonging to a particular cost account must equate to the cost and resources assigned to that cost account. In turn the sum of the cost and resources of the cost accounts belonging to the lowest level WBS or OBS elements must sum to that of the element. This must be repeated throughout both structures until the cost and resources for the project as a whole are obtained. This ensures that all costs and resources are identified at the lowest levels and that they can be systematically and reliably consolidated into the larger project and organizational elements.

The cost breakdown structure (CBS)

The cost breakdown structure (CBS) follows the same method of structure development, with Level 1 being the total cost of the project as shown in outline in Figure 6.8. Level 2 is then the major CBS elements, or primary code of accounts of the following:

- Bulk material.
- Equipment (EBS).
- Direct labour.
- Indirect labour.
- Sub-contracts.
- Other costs.

Level 3 is then the further breakdown, or explosion of these primary cost elements into their secondary code of accounts, as shown for the equipment:

- Electrical equipment.
- Instrumentation.
- Heating and ventilation.
- Mechanical equipment.

Level 4 is the further breakdown into the tertiary code of accounts as is shown for the electrical equipment:

- Diesel generators.
- Transformers.
- Batteries.
- Lighting.

This structure enables costs to be collected, analysed and reported for any cost generating item and consolidated in a similar manner to the other structures, for example equipment cost for a cost account, WBS project element or the total project, as shown for the three dimensional structure in Figure 6.9

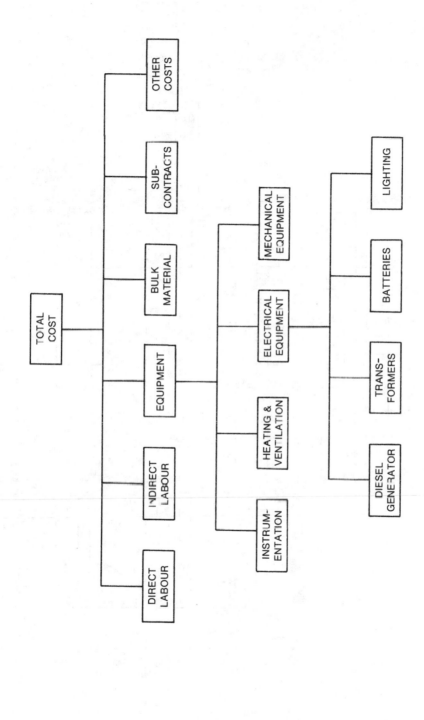

Figure 6.8 Cost breakdown structure (CBS)

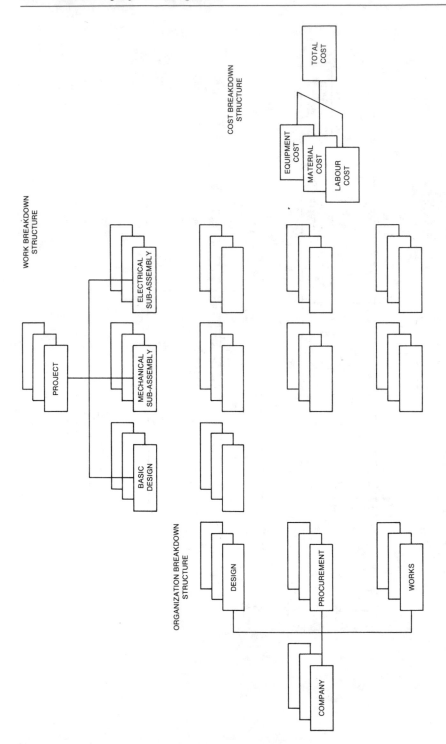

Figure 6.9   The three-dimensional WBS–OBS–CBS structure

Note

1. *Cost Management of North Sea Construction Projects*, AOC International.

Chapter 7

THE MODERN
APPROACH TO
PROJECT CONTROL

Planning and control of a project using the structured approach is hierarchical, multi-level, rolling wave, increasingly two dimensional and distributed, but integrated. This is a tongue twisting description of how planning and control of large projects is carried out today.

A large project may require thousands, or tens of thousands of activities effectively to plan and control it. In earlier decades this could result in project plans covering the walls of a very large room, or rooms. Such plans were totally unworkable, unintelligible, took far too long to create, could never be kept up to date and were generally not used to manage, plan and control the project. As a result projects were not effectively planned, could certainly not be controlled and therefore took longer and cost more then necessary.

One of the problems was also that different people required different levels of detail to carry out their functions. Senior management required a very coarse level of detail, or summary plan, first line supervisors required very detailed plans to organize, plan and control their day-to-day, week-to-week work, and middle managers required an intermediate level of detail.

Hierarchical, multi-level planning and control

As a response to these problems, although such single 'level' plans may be sufficient for the smaller project, modern methodologies use hierarchical, multi-level planning to overcome the problems of dimensionality and detail in larger projects. However, this multi-level approach does not apply only to the larger project with thousands of activities. As soon as the number of activities on a project begin to be counted in the hundreds, or even less, it is necessary and worthwhile to implement a multi-level planning approach. The number of levels of planning will be fewer than with the larger project, but the principles are the same.

All the project planning software packages use this concept, if only in their outlining facilities, or indenting of activities. They identify main summary activities, which in turn are expanded into their component, more detailed activities, which in turn are expanded into theirs, and so on. Summary plans can then be produced for each level of 'indentation' and thus you have hierarchical, multi-level planning. Hierarchical, multi-level planning is just the development and use of the plans for the project in differing levels of detail, or planning levels. These are accompanied by the resource and expenditure budgets to match each level of detail, and control information, analysis and reporting. Where the WBS approach is used, the levels of planning and individual plans are based on the structures and elements used.

Differing numbers of planning levels are used by different methodologies, companies and sizes of project. In many projects, four levels of planning are used:

- Level 1 – A summary plan.
- Level 2 – Intermediate level plans.
- Level 3 – Detailed plans.
- Level 4 – Short term detailed work plans.

These levels of plans are used formally and systematically to expand the project into its component activities, using the work breakdown structure. Each single activity or group of activities, in the higher levels of planning, is expanded into several activities or complete plans in the lower levels of planning. The different levels of plans are linked, together with the events or milestones as shown in Figures 7.1 and 7.2. In medium sized projects a summary level plan and one other level only would be required, while on larger projects four or more levels may be necessary.

Level 1 plan

A Level 1 plan is a summary plan which outlines the project in skeleton form. It is used throughout the project as a top management reporting and review document, but it is also the only plan possible in the early stages of the evolution or conception stage. It is thus also the initial project plan. At the conception stage of the project, it is only possible to build this highly aggregated plan, with the activities being large sizeable increments of work, such as WBS elements or cost accounts.

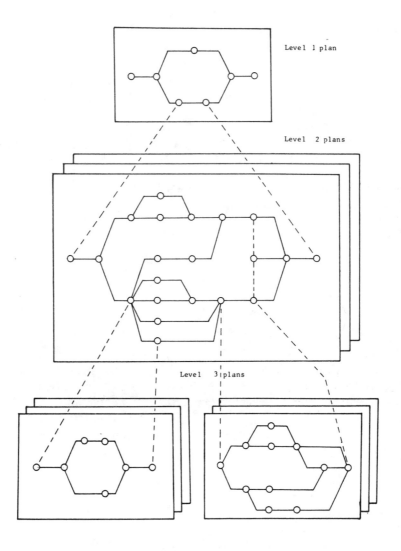

Level 1 plan

Level   2 plans

Level   3 plans

Figure 7.1   A hierarchy of network plans

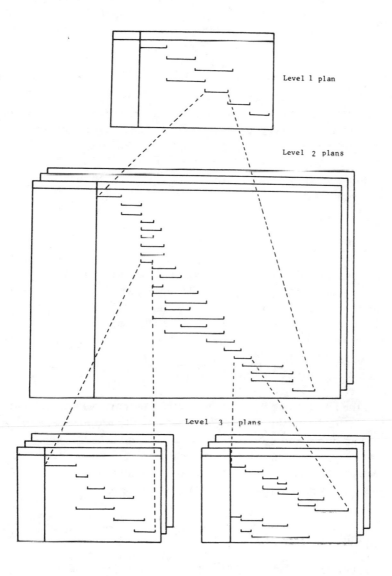

Level 1 plan

Level 2 plans

Level 3 plans

Figure 7.2 A hierarchy of bar charts

Such a plan shows only highly consolidated activities and the milestones associated with the project. It is a broadscale plan embracing design, procurement, manufacturing and/or construction, and commissioning. It contains the first approximate estimates of the timing of each of the stages, rough estimates of the resources required and the costs, and permits certain key points in the schedule and important interrelationships to be estimated approximately. It should highlight which parts of the total project should be emphasized and gives the first indications of requirements for material and equipment delivery dates. In the intial stages it acts as a strategic planning tool to establish the project objectives and strategies and can be quickly constructed and modified to show different ways of carrying out the project, yet allows key points to be located and important relationships to be determined. However, it is very coarsely scaled and on large projects cannot be used for the complete integration of the various project stages, which requires the development of a Level 2 plan. In one North Sea oil project, the Level 1 plan contained only 70 activities for more than a billion pounds of expenditure. In other projects, 15 to 20 activities cover the total project at this level.

Level 2 plan

This plan, or plans, shows the broad sweep of activities with both greater and lesser milestones included. It collects under one description sizeable elements of the project involving several to many detailed activities. It permits detailed examination of the project's structure, and allows relationships which exist between the various parts of the project to be seen and studied. It defines the limits between which individual activities, or groups of activities can move, without affecting project completion. There may be a separate Level 2 plan for every activity in the Level 1 plan.

Thus in the Level 2 plan the activities in the summary plan are expanded and planned in more detail. It is a middle management decision-making and control tool, and identifies responsibilities in the project and organizational structures. It is the first level of planning that requires the use of formalized and computer-based planning techniques. The activities in this plan are not of a size to permit day-to-day, or even week to week scheduling and control of work.

Level 3 plans

These will be the detailed plans of the work to be done, and are likely to be structured in several ways, particularly on a discipline basis. They thus tend to be modular plans, each module covering an element of the project, or the work of an individual group. Often, this level of planning is the lowest level of integrated planning and scheduling of the complete project.

Level 4 plans

The day-to-day, week-to-week work of individuals and groups must be planned and controlled within the overall framework of the higher levels of planning. This planning must take into account actual progress up to that time, actual resources available, material and information availability at the point of work. Thus the Level 4 plans tend to be short term, for example two to six weeks ahead, updated weekly, and produced for each small group, or element of work.

The use of job cards

Level 4 plans, in the past, were typically simple bar charts, but there is a growing trend to use job cards to communicate short-term plans to first line supervisors. Job cards are used in projects ranging from the repair of empty public authority housing to North Sea projects. Job cards detail a unique construction task of a single discipline, with its own material, engineering and quality requirements defined.

The work required to complete an activity or work package is detailed in a number of job cards, and they are issued to the first line supervisors or tradespeople to carry out the work. Job cards contain all the information required to complete the work, as shown in Figure 7.3, including the scheduled start and finish dates, drawing numbers, material quantities, codes and requisition numbers, and quality/inspection details. Job cards are sometimes combined into work packs associated with a particular entity to improve control of work. They thus represent the lowest level of short-term detailed planning, but are also a principal source of control information. Completed job cards confirm the completion of the work and can contain details of the labour and materials actually used and completion dates.

The use of job card systems is not confined to high-tech industries. Figure 7.4 shows the job card system used in an integrated project control and information system in the refurbishment of empty public authority housing. This handled 30 to 50 houses per week, requiring refurbishment at a cost of £2,000 to £5,000 each. These houses came into the contract on a random basis across a city's housing stock of 165,000. Figure 7.4 shows how the march-in documents were processed through the computer to generate work instructions, bonus targets, operational data for the contract supervision, house values for the quantity surveyor, planning data and thereafter cost and manpower performance indices.[1]

Rolling wave planning

Hierarchical planning normally incorporates the rolling wave concept of planning. In many projects it is not practical or possible, because of the lack of the necessary information to plan the complete project in any level of detail in its

JOB CARD (SHEET 1)

Code Number Description	Planned Dates Actual Dates	Discipline Area	
Description of work to be done	Quality Control and Special Requirements	Permit Requirements	Other Requirements
	Drawing Requirements		
Material Requirements	Comments Sign-off		

JOB CARD (SHEET 2)

Code Number Description	Planned Dates Actual Dates	
Supervision Man-hours	Direct Labour/ Trade man-hours	Indirect Labour/ Trade Man-hours

Figure 7.3   Typical job cards

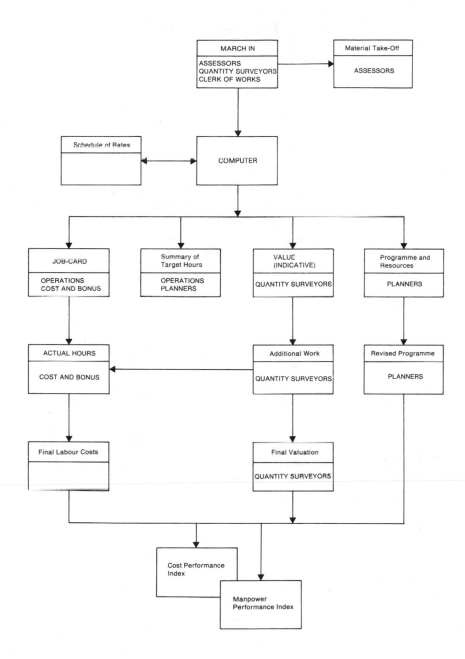

Figure 7.4   Refurbishment – job card system

early stages. Often the necessary information to plan the later stages of the project in detail is actually generated in these earlier stages. In such projects the use of the rolling wave concept overcomes this problem.

At the start of a project it is generally possible to create only a Level 1 summary plan outlining the complete project, with more detailed Level 2 or 3 plans for the early stages of the project. Then as more information is generated by these earlier stages, it may be possible to create a Level 2 plan for the complete project, and a Level 3 plan for the middle stages of the project. Later, as the middle stages generate more information, the Level 3 detailed plans for the final stages can be created.

This can be likened to a rolling wave, moving from left to right, that is from the start of the project to its finish. The work in front of the rolling wave is only planned in coarse detail to Level 1, or perhaps Level 2, with the crest of the wave being the development of Level 3 or 4 plans. Within cost accounts, or larger packages of work, the same concept can be used. The earlier activities are fully defined work packages or job cards, and the later are larger 'planning packages', in which the work is not fully defined and detailed. The Level 1, and later the Level 2 plans, integrate the Level 3 and 4 plans and provide a framework for this rolling wave planning.

Project control methodolgies and hierarchical planning

Different modern methodologies use the hierarchical planning approach in different ways and the following descriptions outline some of these applications:

- An individual project for a module or link up in a North Sea oil platform.
- A large US project management contractor.
- PRINCE methodology.
- C.Spec. applications
- Mega-project applications.
- Multiple projects.

North Sea project

Level 1

The top tier, or Level 1 network, will often be a simple linked bar chart in logical structure, containing only milestone events, and will be used for reporting to the client or the contractor steering committee. It will usually equate to a similar Level 1 budget dataset within cost control.

Level 2

The Level 2 network is the overall master schedule which is used to record intermediate milestones by stage and the main system interfaces. Line management will use this schedule to identify problem areas and trends and react to them.

Level 3

Level 3 networks are the detailed construction schedules. There may be several, perhaps one for each stage with sub-nets for specific activities within a given sub-system and discipline. They are the basic control documents for control of offshore construction and are the lowest level at which formal scheduling is carried out.

Level 4

Level 4 planning is represented by job cards, organized into sequence within their parent activity schedule dates.

The method of linking these levels allows consistent planning and progress data to be summarized upwards from the Level 4 job cards into condensed reports which are suitable for use at various project management levels. In the reverse direction early start and finish dates are passed to the dependent reports and thence to the material registers. This allows 'lookahead' reports to be produced of, say, 14- and 56-day timespans and features the job cards in these windows as well as lists of materials to be expedited.[2]

A large US project management contractor

Level 1

Milestone schedule.

Level 2

Project summary schedule, covering engineering, procurement and construction.

Level 3

Intermediate schedules structured by phase, system, discipline, facility, module and commodity.

Level 4

Detailed schedules covering such items as specification, drawing and task control, and rolling wave schedules for six months, detailed two-week schedules and start-up.

PRINCE

The PRINCE methodology for UK government-sponsored information technology projects uses the hierarchical, multi-level approach based on product breakdown structures, that is WBS. In addition it emphasizes the division of the project into stages, which are key control or decision points and usually involve the completion of a main product or products. Each of these stages has appointed a stage manager who is accountable and responsible for that stage. It uses a 'set' of of two linked plans: the technical plan, or work schedule, and the resource plan. The following levels of planning are used for both plans on a linked basis.

Level 1

A top level technical and resource plan produced at the initiation stage, showing the main products, activities and resources.

Level 2

Technical and resource plans for each 'stage' of the project showing all products, activities and resources for that stage. This may only be developed towards the end of the previous stage.

Level 3

Detailed technical and resource plans for work within a stage, used for the detailed planning and control of the main activities.

Level 4

Individual work plans detailing activities to specific people. These do not generally have accompanying resource plans.

In addition, Exception plans are produced at any point or level, when a deviation in cost or time is identified which exceeds a certain level of tolerance. These show the appropriate actions to deal with the deviation and the knock-on effects.

The above description of hierarchical multi-level planning covers its application to single dimensional structuring. This structuring may be explicit with a WBS defined, or simply implicit in the way the plans were made. However hierarchical, multi-level planning also applies to the classical, two dimensional approach in structuring a project.

Hierarchical multi-level planning in a structured project (C.Spec.)

Traditionally projects have been planned along the project axis or 'dimension', that is the plans were implicitly structured to outline what was required to complete the project deliverable and its component parts. In the simple example given in Chapter 6 (p.125) this would involve planning the work required to complete the basic design, mechanical sub-assembly, electrical sub-assembly and the final assembly. Planning and control in this project dimension is necessary to integrate the work of all the organizational groups who contribute to the project and to its individual elements, as defined in the WBS.

Sometimes, in addition, somewhat as an afterthought, responsibilities for the work or disciplines involved are assigned, and 'sorted output' used to produce plans for the principal organizational elements or disciplines involved. In the simple example this would be design, procurement and works, or at a lower level electrical design, drawing office, etc. This results in plans structured in an organizational dimension as well as the traditional project dimension, but more or less on an ad hoc basis. Yet, this organizational dimension is the one in which people and groups are managed, and organized. It is critical that not only is the work of these groups planned and controlled, but also that their performance is measured and reported.

After all, planning is concerned with who does what, when; manpower planning on an ad hoc sorted resource output is inadequate to manage the groups, departments and companies involved. Although there may be managers in charge of project elements, the resources, that is the skilled staff and labour employed, are more likely to be managed on a functional discipline or trade basis, and their work must be planned and controlled on that basis, as well as on a project element basis.

Thus planning and control in this organizational dimension is also necessary to integrate the work carried out by each organizational element on all of the project elements to which it contributes. In addition the move towards emphasizing personal accountability and responsibility of group managers at all levels, and the use of the contractor/consignee concept necessitates planning and control oriented to this organizational dimension.

The principal differences between planning based on the OBS and the more traditional ad hoc discipline planning, are that it is systematic and produces a consolidated hierarchy of plans. Thus the plans for individual functional groups or disciplines are consolidated into departmental or company plans, which in turn are consolidated into higher level organizational element plans.

Therefore, if it is to be fully effective, planning and control of a project should be carried out in two dimensions, namely that of the project and its WBS elements, and that of its organization and its OBS elements. Although the use of hierarchical, multi-level planning and control can be applied independently of the use of a structured approach, it finds its full expression when this approach is used. The levels of planning used are then the levels in both of the structures, and the individual plans used at each level are those for each of the elements at that level.

In order to illustrate hierarchical planning in two dimensions in a structured situation, consider the simple example. The common foundation block, or planning module is that of the cost account. The plans, that is the schedule, resource budget and expenditure budget, of the individual cost account are integrated and consolidated in the vertical dimension to give the plans for the lowest level WBS element. Similarly the plans of the individual cost accounts are integrated and consolidated in the horizontal or organizational dimension to give the plans for the lowest level OBS elements. Thereafter the plans for these lowest level elements in both dimensions are integrated and consolidated to give the plans for the higher level WBS and OBS elements right up to the complete project and organization plans.

Figure 7.5 shows the hierarchy of plans in Gantt chart form for the simple example, structured in the project dimension. The foundation blocks of these plans are the individual cost account plans, as shown for the work of the electrical design group on the electrical sub-assembly, that is cost account 311-43. These cost account plans are each a discrete planning and reporting module for the work of one organizational group on one WBS element. This planning module would be accompanied by its associated resource and expenditure budgets.

The plans for its parent lowest level WBS element, that is, the electrical sub-assembly, integrates and consolidates the plans of all the organizational groups contributing to its completion. This includes the cost account plan plus the plans for these other cost accounts:

- 311-43 Electrical design.
- 313-43 Instrument design.
- 314-43 Drawing office.
- 321-43 Purchasing.
- 321-43 Expediting.
- 331-43 Fabrication.
- 332-43 Assembly.

The process is repeated for the next level of the WBS structure, which in this case is the complete project, by integrating and consolidating the plans, resource and expenditure budgets of all WBS Level 2 elements. This creates a hierarchy of plans on the project dimension as shown in Figure 7.5:

- Level 1 is the summary plan for the project.

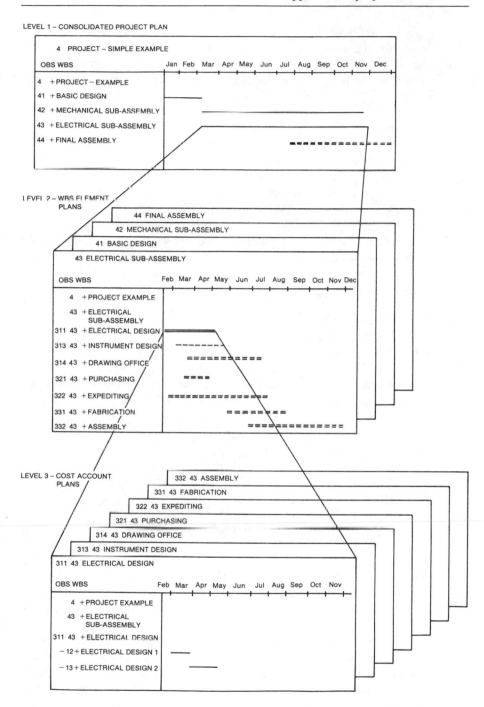

Figure 7.5   Hierarchical planning based on the work breakdown structure

- Each Level 2 WBS element will have its own Level 2 plan, as shown for the electrical sub-assembly.
- The individual Level 3 plans will be the plans for each cost account, as shown for the work of the electrical design group on the electrical sub-assembly.

Figure 7.6 shows the hierarchy of plans for the simple example structured in the organization dimension. The foundation block planning modules are the same cost account plans as in the hierarchy of plans structured in the work or project dimension, but they are arranged differently. For example, the work of the electrical design group on the electrical sub-assembly, coded 311-43, is the same planning module as shown in Figure 7.5, and is a foundation block for both planning hierarchies.

The schedule, resources and expenditure budgets for its parent Level 3 OBS element, that is the total work on this project of the electrical design group, are then obtained by consolidating the plans for the cost account it is responsible for, as shown below:

- 311-41 Basic design.
- 311-42 Mechanical sub-assembly.
- 311-43 Electrical sub-assembly.

Similarly the plans for the design department consolidate the plans of the Level 3 OBS elements, that is the various design groups which make up the department:

- 311 Electrical design.
- 312 Mechanical design.
- 313 Instrument design.
- 314 Drawing office.

This process is repeated for each level of breakdown until the consolidated plan, structured on an organizational basis, is obtained. At each level, these consolidated plans can be exploded into greater detail, when required. Although this is somewhat elaborate for the simple example, it is shown to demonstrate the application of two dimensional hierarchical planning. This creates the hierarchy of plans for the project in the organizational dimension, as shown in Figure 7.6:

- Level 1 is the summary plan for the total organization.
- Level 2 plans are the consolidated plans for the Level 2 OBS elements, that is for each department involved, as shown for the design department.
- Level 3 plans are those for Level 3 OBS elements, as shown for the electrical design group, that is for the groups which make up the department.
- Level 4 plans are the plans for each cost account, as shown for the

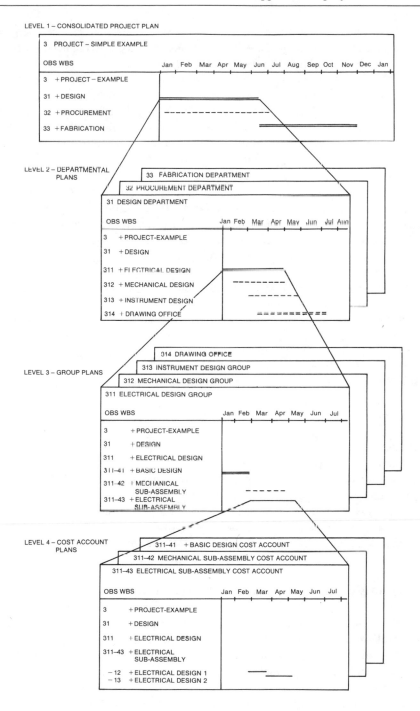

Figure 7.6   Hierarchical planning based on the organization breakdown structure

electrical design on the electrical sub-assembly. This is of course, identical to the Level 3 Plans for the WBS dimension, that is, the cost account plans are the basic building blocks.

This permits consolidation and summarization for each level, yet also permits a full expansion of all plans when required. The mechanism for carrying this out is the coding system based on these structures, which automatically consolidates the cost account plans and the control analysis and reporting on both the WBS and OBS structures, such that each is consistent with the other and they are totally integrated. All that is required is that the basic project plans – schedules, resource and expenditure budgets – are created using a modular approach based on the cost account plans within the project WBS and OBS structures. Modern software and the coding system enables the user to produce plans and reports which are structured, integrated and consolidated or exploded in any way that the coding system is designed, at any level of detail, with only a few key strokes on the terminal. A summary plan or report can be produced for any element, and if there are problems it can be exploded into greater detail for the total element, or any component part of it.

Thus the cost accounts, each WBS and OBS element, and their managers have the factors defined for them in the same manner as the cost account and the overall project, with in particular one person totally accountable and responsible for each. Each group, department, division, or company, and each project WBS element, and organizational unit can have its own real or pseudo-contract on the contractor/consignee principle.

Planning the very large project

The planning of the very large project, sometimes termed a giant or mega-project is more critical than ever to its efficient management and control. A very large project is generally viewed as a number of separate medium-sized to large projects, and represents a special case of multi-project management. In the following discussion, for the sake of simplicity, a very large project will be termed a 'programme' , though in practice programme and project are inter-changeable.

There are two principal variations in how such a large project can be planned:

- Where resources are shared between projects, planning is integrated in whole or in part, as will be described later in relation to multiple projects.
- Planning is decentralized, with parts of the project being planned separately, and integration occurring at Level 1 plans, or perhaps Level 2 plans.

Typically the owner company, or its project management contractor, would carry out the overall programme planning and control, involving the integration of every contributing company's work, and the bulk of the work on the programme will be carried out by a number of construction or manufacturing companies who will have contracts for the various projects which make up the programme. Each of these companies will have their own project management staff and will be supervised by either or both of the owner's and the programme manager's staff. These companies will view their contracts as completely separate projects, and the programme manager's staff will supervise them, both as separate projects and as part of the interlinked programme.

It is in the planning of these very large projects that the hierarchical and rolling wave principles of project planning are essential. The number of levels of planning used can be greater than the three or four outlined previously, but not all would have to be integrated. The interrelationships required between the individual project plans which make up the programme are generally limited to key decision points or milestones, and the programme plans need only include these to give the necessary overall integration of the programme. The number of levels of plans and their integration will vary from one programme to another, and one example of such a hierarchy is as follows:

- Level 1 programme plan
  This will be a skeleton plan of the programme showing only the key programme decision points or milestones, with most of the activities being individual projects, contracts or phases of projects.
- Level 2 programme plan
  This is the consolidation of the individual Level 1 project plans into one integrated programme plan, and identifies the key programme interrelation points or milestones between projects.
- Level 2/3 programme plans
  It may be necessary in some cases, where there is much interrelationship between projects, to use another intermediate integrated plan, showing the minor key programme interrelation points or milestones between projects. This would be the consolidation of individual project plans, somewhere between their Levels 1 and 2.

Individual project plans

Below the above levels, separate project plans can be built for each project using hierarchical principles as described previously, and showing the programme's major and minor key milestones. Progress between milestones can be transferred from the individual project plans to the higher level programme plans to monitor and integrate the total programme. This system can work effectively when each project is handled by separate companies, each with its own manpower resources. Integrating the manpower plans of the individual projects into one programme manpower plan is only required where there are resources shared between projects. For example, in the owner or programme management company, the regional availability of labour, or where space and accomodation are limited, such as on an off-shore oil platform, or where the programme is nearing completion. In such cases, integrated functional planning must be carried out for the programme as a whole.

Multi-project planning and control

Where a company or a manager is handling several projects at the same time, and particularly where resources have to be shared between projects, it is essential that the planning and control of these multiple projects be integrated. The portfolio of projects being managed must be then looked on as one project. Thus many junior project engineers, who are handling several minor projects, are in fact handling what is, for them, a larger project, with many of the problems outlined in this chapter. Common examples of this situation are as follows:

1.   An owner company, for example, a major chemical company, which has several important projects underway at any one time, each at various stages of its life cycle and each probably with a different contractor.
2.   A contractor who has several projects each with a different client company.
3.   A factory with a mix of small and medium-sized projects, using its own resources and occasionally, when handling large projects, using subcontractors or contractors.
4.   A local authority with a large number of minor projects and a few medium-sized projects, using a mixture of direct labour and contractors.
5.   A junior project manager/engineer responsible for several minor projects, primarily using in-company resources, in a company where projects are secondary activities.

The major problem in such situations is the sharing of resources between the following projects:

1.   Key management personnel, i.e. project managers, design managers and supervisors, construction managers, and foremen.
2.   Design engineers, particularly specialists.
3.   Drawing office personnel.
4.   Directly employed construction labour, in the last two examples.
5.   Floating construction labour available on a regional basis.

Where resources have to be shared, it is necessary to carry out integrated planning of multiple projects in some form or other. The total availability of these key resources become constraints which must be recognized in the planning of the individual project. This integrated planning could be carried out in two ways: the plans for all the projects are integrated into one multi-project plan, or the sub-plans for each project for only the resources being shared are integrated in one multi-project functional plan.

When the projects are small there are few problems in integrating into one the plans for all the projects and in carrying out manpower planning. Simply by using artificial activities to impose delays on the starting of each project, or each stage of a project, multi-project planning can be carried out. Another level is added to the top of the work breakdown structure, for control purposes, which represents the multi-project, with the first level of breakdown being the individual projects. Even with larger projects it is physically possible, using computer systems, to integrate these plans together. These systems have multi-project options which can deal with the individual project with its own data file, but which can also consolidate these files and plans into one multi-project plan.

The principal difficulty with integrating large projects is that the total plan becomes very large and cumbersome and in practice it is not really necessary. The only integration between projects that is required is where resources are shared. Therefore it is simple, quicker and more flexible to integrate planning only for those functions which are shared. For example, a firm may be handling three projects at the same time, each requiring an average of 40 draughtsmen for five months, that is, a total load of 600 man-months, with a peak requirement for each project of, say 70 draughtsmen. If it only has 90 draughtsmen available and if it attempts to push all three projects through the drawing office at the same time, there will be total chaos and in-fighting between project managers for priority for their projects. If no other draughtsmen can be obtained, for example, by subcontracting or hiring temporary labour, there is no way that the drawing office work on these projects can be completed in less than approximately six and a half months.

If it is left to the system to muddle through there will be complete disorganization and it will probably take considerably longer to complete the work. The drawing office plan for all three projects has to be constructed on a logical and top management-imposed priority basis, with a significant constraint being the availability of draughtsmen.

Individual project plans would be constructed and the drawing office work for all three projects integrated into one functional plan, which would then be adjusted to level the drawing office resource requirements to that available, by establishing a priority for each project. The rest of the work on each project could then be planned around the drawing office constraint by inputting the necessary scheduled starts and scheduled finishes for drawing office work determined in the integrated drawing office plan. It may then be possible to expedite the highest priority project through the work prior to the drawing office stage, such that the bulk of the drawing office workload arrives earlier than previously planned. If this can be achieved the planning and balancing process is repeated so that the completion dates for the drawing office work would be staggered but not significantly delayed.

The same principle can be applied to any function which shares it resources between projects or parts of a project. When a large number of resources is shared between multiple projects, it will be necessary to carry out fully integrated planning as there will be many complex interactions between projects and resources. If this was attempted on an individual function basis it would require many iterations and people would become confused. Automatic computer-based resource levelling would have to be carried out with project priorities set by the planner, with limited man-machine interaction. This would produce a final integrated multi-project plan which makes sensible use of priorities to achieve the objectives of all the projects and the company as a whole.

Multiple projects in the minor project situation

The junior project manager/engineer responsible for several minor projects in a situation where projects are of secondary importance is a somewhat special case of multi-project planning and control. In the other examples quoted, projects, if not the primary activity of the organization, are of major importance and thus organization, systems and resources are project-biased. In this example the minor projects are of very much secondary importance. The contributing functional departments' primary activities are probably not projects, for example, they may be maintenance or manufacturing, the organization's information systems are not project-oriented and the project manager is probably in a weak matrix organization and is acting more as a project coordinator whose responsibilities far outweigh his or her authority.

In such situations the contributing organizations are primarily concerned with their mainstream activities and allocate only to projects resources not required for these activities. These projects are then generally under-resourced and only worked on intermittently, with resources being withdrawn every time there is a surge in demand from the mainstream activities.

These projects often take a long time to complete and are carried out inefficiently, with parts perhaps being completed quickly, if one department has spare resources and other parts taking forever, if the reverse is the case. Work is uncoordinated, both on the total project portfolio and for the individual project, and life is full of frustrations for the project manager.

The same principles that apply to the larger project and the multi-project situation, as outlined above, apply equally if not more so to this situation. The portfolio of minor projects must be considered as one larger project, with minor projects being completed and started as required, but all integrated together as follows:

1. A work breakdown structure must be established, with the first level of breakdown being the individual minor project. Often no further breakdown will be required.
2. The work breakdown structure and organizational breakdown structure must be integrated and cost accounts established, albeit in many cases these cost accounts may be quite small.
3. A hierarchical work plan must be made for the total project portfolio, with the first level plan made up of individual projects.

4. The overall manpower plan and budget must be established.
5. The individual contributing organizations' work plan, manpower plan and budget must then be established and agreed.
6. The control system must work in two dimensions, i.e. up the work breakdown structure for the projects and up the organizational breakdown structure for the contributing organizations.
7. A matrix of responsibilities can be established.

Each contributing organization will then know its total resource commitment to project work, which can then be compared to the forecast resources available in the light of past experience. If project requirements exceed the expected resources available then the work on the portfolio of projects would have to be rescheduled and balanced between departments. Once a resource commitment was agreed with each department and a period plan completed based on this, this level would be considered a contractual commitment. In some cases this may take the form of a minimum contracted resource level, with a variation above this level dependent on mainstream levels. Any planning would have to be adaptive, but coordinated between projects and departments to take advantage of increased resources available.

The project manager would then be able to manage a portfolio of projects and coordinate the work on individual projects and this portfolio, balancing the resources available with the resources required for any mix of project work. For example, if department A has resources above the minimum agreed level, which projects should it work on, what demands will it make on other contributing departments and how can they be met? The project manager will better be able to allocate priorities, identify bottlenecks, forecast completion dates and accept or reject new minor projects, or conversely forecast completion dates for them.

The monitoring of individual contributing departments' actual resource commitments and performance will enable the project manager to exert authority over them and to control their activities. For example, a department may have agreed to a minimum resource allocation to projects of 6,000 man-hours per month, with an expected average of 8,000 man-hours. Control information may show it committing only 4,000 man-hours per month, contrary to an agreed plan and senior management can then be brought to exert pressure to increase this, or conversely replan the work and forecast completion dates based on a new contract. Similarly, if 6,000 hours have been worked and only the equivalent of 4,000 man-hours of budgeted work have been completed. Thus even the most junior project manager/engineer in this situation is faced with the problem of handling the larger project and can benefit from the use of this other dimension of advanced project management.

Distributed, but integrated planning and control

There is some debate about whether planning should be centralized or decentralized; whether planners should be in a central staff group, or department, or decentralized to individual project units. In the early days of project planning, planning had to be centralized because knowledge of the specialist planning techniques was limited and computing was centralized. There are still strong arguments for the centralisation of planning including the following:

- There is a need for the standardization of systems and methodology across all groups and elements of the project.
- Planning needs to be coordinated and integrated across the project.
- Project managers have a central role in the planning and control of their projects, and planning must be under their direct control.
- There should be a top-down approach to planning a project, i.e the project manager or central group undertakes the planning and it is not left to uncoordinated and unskilled group and element managers, in a bottom-up approach.
- Grouping planners together in a functional staff group gives all the benefits of functionalization.
- The management, planning and control of a portfolio of projects requires centralized planning so that the projects can be managed and resourced as one large project.

Nevertheless, there are also strong arguments for decentralized planning:

- Human factors.
- Encouraging individual accountability.
- Planning cannot be considered in isolation from other factors.
- Problems of centralized planning in large multi-company projects.

Human factors

Unless the people responsible for the preparation of the plan have made a thorough and logical analysis, the plan will not be realistic. Similarly, unless the people responsible for executing the plan work in accordance with the information outlined in it, nothing will have been achieved by planning.

Centralized planning tends to emphasize the role of the specialist planner and the techniques used, to the detriment of the human factors involved. When plans are made by centralized planners acting on their own, there is a high probability that they will be unrealistic, as it is just not possible for the planner to be fully informed and to exercise critical judgement on what is said in the many areas and functions of a project. More importantly, the plans will be unlikely to be carried out, as human nature being what it is, most managers have their own way of doing their job, and dislike being told in detail how to do it. Effective planning requires the involvement of all those concerned, both to ensure the correctness of the plan, and to obtain their commitment to it. If this participation and commitment is not achieved, plans are unlikely to be realistic and they will not be used.

Encouraging individual accountability

If planning is centralized, then control and reporting also tend to be centralized. Centralized planning and control are not compatible with an emphasis on individual accountability, responsibility and the contractor/consignee concept. Each cost account, group and higher level WBS and OBS element manager must at the very least be involved in, but preferably carry out the planning and control of their individual responsibilities. Control must also start at the individual manager level, that is self-control of their own area of responsibility.

Mode of planning and organization

Whether planning and control are centralized or decentralized is only one facet of the decision. If planning is centralized, this almost inevitably means that the organization and management of the project, or portfolio of projects, is centralized, with all that entails. This may be effective for the smaller project but has many problems in the larger project, as discussed previously.

Multi-company large projects

The concept of totally centralized planning in a multi-company large project is not practical, and this is not solely due to the large number of activities and groups involved. Each company will tend to have its own methodology, systems and techniques, and it will simply not be possible to have totally centralized planning and control.

Distributed, but integrated project control

Project control should be neither centralized or decentralized, that is a top-down or a bottom-up approach; it should be both. Project planning and control does need to to be integrated, but it is also required to be distributed. Individual managers should plan and control their individual areas of responsibility, assisted by staff planners. However, these plans should be integrated into the overall project control system. The terms distributed and integrated are more appropriate than decentralized or centralized.

Planning and control should be a combination of the top-down, bottom-up approaches, with the emphasis changing as the form of organization changes through the life cycle of the project. Thus on a large project, there will be an emphasis on centralized planning and control at the early and later stages of the life cycle, with an emphasis on distributed planning and control in the middle, work intensive stages. In the hierarchical, multi-level planning approach, the Level 1 and possibly Level 2 plans may be made centrally, but the Level 3 and 4 plans may be made on a distributed basis.

Distributed planning requires the establishment and use of standardized methodology, systems and techniques, either throughout the project or at the top two or three levels of planning. This is backed up by the training of all the managers involved in their application and use. This is not to say that these managers need actually to do all the work involved in the planning process. They are unlikely to have the time available, or the same skills and speed in the use of the systems as the specialist planners. Specialist planners have an important role in assisting, or actually making the plans, but the plans made must be the individual manager's plans, prepared within the framework of the overall Level 1 or 2 plans, structures and coding.

In a multi-company situation, standardization of methodology, systems and techniques may or may not be possible. This is where the hierarchical multi-tiered WBS and CRT methods are applicable. When the overall project organization is divisionalized, has multiple organizational units, each perhaps using a different contractor, the WBS/OBS framework becomes multi-tiered. Each project division or organizational unit will be responsible for an individual major or minor WBS element, which will have its own dedicated OBS, or organizational structure.

There will be an overall WBS/OBS framework, and each division or unit will have its own WBS/OBS framework for the element in the overall structure for which it is responsible, as shown in Figure 7.7. This concept can easily be extended to include the common situation where the client company has a mirror image organization spanning all the WBS/OBS frameworks, where each separate structure is that of a separate contract. This is in fact multi-dimensional structuring and can be implemented using data base principles. This permits the integration of different structures into one system, with project data completely traceable through the hierarchy of structures. It allows multiple contractor structures to be mapped, chained and merged into one project wide WBS, and gives great flexiblity in the use of alternative structures for integration, planning, control and reporting. The main advantage of the approach is that it can handle multiple company control using different structures, different methodologies and techniques, yet can integrate them into one system. Standardization and integration are possible at Levels 1, 2 or sometimes even Level 3 in the overall WBS, and this integrates the distributed planning and control.

In this database approach the key components are as follows:

- Control elements
  These are the elements of the work which makes up the project, e.g. work breakdown elements, cost accounts or work packages.
- Relational data
  This defines the relationships between control elements, i.e. the parent-

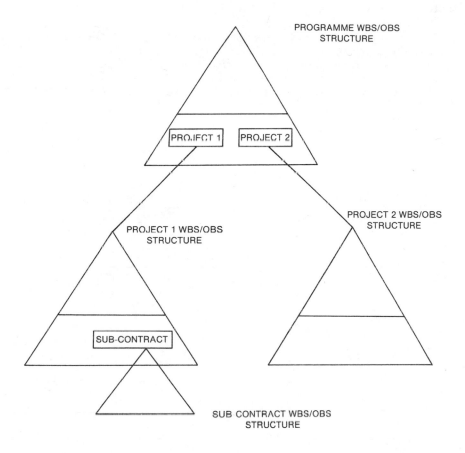

Figure 7.7   Multi-tired WBS/OBS structures

child relationships; this may involve multiple coding references, each of which may belong to a separate hierarchical structure
- Control data
  This is the usual control data, such as cost.
- Project structure hierarchy
  This is the set of parent-child relationships used for summarizing control elements.[3]

Thus, both on the smaller and the larger project, distributed, but integrated planning and control is feasible and should be used to combine most of the advantages of both centralized and decentralized planning in a modern methodology of structured project management, planning and control.

Notes

1. F.L. Harrison (1989) 'Structure and the Project Control and Information System', *Quantity Surveyors, Computers and Project Management Conference.*
2. *Cost Management of North Sea Construction Projects*, AOC International.
3. T.J. Calnan (1988) 'The use of structures in today's program management environment', *From Conception to Completion*, 9th World Congress on Project Management.

Chapter 8

PERFORMANCE ANALYSIS BASED ON EARNED VALUE – CHANGE CONTROL

Variance analysis

In the past the conventional method of control analysis was variance analysis. This measures the difference between two factors by subtracting one from the other to give a positive or negative variance. It can be used to show differences between actual progress and planned, and resources used against estimate or budget for example, the following are common variances in the control of projects:

- Scheduled start versus actual start.
- Scheduled finish versus actual finish.
- Scheduled time for an activity versus actual time.
- Scheduled date of a milestone versus the actual date when the milestone was reached.
- Budgeted cost versus actual cost.
- Measured value versus actual cost.
- Budgeted man-hours versus actual man-hours.
- Budgeted unit cost versus actual unit cost.
- Budgeted percentage complete versus actual percentage complete.

Although still used extensively today, variance analysis must be supplemented by other methods as it is an inadequate, often misleading, and sometimes meaningless, guide to progress and performance. For example, consider a simple case where the budgeted expenditure to date on a project is £820,000 and the actual expenditure is £850,000, giving a positive variance of £30,000. All this tells you is that expenditure is ahead of budget. It does not give you any of the following information:

- Whether you are on, above or below the expected cost performance.
- What will be the likely final cost of the project.
- Whether you are on, behind or ahead of schedule.
- What will be the likely completion time of the project.

In order to arrive at these factors a subjective assessment of the 'percentage complete' is often made to compare against these figures. Almost inevitably this is optimistic and is influenced by the actual figures. These subjective estimates are extremely unreliable, to say the least.

Thus variance analysis, when used on its own, suffers from the following problems:

- It is purely historic and not forward looking.
- It does not indicate performance clearly and simply.
- It is not sensitive enough to identify problems at an early stage.
- It does not use effectively all the data available.
- When used with 'percentage complete' it tends to be highly subjective and unreliable.
- It does not indicate trends.
- It does not integrate schedule and cost and thus it confuses the effect of schedule and cost variances, and their interaction.
- It is not generally structured and personalized to support individual accountability and responsibility.

Thus when the traditional variance analysis is used on its own, it is an ineffective way of analysing and reporting project progress and performance.

Performance analysis based on earned value

The modern methodology used in analysing project progress and performance uses 'performance measurement' based on 'earned value' concepts, which integrate cost and schedule on a structured and personalized basis. There are actually three elements of data required to analyse performance, from which much more information can be extracted than from the two element variance analysis. These elements are the budgeted, actual and 'earned value'. The earned value is simply the budgeted value, in terms of cost or man-hours, of the work actually completed.

The problems of subjectivity in the measurement of earned value are avoided by the use of the structured approach, whereby the work is broken down into WBS elements, cost accounts, work packages or job cards. The earned value of the work completed is then based on the budgeted value of these completed segments of work, plus an estimate of open, that is started but not yet completed, work packages or job cards. The level of subjectivity is thus much reduced, and quickly corrected as open work packages or job cards are completed.

In the simple case used for variance analysis, the three elements of data might then be as follows:

- Budgeted expenditure = £820,000
- Actual expenditure = £850,000
- Earned value = £750,000

If in addition the total budgeted cost of the project was estimated at £2,000,000, with a completion time of 50 weeks, this data can be used to generate the following control information to guide management decision-making and action:

Cost

Variance = £750,000 – £850,000
= – £100,000

The project is £100,000 over budget!

$$Performance = \frac{£750,000}{£850,000}$$
$$= 0.882$$

The project is obtaining 88p of earned value for every pound expended, that is, cost performance is 88% of that planned.

Forecast final cost = £2,000,000 ÷ 0.882
= £2,267,000

The project will be £267,000 over budget, if there is no change in performance.

Schedule

Variance (in cost terms) = £750,000 – £820,000
= – £70,000

The project is the equivalent of £70,000 behind schedule.

$$Performance = \frac{£750,000}{£820,000}$$
$$= 0.915$$

Schedule performance is only 91.5 per cent of planned.

Forecast final completion time = $\dfrac{50 \text{ weeks}}{0.915}$

$= 54.6$ weeks

The project will be 4/5 weeks late if there is no change in performance.

S-curve analysis

Additional information can be obtained, particularly on trends, by the interpretation of S-curve graphs of budgeted, actual and earned value as shown in Figure 8.1. These curves show that the work progressed as planned up to the end of Period 3. The rate of working then accelerated in Periods 4 and 5, but it did not achieve the planned rate of working. In particular the slope of the earned value curve is significantly less than the slope of the budgeted or actual expenditure. Unless the slope of the earned value curve can match that of the other factors, over-expenditure and schedule slippage will continue to increase.

Period to period analysis

There is a danger of underestimating trends if cumulative analysis only is carried out. Figure 8.2 shows the period to period data and the graphs of period to period cost and schedule performance. These show the position in this project to be more serious than shown in the cumulative analysis. The cost performance in Period 5 was only 0.82, indicating a final cost of £2,374,000, that is 18.7 per cent over budget if performance remains unchanged. Similarly the Period 5 schedule performance indicates that the project will be approximately 8 weeks late.

Although this simple case uses project expenditure as a basis, the same methodology can be applied to labour cost on its own, or often simply to the man-hours worked, which are often the alternative currency used in analysis.

C.Spec. performance analysis

Performance analysis based on earned value provides an effective way of analysing project data to produce information for management. Each manager and group can quickly and reliably receive measures of their performance. This can be used to increase motivation considerably, particularly when comparisons can be made with other groups working on the project. Performance measurement can be used with any structured methodology of project control but finds its fullest expression with the C.Spec. cost/schedule control systems methodology. This uses a jargon of its own which is increasingly being incorporated in project

EXPENDITURE

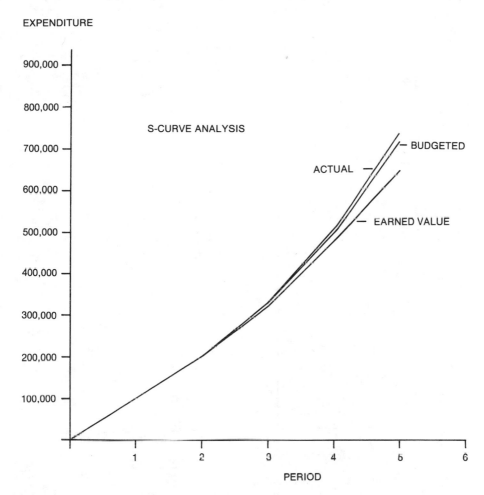

Figure 8.1 S-curve analysis

control software packages and with which all project managers should become familiar.

The terms used for the three basic elements of data, which can be applied to cost or man-hours, are as follows:

- BCWS – Budgeted cost for work scheduled.
- BCWP – Budgeted cost for work performed (earned value).
- ACWP – Actual cost of work performed.

Using these three data elements, it is possible quickly to evaluate the following for each cost account and WBS/OBS element:

- Cost variance   = BCWP − ACWP

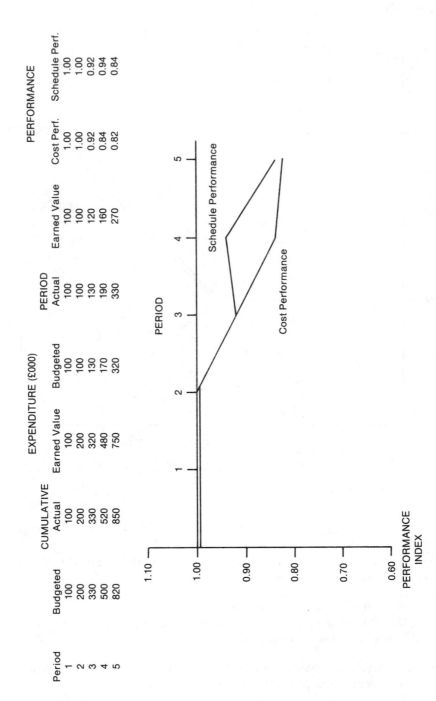

Period	CUMULATIVE EXPENDITURE (£000)				PERIOD			PERFORMANCE	
	Budgeted	Actual	Earned Value	Budgeted	Actual	Earned Value	Cost Perf.	Schedule Perf.
1	100	100	100	100	100	100	1.00	1.00
2	200	200	200	100	100	100	1.00	1.00
3	330	330	320	130	130	120	0.92	0.92
4	500	520	480	170	190	160	0.84	0.94
5	820	850	750	320	330	270	0.82	0.84

Figure 8.2   Period to period performance analysis

- Schedule variance (in cost terms) $\quad = \text{BCWP} - \text{BCWS}$
- Cost performance index (CPI) $\quad\quad = \dfrac{\text{BCWP}}{\text{ACWP}}$

- Schedule performance index (SPI) $\quad = \dfrac{\text{BCWP}}{\text{BCWS}}$

- Estimate to complete the project (ETC) $\quad = \dfrac{(\text{BAC} - \text{BCWP})}{\text{CPI}}$

 (BAC is budget at completion)
- Estimate at completion (EAC) $\quad\quad = \text{ACWP} + \text{ETC}$
 (forecast total cost)

In order to illustrate the terms used and this form of analysis, a 'simpler' simple example will be used, the details of which are shown in Figures. 8.3 and 8.4.

Budgeted cost for work scheduled (BCWS)

BCWS is simply another name for the time-phased budget against which performance is measured for the project and for the individual cost account. It is generally determined for each individual cost period and on a cumulative basis, though in small projects it may be determined on only a cumulative basis. For any given time period, budgeted cost for work scheduled is determined at the cost account level by totalling the budgets for all work packages scheduled to be completed, plus the budget for the portion of in-process work (open work packages) scheduled to be accompalished, and the budgets for the overheads for that period. Table 8.1 shows the BCWS for each period for the simple example.

Budgeted cost for work performed (BCWP)

The budgeted cost for work performed consists of the budgeted cost of all the work actually accomplished during any given time period. This can be determined by individual time period, and on a cumulative basis. At the cost account level BCWP is determined by totalling the budgets for work packages actually completed, plus the budget applicable to the completed in-process work with open work packages, and the overhead budget.

 The main difficulty encountered in the determination of BCWP is the evaluation of work in progress (work packages which have been started but have not been completed at the time of cut-off for the report). As discussed previously, the use of short span work packages, or the establishment of value milestones within work packages will significantly reduce the work in progress evaluation problems, and the procedures used will vary depending on work package length. For example some contractors prefer to take 50 per cent of the BCWP credit for a work package budget when it starts and the remaining 50 per cent at its completion. Other contractors use formulae which approximate the time phas-

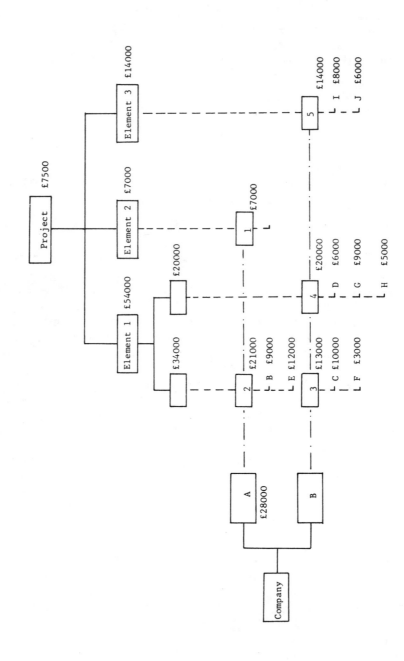

Figure 8.3   WBS and estimates for simple project

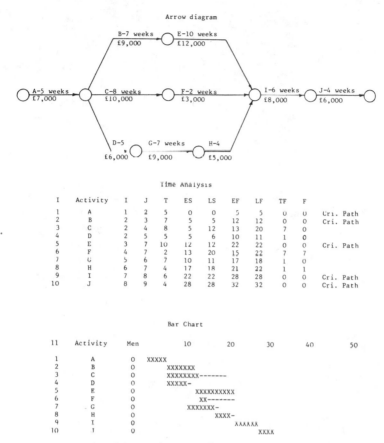

Figure 8.4 Project plan for simple example

ing of the effort, while others prefer to make physical assessments of work completed to determine the applicable budget earned. For longer work packages many contractors use discrete milestones, with pre-established budget, or progress values to measure work performance. The method used largely depends on work package content, size and duration. However, the use of arbitrary formulae should be limited to very short work packages. Table 8.2 shows the manual calculation of BCWP for Period 3 in the simple example.

Actual cost of work performed (ACWP)

This is simply the costs actually incurred and recorded in accomplishing the work performed within a particular time period. These may be collected at cost account level, though more commonly they are collected at work package level, or individual activity level, depending on the size of the activity.

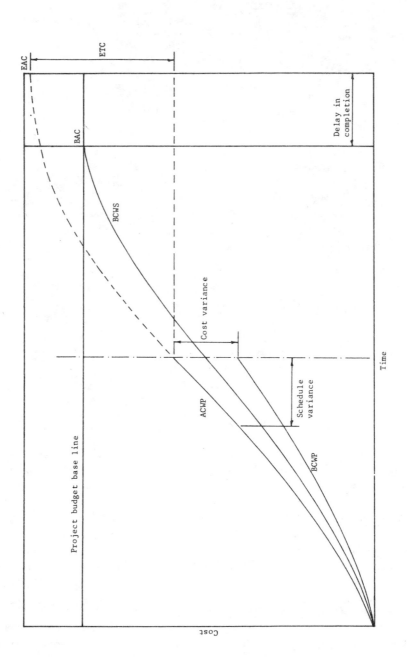

Figure 8.5   Typical project S-curve

Table 8.1   Manual calculation of project budget for cost accounts

Control centre	Estimate	Monthly budget (£) period							
		1	2	3	4	5	6	7	8
Cost Account No. 1									
Work package A	7,000	5,600	1,400						
Total	7,000	5,600	1,400						
Cost Account No. 2									
Work package B	9,000		3,857	5,143					
Work package E	12,000				4,800	4,800	2,400		
Total	21,000		3,857	5,143	4,800	4,800	2,400		
Cost Account No. 3									
Work package C	10,000		3,750	5,000	1,250				
Work package F	3,000				3,000				
Total	13,000		3,750	5,000	4,250				
Cost Account No. 4									
Work package D	6,000		3,600	2,400					
Work package G	9,000			2,571	5,143	1,286			
Work package H	5,000					3,750	1,250		
Total	20,000		3,600	4,971	5,143	5,036	1,250		
Cost Account No. 5									
Work package I	8,000						2,667	5,333	
Work package J	6,000								6,000
Total	14,000						2,667	5,333	6,000
Department A									
Cost Account No. 1	7,000	5,600	1,400						
Cost Account No. 2	21,000		3,857	5,143	4,800	4,800	2,400		
Total	28,000	5,600	5,257	5,143	4,800	4,800	2,400		
Department B									
Cost Account No. 3	13,000		3,750	5,000	4,250				
Cost Account No. 4	20,000		3,600	4,491	5,143	5,036	1,250		
Cost Account No. 5	14,000						2,667	5,333	6,000
Total	47,000		7,350	9,971	9,393	5,036	3,917	5,333	6,000
Total Project	75,000	5,600	12,607	15,114	14,193	9,836	6,317	5,333	6,000

Cost/performance analysis

Using these three elements of data, it is possible to carry out an analysis of performance which integrates schedule and cost. Combining this with the work breakdown structure permits this analysis to be carried out at will, for any part of the project, for any contributing organization and for the project as a whole. On larger projects, these comparisons are carried out for the latest time period, and on performance to date, that is, on a cumulative basis, whereas on smaller projects they are sometimes carried out on only a cumulative basis.

Cost variance shows whether the work done costs more or less than was estimated, and schedule variance will give a cost measure of how far behind, or ahead of schedule is the cost account, work breakdown structure item or the project. Estimates to complete (ETC) and estimate at completion (EAC) produced by this method are mechanistic methods of forecasting final costs, but do tend to show the outcome if no improvement is made or action is taken. In essence they challenge 'Show why we should not take these as the likely outcome'.

This form of analysis can also be shown graphically using S-curves, both for the total project and for individual cost accounts. Figure 8.5 shows an S-curve for a typical project. The cumulative data elements are plotted as shown, and both the cost and schedule variances are clearly shown. In addition it can graphically show the estimate to complete (ETC) and estimate at completion (EAC). Figure 8.6 shows a similar analysis for a cost account in the simple example.

Cost variance and schedule variance when considered together, give an integrated picture of the position of the project, or individual cost account, as shown in Table 8.3.

Tables 8.4 and 8.5 show the performance analysis reports for Periods 2 and 3 for the simple project shown in Figure 8.3. To illustrate the terms used, consider the cumulative performance analysis for Cost Account 2 in Period 3 as shown in Table 8.5.

Cost variance analysis

The comparison of BCWP and ACWP shows whether completed work has cost more or less than was budgeted for that work, for example:

$$\begin{aligned} \text{Cost variance} &= \text{BCWP} - \text{ACWP} \\ &= 7650 - 8370 \\ &= -720 \end{aligned}$$

Thus the cost account is costing more than budgeted. Analysis of the differences should reveal the factors contributing to the variances, such as poor initial

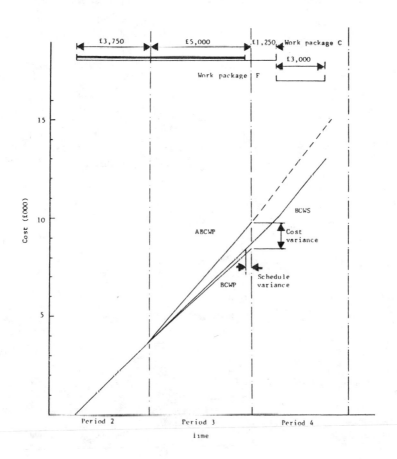

Figure 8.6   S-curve for Cost Account 3

Table 8.2   Calculation of budgeted cost of work performance (BCWP) for Period 3

	Estimate	% complete	Cumulative BCWP	Previous BCWP	BCP for period
Cost Account No. 1					
Work package A	7,000	100	7,000	7,000	0
Total	7,000	100	7,000	7,000	0
Cost Account No. 2					
Work package B	9,000	85	7,650	3,240	4,410
Work package E	12,000	0	0	0	0
Total	21,000	36	7,650	3,240	4,410
Cost Account No. 3					
Work package C	10,000	85	8,500	3,800	4,700
Work package F	3,000	0	0	0	0
Total	13,000	65	8,500	3,800	4,700
Cost Account No. 4					
Work package D	6,000	100	6,000	3,600	2,400
Work package G	9,000	0	0	0	0
Work package H	5,000	0	0	0	0
Total	20,00	30	6,000	3,600	2,400
Cost Account No. 5					
Work package I	8,000	0	0	0	0
Work package J	6,000	0	0	0	0
Total	14,000	0	0	0	0
Department A					
Cost Account No. 1	7,000	100	7,000	7,000	0
Cost Account No. 2	21,000	36	7,650	3,240	4,410
Total	28,000	52	14,650	10,240	4,410
Department B					
Cost Account No. 3	13,000	65	8,500	3,800	4,700
Cost Account No. 4	20,000	30	6,000	3,600	2,400
Cost Account No. 5	14,000	0	0	0	0
Total	47,000	31	14,500	7,400	7,100
Total Project	75,000	39	29,150	17,640	11,510

Table 8.3   Cost and schedule variance

BCWS	BCWP	ACWP	Cost variance	Scheduled variance	Analysis
4	4	4	0	0	On schedule, on cost
4	4	3	1	0	On, schedule, under cost
4	4	5	−1	0	On schedule, over cost
3	4	4	0	1	Ahead of schedule, on cost
3	4	3	1	1	Ahead of schedule, under cost
3	4	5	−1	1	Ahead of schedule, over cost
5	4	4	0	−1	Behind schedule, on cost
5	4	3	1	−1	Behind schedule, under cost
5	4	−5	−1	−1	Behind schedule, over cost

estimate for the task, technical difficulties requiring additional resources, the cost of labour and materials different from planned, or a combination of these or other factors.

Schedule variance analysis

Comparisons of BCWS with BCWP relate work completed to work scheduled during a given period of time, for example:

$$
\begin{aligned}
\text{Scheduled variance (in terms of cost)} &= \text{BCWP} - \text{BCWS} \\
&= 7650 - 9000 \\
&= -1350
\end{aligned}
$$

Thus this cost account is significantly behind schedule.

Although this provides a valuable indication of schedule status in terms of monetary value of work accomplished, it may not clearly indicate whether or not schedule milestones are being met, since some work may have been performed out of its planned sequence. A formal time scheduling system must therefore be used to provide the means of determining the status of specific activities or milestones. For example, Figure 8.7 shows the integration of the cost and schedule analysis at the end of the third month in this example.

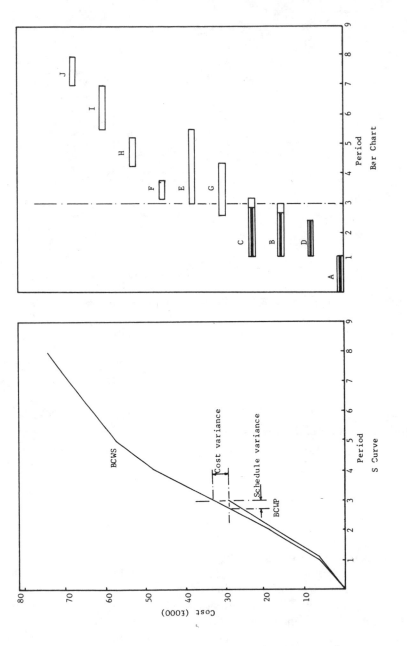

Figure 8.7   Integration of cost and schedule

Table 8.4 Performance report for Period 2

a) PERFORMANCE ANALYSIS FOR PERIOD 2

Cost acc. number	Budgeted cost Work sch.	Work pe.	Actual cost Work pe.	Variance Schedule	Cost	Perf. index Schedule	Cost
1	1400	1450	2150	50	−700	1.03571	0.674418
2	3857.13	3240	3270	−617.13	−30	0.840002	0.990825
3	3750	3800	3825	50	−25	1.01333	0.993464
4	3600	3600	3672	0	−72	1	0.980392
5	0	0	0	0	0	0	0
PROJECT	12607.1	12090	12917	−517.1	−827	0.958993	0.935875

b) CUMULATIVE PERFORMANCE ANALYSIS FOR PERIOD 2

Cost acc. number	Budgeted cost Work sch.	Work pe.	Actual cost Work pe.	Variance Schedule	Cost	Perf. index Schedule	Cost			
1	7000	7000	7700	0	−700	1	0.90909	7000	7700	−700
2	3857.13	3240	3270	−617.13	−30	0.840002	0.990825	21000	21194.4	−194.4
3	3750	3800	3825	50	−25	1.01333	0.993464	13000	13085.5	−85.5
4	3600	3600	3672	0	−72	1	0.980392	20000	20400	−400
5	0	0	0	0	0	0	0	14000	14000	0
PROJECT	18207.1	17640	18467	−567.1	−827	0.968852	0.955217	75000	78516.2	−3516.2
DEPT. A	10857	10240	10070	−6.7	−730	0.943	0.933	28000	30010	−2010
DEPT. B	7350	7400	7497	50	−97	1.001	0.987	47000	47610	−619
PROJECT (BY DEPT.)								75000	77679	−2629

c) WORK PACKAGE ANALYSIS

WP	Budget	Actual	Variance
1	7000	7700	−700

Table 8.5   Performance report for Period 3

a)   PERFORMANCE ANALYSIS FOR PERIOD 3

Cost acc. number	Budgeted cost Woek sch.	Work pe.	Actual cost Work pe.	Variance Schedule	Variance Cost	Perf. index Schedule	Perf. index Cost
1	0	0	0	0	0		
2	5142.84	4410	5100	−732.84	−690	0.857502	0.864705
3	5000	4700	6000	300	−1300	0.94	0.783333
4	4071.42	2400	3540	−2571.42	−1140	0.482759	0.677966
5	0	0	0	0	0	0	0
PROJECT	15114.2	11510	14640	−3604.2	−3130	0.761535	0.786202

b)   CUMULATIVE PERFORMANCE ANALYSIS FOR PERIOD 3

Cost acc. number	Budgeted cost Woek sch.	Work pe.	Actual cost Work pe.	Variance Schedule	Variance Cost	Perf. index Schedule	Perf. index Cost			
1	7000	7000	7000	0	−700	1	0.90909	7000	7700	−700
2	8999.97	7650	8370	−1349.97	−720	0.850002	0.913978	21000	22976.4	−1970.4
3	8750	8500	9825	250	−1325	0.971420	0.865139	13000	15026.5	−2026.5
4	8571.42	6000	7212	−2571.4	−1212	0.7	0.831946	20000	24040	−4040
5	0	0	0	0	0	0	0	14000	14000	0
PROJECT	33321.4	29150	33107	−4171.4	−3957	0.874813	0.880478	75000	85181	−10181
DEPT. A	1600	14650	16070	−1350	−1420	0.916	0.912	28000	30702	−2702
DEPT. B	17321	14500	17037	−2821	−2537	0.837	0.951	47000	55229	−8229
PROJECT (BY DEPT.)								75000	85931	−10931

c)   WORK PACKAGE ANALYSIS

WP	Budget	Actual	Variance
1	7000	7700	−700
4	5000	7212	−1212

Performance indices

On quickly scanning such a report, varying figures for cost and scheduled variance may at first glance not show up significant deviations clearly enough because of differences in magnitude of the figures involved. For example, a cost variance of £20,000 on one cost account with a BCWP of £200,000 is not as important as the cost variance of £20,000 on a cost account with a BCWP of £100,000. The use of cost scheduled performance indices overcomes this problem and provides at a glance a reliable indication of danger spots.

Cost performance index (CPI) $= \dfrac{BCWP}{ACWP}$

Schedule performance index (SPI) $= \dfrac{BCWP}{BCWS}$

A performance index of 1 then represents 'par' performance; an index performance of less than 1 represents performance poorer than planned; an index greater than 1 represents a better performance than planned. Thus in the above examples, the first cost account would have a cost performance index of 0.91 and the second cost account would have a cost performance index of 0.83, clearly a greater problem. In the case of Cost Account 2 in Table 8.5.

$$CPI = \frac{7650}{8370}$$
$$= 0.914$$
$$SPI = \frac{7650}{9000}$$
$$= 0.85$$

These variances and performance indices are required at the cost account level and at higher levels. Performance analysis of higher level cost accounts consists of direct summaries of the results of such comparisons at the basic level. It is thus relatively simple to determine project status and organizational performance at all levels of both the work breakdown structure and organizational structure from the cost account level. Cost favourable variances in some areas may be offset by unfavourable vaiances in other area, and higher level managers will normally see only the most significant variances at their own level. However, the accumulation of many small variances which may be adding up to a large overall cost problem, not attributable to any single difficulty, will also be evident.

In this simple example, the project is the only higher-level cost account, on the vertical consolidation axis, for which performance analysis is carried out. On the horizontal axis, performance analysis is carried out for the two departments involved. Table 8.5 shows this analysis carried out for these three higher-level cost accounts.

Forecasting the final cost

Forecasts of the final cost of the project and parts of it, that is, cost accounts and work breakdown structure level items, are pieces of information often requested of project managers by anxious senior management and are vital to the project cash flow, the viability of the project and sometimes decisions on whether to cancel the project after it has started. No matter what the reason, as soon as work has started, this information is frequently and urgently requested.

A great deal of management judgement should go into these estimates, but this system does provide a mechanistic way of estimating these final costs, as there is a danger of relying too much on subjective estimates. This analysis provides a starting point for more judgemental estimates and a benchmark with which to compare them. The method used is a simple extrapolation of performance to date. The forecasts are calculated for each cost account and higher-level accounts, including the project, for which a full performance analysis is carried out. They are calculated by dividing the budget for the remaining work to be carried out by the CPI and adding it to the actual cost of work performed, for example:

Performance to date (CPI) $= \dfrac{\text{BCWP}}{\text{ACWP}}$

Budgeted cost for the remaining work $= \text{BAC} - \text{BCWP}$

Estimate to complete (ETC) $= \dfrac{\text{BAC} - \text{BCWP}}{\text{CPI}}$

Forecast cost at completion (EAC) $= \text{ACWP} + \text{ETC}$

Using this method forecasts of the final cost for segments of the project can be made for the following:

1. Individual cost accounts that have been started.
2. Work breakdown structure items that have been started.
3. Organizational cost accounts that have been started.

Thus, forecasts of the final cost of all activities and cost accounts that have been started can be made, based on performance to date. In addition, using average performance to date, forecasts for the expected total cost of the project can also be made. In the example:

Performance to date (CPI) $= 0.88$

Budgeted cost for the remaining work $= £75,000 - £29,150$
$= £45,850$

Estimate to complete (ETC) $= \dfrac{£45,850}{0.88}$
$= £52,073$

Forecast cost at completion (EAC) $= £52,073 + £33,107$
$= £85,180$

One drawback is that at first sight no forecast can be made for those segments not started, except to take into account the average overall performance. This is where the hierarchical cost account structure permits a logical extrapolative forecast for many cost accounts not yet started. For example, where an organization is responsible for several cost accounts, performance on their initial cost account can be used to forecast performance in later cost accounts. Admittedly there are many factors to take into account, but the extrapolative forecast is a good starting point and any change in it must be justified. Similarly forecasts of final cost on higher level breakdown structure items, can be based on performance on the early work.

In this example Cost Account 5 is not started but the CPI for the department involved is 0.85. Using this as a measure of future performance the EAC for Cost Account 5 can be forecast at £16,451.

There are thus three methods of forecasting the final project cost:

1. The average overall performance to date.
2. Organizational performance.
3. Work breakdown structure performance to date.

In this example, only two methods are used, namely average performance to date on the overall project, and performance by the individual organization. This gives an EAC of £85,180 and £85,931, respectively, compared to a budgeted figure of £75,000.

A hypothetical analysis for the first three periods in the simple example might proceed as follows.

Period 1

The performance report for Period 1 is not shown, as the only work done was on Cost Account 1. The budgeted expenditure (BCWS) was £5,600; the actual expenditure (ACWP) was £5,500; and the package was estimated to be 80 per cent complete. Thus, earned value was £5,600 (80 per cent of £7,000, the total estimated cost) that is, BCWP. Work is thus estimated to be on budget and on schedule.

Period 2

The performance report for Period 2 is shown in Table 8.4, both for the individual period and on a cumulative basis. In both, the expenditure is approximately as budgeted and the performance indices are only marginally below par. The forecasted final cost, that is, estimate at completion (EAC) is only slightly more than the budget at completion (BAC). Apparently there is no cause for alarm. In fact there are several small signs of problems:

1. Schedule performance index (SPI) for Cost Account 2 is low at 0.84. This is

caused by the late completion of cost accounts which delay its start. However, the momentum of work seems to be approximately as planned and budgeted, so that this slow start appears to have been overcome.

2. The cumulative cost performance index (CPI) for Cost Account 1 is now reliably estimated at 0.91, being based on a completed work package. If this is used for Department A's performance, it raises the EAC for its work to £30,010; if used for the project as a whole it forecasts an EAC of £82,417 which is rather more worrying.

3. The CPI in Period 2 is 0.67 and this abnormally low value is caused by the system correcting for the previous period's optimistic estimate of percentage complete of 80 per cent, as against a more realistic value of 72 per cent as can now be estimated with 20-20 hindsight. This demonstrates how the system rapidly corrects and highlights previous optimistic subjective estimates of progress. It also calls into question the reliability of the percentage complete estimates of the three work packages that are open in this period. If they are similarly overestimated, then the project is heading for an overrun. However, it is early days yet, the signs are not conclusive, and the project manager would have difficulty in persuading other people, but at least would be alerted.

Period 3

The performance report for Period 3 is shown in Table 8.5 and the problems are now more obvious. Though the rate of expenditure is only slightly below budget, the work achieved for this expenditure is much less than expected. The significant pointers are as follows:

1. Both the SPI and CPI for the work done during the period are very low, indicating both that the work on the project is not going well and that the previous period's estimates of completion were highly optimistic.

2. The forecast final cost of the project (EAC) is now £85,181 based on overall performance, or £85,931 based on departmental performance.

3. Both departments' performances are well below par, with Department B's being especially low at 0.837 for schedule and 0.851 for cost.

4. Work on Cost Account 4 is well behind schedule and well over budget, that is an SPI of 0.7 and a CPI of 0.83.

Thus performance analysis using the earned value concept on cost centres, termed work packages, each looked on as a discrete sub-contract, and structured into cost accounts using the work breakdown structure, can provide effective control of projects. The size of the work package can be varied, according to the size of the project and the sophistication of the information system used. The schedule and cost variances, coupled with schedule and cost performance indices give sensitive and reliable indicators of progress achieved against plan and budget. The system also automatically produces forecasts of final cost for parts of the project and the project as a whole. The performance of contributing organizations is automatically monitored and gives an effective feedback to those involved. Hopefully the use of performance analysis will lead to more effective control of projects in the future than in the past.

Reports

Data overload

The presentation of the performance analysis reports shown previously is satisfactory for the simple example used, but obviously inadequate for the larger project where hundreds of cost accounts may be involved. In such cases the project manager is faced with a common problem of project management, data overload. In larger projects there is so much data required and produced for control that the project manager can be faced with iterally hundreds of pages of computer output each month, which there is no time to assimilate.

There is an important difference between data and information, and what may be information at one level of management, may be data at a higher level. Thus it is necessary to have a clear understanding of the difference between the two terms. Data can be defined as groups of non-random symbols which represent quantities, actions, things, etc. Information is data that has been processed into a form which is meaningful to the recipient and which is of real or perceived value in current or prospective decisions and actions.

Data analysis for information

Thus the project control and information system must be able to analyse the project data to produce meaningful information to all those involved. This implies that each manager involved on the project receives the informtion that is relevant to their responsibilities on the project, no more and no less.

Even if data are effectively analysed to produce this information, on the larger project this will still produce a mass of detailed information which needs to be consolidated and filtered or reported by exception.

If the project, all the component elements of it and all the functions involved are performing satisfactorily, that is, the project is progressing to plan and budget, there is no need to report additional detail. Similarly, if only one element or organizational function is showing a signficant variance, then only that element needs to be fully analysed and reported. In addition each manager involved on a project requires only that information relevant to thier area and level of responsibility.

Performance analysis information must be consolidated and summarized to provide the relevant information to each manager in the work breakdown structure and the organization breakdown structure. It must also be filtered, that is, significant variances must be highlighted by exception reporting, and narrative reports made as to the reasons for them and the correction action taken. Trouble-shooting time and effort need then be concentrated only on problems having a significant impact on cost and schedule.

Coding

The project control and information system thus depends on a coding system to identify the structure of cost summarization for both the work breakdown structure and the organization breakdown structure. The coding system must also be able to handle both the cost account or work breakdown element itself, for example, electrical drawing office – the cost elements involved are labour, materials, etc. This permits consolidation by work element or cost element, for example, higher level reports could examine consolidated labour performance as well as overall performance on major parts of the project.

Thus a coding system may have three reporting structure/summarization tables to facilitate this:

1. Work breakdown structure.
2. Organization structure.
3. Cost element structure.

The consolidation procedure should then be able to summarize data and information of any of these reporting structures, either separately or in combination. The work breakdown structure permits reporting in the way that work is planned and carried out while the organizational structure permits reporting on functional department or organizational performance. Reports at different levels would then give different amounts of detail from senior management to cost account manager.

Cost account report

The basic building block of the control and information system reports is thus the individual cost account performance report, as shown in Figure 8.8. This is sent to the manager of the cost account and shows the general performance analysis information, as described previously.

Higher level reports

The individual cost account reports can then be consolidated into the reporting structure as shown in Figure 8.9. Thus the senior management will receive the consolidated reports for all projects in which the company is involved; the client and contractor project manager will receive the consolidated reports for the

Cost Performance Report

Date : May 25 1984

Project	:Modular Robot	C.A.Name
Company	:A.N.Other	C.A.Manager_Title
Department	:Design	_Name
Rev. Date	:Jan.1984	

Cost Account:
:Electrical Drawing Office
:D.O.Manager
:F.L.Harrison

WBS Code : 1012104
CBS Code : 231401

Cost Element	Current Period					Cumulative to Date					At Completion		
	Budgeted W.S.	Cost W.P.	Actual A.	Variance WP-WS	WP-A	Budgeted W.S.	Cost W.P.	Actual A.	Variance WP-WS	WP-A	BAC	EAC	BAC-EA
D. Labour	35200	45000	54000	9800	-9000	70400	89750	108045	19350	-18295	105600	127126	-21526
L. O/heads	24640	29411	35293	4711	-5882	48280	58666	70617	9396	-11941	73920	88978	-15058
Material	2000	2500	2500	500	0	4000	5000	5030	1000	0	5000	7000	0
Services	10000	12000	12000	2000	0	25000	29000	29000	4000	0	30000	30000	0
Sub-Cont.	0	0	0	0	0	0	0	0	0	0	0	0	0
G&Admin.	10000	10000	10000	0	0	20000	20000	20000	0	0	30000	30000	0
Total	81840	98911	113773	17071	-14882	168680	202416	232662	33736	-30246	244520	283104	-38584
Man Hours	3200	4090	4909	898	-14882	6400	7618	9178	1218	-1560	9600	11566	-1966

Period- C.P.I.=0.87 S.P.I.=1.21 M/Hour P.I.=0.83

Cumulative- C.P.I.=0.87 S.P.I.=1.2 M/Hour P.I.=0.83

Figure 8.8 Cost account report

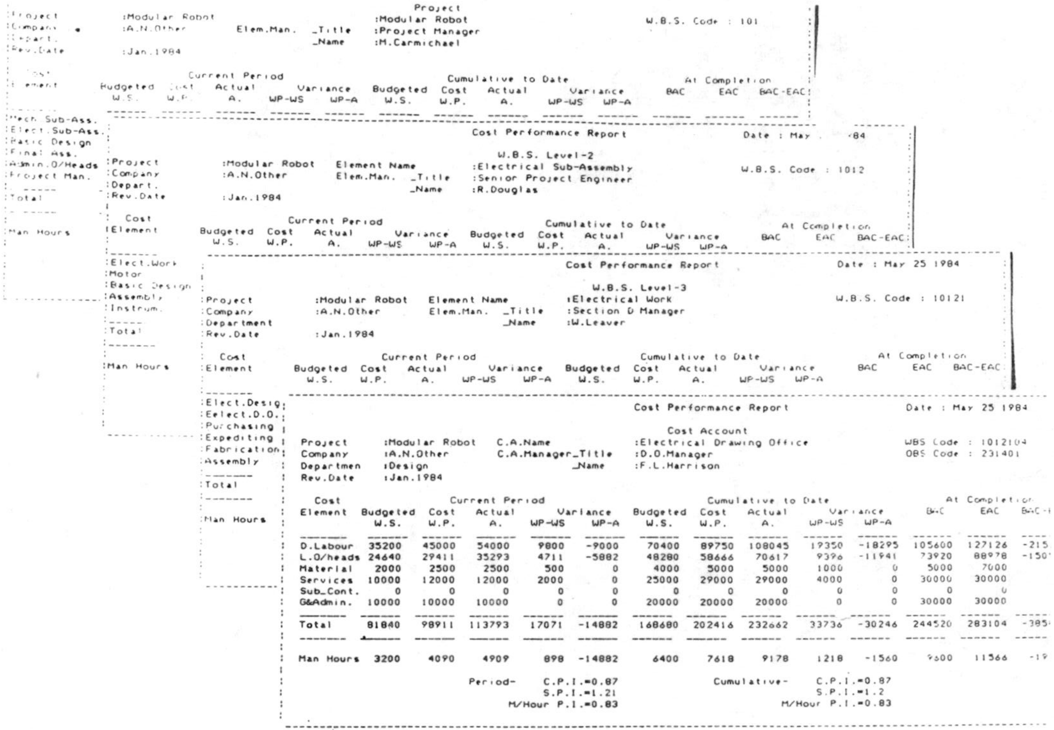

Figure 8.9   Hierarchy of reports

individual project; the drawing office manager will receive the performance report for the department's performance for all the projects going through the drawing office and the individual project; and the manager in charge of a WBS element will receive a performance report on that WBS element, and so on. Individual managers will receive reports for their span of responsibility at a level of detail appropriate to their level of operation.

Exception reports can be produced at any level by setting threshold levels for size of variance or deviation from the norm in performance indices.

Traceability

Hand in hand with this process of consolidated reporting must go the principle that variance or deviation from the norm of performance indices must be able to be traced downwards to their sources. Thus if a project is seen to have problems, it must be possible to look at the next level of breakdown, to see which Level 1 element is causing it. This process must be able to be continued to cost account level and the cost elements involved, and then if functional performance is seen to be in question, it should be possible to trace up the organizational breakdown structure to examine performance on other cost accounts and higher level elements. A simple example is shown in Figure 8.10.

If interactive computing systems are employed it is quite possible to sit at a visual display unit and carry out the tracing operation quickly and easily. However, no matter what system is used, this traceability is inherent in the coding structure used, together with the work breakdown structure integrated with the organizational breakdown structure. In the example shown in Figure 8.10, the project has a schedule performance index of 0.89 and a cost perform ance index of 0.95. If it is chosen to trace down the source of the deviation on the CPI the following become apparent:

1. The project report shows the problems are in basic design and the electrical sub-assembly. If it is chosen to trace down the electrical sub-assembly structure:
2. The next level shows the problem is confined to the electrical work element.
3. The next level shows the problem is in the electrical design and electrical drawing office. If it is then possible examine the electrical drawing office cost account report, as shown in Figure 8.8.
4. It is then possible to trace up the organization breakdown structure and examine performance on all drawing office work. This shows that schedule performance on the electrical drawing office cost account has been completed at the expense of schedule performance of mechanical and instrument work. It also shows an important cost performance problem in the mechanical drawing office which can be traced up its structure.

Project	S.P.I.	C.P.I.
Basic Design	1.0	0.9
Mechanical Sub-Ass.	0.7	1.02
Electrical Sub-Ass.	0.98	0.85
Final Assembly	-	-
Project Management	1.0	1.1
Central Admin.	1.0	1.0
Total Project	0.89	0.95

Electrical Sub-Ass.	S.P.I.	C.P.I.
Electrical Work	1.2	0.88
Design	2.0	1.0
Motor	1.0	1.1
Assembly	-	-
Instrumentation	0.89	0.95
Total Elect. Sub-Ass	0.98	0.85

Electrical Work	S.P.I.	C.P.I.
Electrical Design	1.0	0.82
Elect.Drawing Off.	1.2	0.87
Purchasing	1.0	1.03
Expediting	1.0	0.95
Fabrication	-	-
Assembly	-	-
Total Elect.Work	1.15	0.88

Work Breakdown Structure

Drawing Office	S.P.I.	C.P.I.
Mech.Drawing Off.	0.5	0.7
Elect.Drawing Off.	1.2	0.88
Inst.Drawing Off.	0.75	1.03
Total Drawing Off.	0.85	0.85

Organisation Breakdown Structure

Figure 8.10   Traceability of reports

Control of changes to a project

One of the identifiable common causes of delay, cost escalation and low labour productivity are changes to the project. Many, many projects take longer and cost more than necessary because of changes and additions to the original scope. It is quite common for changes to a project to add anything up to 50 per cent to the project cost and not unusual for them to add more. Thus one of the most important and, unfortunately, unpleasant and troublesome functions of a project manager is to control the changes to the project. Changes have the following detrimental effect on performance in project work:

1. They increase the cost.
2. They cause delay.
3. They reduce morale and productivity.
4. They worsen relationships among those involved.

Changes in design in project work typically lead to additional cost and time to completion. In addition to this extra cost and time, which may or may not be justified, design changes during the engineering and construction phases cost more and the work takes longer than the same work would have if it had been included in the original project specification. This is because, in addition to work having to be redone, the sequence of work is disrupted; not only must the design of the particular item concerned be changed, but all those items interrelated to it must be changed too. At the construction stage, changes are more costly still, because work, materials and equipment may have to be scrapped and design, materials purchasing and construction work must often also be done on a rush basis.

Though changes have a detrimental effect on morale and efficiency in general, this effect is multiplied in the manufacturing and construction phases. Whenever work has to be torn down or scrapped and repeated, labour morale and productivity is affected and this can lead to long-term effects not least in the area of industrial relations.

One of the worst effects of change is on relationships between the project manager or managers, and other managers on the project. It is the project manager's responsibility to resist changes unless they are absolutely essential to the objectives of the projects and in the company's interests. This forces the project manager into conflict in two ways. If the project manager is in the owner company, changes must be resisted which arise from that company's managers, and also changes must be negotiated with any contractors involved. Changes, as mentioned previously, disrupt design and construction work and are more costly than just the work directly involved. Thus the actual cost of changes is much higher than the work itself would make them, and they are very difficult to estimate accurately and to negotiate. In addition, there are often legitimate differences of opinion as to what is a change to the contract, or as to what are the cause and effect. Some contractors also tend to overcharge for extras, and make a significant percentage of their profits in this way. It is therefore often very difficult to disentangle these factors, and this uncertainty can cause differences of opinion and hence conflict. Probably the worst of these effects is on project managers' relationships with other managers in their own company, be it client or contractors. The differences of opinion and conflict that occur have often to be resolved at a very senior level in the companies involved.

Changes in a project can also lead to a breakdown of the control system. Sometimes actual progress, resource usage and cost are compared to planned values of these factors which have not taken into account changes and this leads to a totally misleading assessment of performance.

Changes may occur at any stage during the project and can arise for several reasons:

1. Changes in the specifications or scope of the project during the development stages. Changes to design occur legitimately in these stages, but often complex changes in scope or specification are proposed and accepted implicitly without adequate evaluation of the consequences in terms of time and money. Once the project specification and cost have been approved, changes in scope are very expensive and have a questionable value.
2. Late design changes are the most troublesome and expensive changes. They typically arise out of errors and omissions in the original design work, afterthoughts, and from the client company's attempts to keep up to date and incorporate the latest developments in technology. There is little alternative but to incorporate changes to correct errors and omissions, but afterthoughts and changes to keep up to date are a bone of contention in project work.
3. Changes due to safety or legal requirements. Here again there is little alternative but to include these changes in the project.
4. Changes which are justified or appear to be justified to improve the rate of return. The advisability of these kinds of change is debatable. The fact that a certain addition to a project is estimated to give a 30 per cent internal rate of return may not be sufficient justification to include it. Whether or not to accept this type of change should be a matter of top company policy. One view is that they are not acceptable because this type of forecast rate of return is often inaccurate and biased; estimates of the cost of changes are very difficult to make, as discussed previously, and thus the rate of return is also difficult to estimate.

   More importantly, if the project is, say, to build an oil refinery at a certain capacity, changes of this kind do not usually add any significant advantage on a company or market basis, and the objective should always be to carry out the company's top level objectives as cheaply as possible, consistent with satisfactory time and technical performance. Many worthwhile projects have been failures because of additions of this nature. If spare capacity is worthwhile, this should be a top level management decision and not some design engineer adding a slightly larger size of equipment.

5. Changes which are thought desirable. This is a significant area of conflict, particularly within companies. Operating managers would like certain additions for various reasons, sometimes worthwhile, sometimes simply luxuries; design engineers would like to add certain features, upgrade others or increase some equipment sizes. The project manager has to resist this type of change, and must establish a clear definition between 'musts' and 'wants', and only accept changes that must be made to meet the original scope and safety standards, that is, 'musts'.

In order to control change, and reduce the conflict within and between companies, the project manager should endeavour to achieve the following:

1. Implicit backing up by senior management of the manager's efforts to resist non-essential changes. The policies on changes to increase the rate of return on projects should be spelled out by senior management. If this is permitted, the rate of return used should be significantly higher than that used as a cut-off point for normal company projects. As far as possible a policy should be established and communicated by senior management on musts and wants.

    In other words, senior management must back up the project manager by saying 'no' to changes which are desirable, but not essential.
2. The original scope and specifications of the project should be as clear as possible. Factors like the policy of whether or not to allow for some spare capacity to allow for expansion should be spelled out by senior management.
3. At some clearly defined stage, no further changes must be permitted, excepting those that are absolutely essential for the success or safety of a project, that is, the project must be 'frozen' at some stage. The project manager would like this freeze to be at the development stage, but other managers would prefer it to be at the construction or manufacturing stage. The earlier the project is frozen, the lower the cost and the delay to the project caused by changes.
4. Finally, a change control system must be set up.

Change control systems

Thus the control of changes to a project is one of the most critical activities of a project manager. Although the number and scale of changes will vary with the stage of project specification, for example, between a fully specified fixed-price contract and a research, development, design and manufacturing project, the importance of the control of change does not. One would think that change would be very limited on a fixed-price, fully defined project, with completed drawings and perhaps bills of quantities, but in practice, this is not the case.

It is in the larger projects that the control or in reality the management, of change really reaches a climax. Although change must be resisted, it is generally impossible to avoid it in the larger project. It must be accepted at the outset that change is going to occur and change control systems must be set up to manage and control change as a way of life.

In order to identify, analyse and control changes to a project, the project manager must set up a system to handle these changes. This system must perform the following tasks:

1. Identify changes from the original scope.
2. Forecast their cost and their effect on other work and the time required for them.
3. Subject them to managerial analysis and decision.
4. Record actual figures on them.
5. Highlight them to senior management.
6. Set up a system for solving disputes with the minimum of conflict.
7. See that the changes are implemented.

The implementation of a change control system, sometimes termed 'trend forecasting', 'deviation control' or 'configuration control', early in the project life is critical. Such systems must emphasize periodic weekly or monthly reviews during the formative design and procurement stages of a project. Control is made effective during these phases by frequent reporting of changes and by the communication of change notices to key people, so that full consideration can be given to the necessity of the requested changes and their effect on cost and time.

This system must be a dynamic technique of estimate and specification revision, by which the effect of departures from the basis of the estimate and specifications are identified as they occur, and adjustments are made to the control estimate being used at that particular stage of the project. This enables those in control of the project not only to see the effect of change on schedules and cost much more quickly than previous techniques allow, but also enables them to consider corrective action, and in many cases to take such action at a time when alternative courses of action are still feasible to counter the effects of adverse variations. Thus a change control system must be considered to be a system of continually identifying changes, or deviations as they occur, from the conditions or facts assumed in the project estimate and specification baselines and of taking corrective action where applicable to counter the effect of adverse change on the cost or schedule.

Change control systems have evolved in different ways and with different jargon in industrial projects and in advanced technology industries, primarily the aerospace weapons industry. In this industry change control is called 'configuration control' and is just one part of what is termed 'configuration management'. Although this is an esoteric term for construction projects, it is widely used in advanced technology projects and implies a formalized discipline for providing uniform product descriptions, status records and reports. Config-uration management is essentially the formalization of a discipline which integrates the technical and administrative actions of identifying, documenting, controlling and reporting the functional and physical characteristics of a product or project during its life cycle and of controlling changes to these characteristics. Thus configuration management is a more embracing term than change control system and puts more emphasis on the initial structuring of a project and on an engineering change control system to ensure the product produced is the product desired. However, configuration control and change control systems are more or less identical processes involving the following steps:

1. Establishing a baseline scope, specification, estimate, and schedule for the project.
2. Identifying changes to this baseline, communicating them to all concerned and determining their consequences.
3. Reviewing, approving or rejecting these changes.
4. Implementing these changes.

Establishing a baseline

A change control system should be implemented as soon as the initial scope, specification and estimate of cost has been defined. It does not matter how preliminary this scope and estimate are, they must be used as a basis for identifying changes, evaluating their consequences and controlling them. As more information becomes available, the project scope, specifications, plan and estimate will become more refined and at each stage will form a baseline for the future control of changes.

The change control system should enable management to trace the reasons for the differences in estimates made at varying stages in the project. Often the question is asked by a client or contractor's management 'How did a £10m estimate at an earlier stage come to be a £15m estimate at this stage?' The quality of an estimate depends to a large extent on the amount of engineering that forms the basis for that estimate. As engineering progresses, better quality estimates can be made. A change control system bridges the time gap between a lower quality of estimate, based on less well-defined engineering, and the higher quality of estimate that results from more detailed engineering. Typically on important projects, a design specification is written at a relatively early stage, to define the particular design that has to be used in the project. An estimate is made of the cost of this plant and approvals are sought and obtained. Let us assume that this point in time is point A. Additional engineering must be put into the project. The detailed process design is developed and mechanical specifications are completed to the point where a fixed price competitive bid can be requested. A new estimate, on the basis of this greater engineering definition, is made at point B in time.

A–B thus represents the time interval during which the detailed design was carried out and could represent anything from several months to several years. Unless there is a good estimating technique, combined with a change control system, the project could easily get out of control. The change control system prevents this happening and makes it possible to trace the reasons for the differences in the two estimates.

Identifying changes

Before changes to the project can be controlled they first must be recognized. A change or deviation is identified as a noticeable departure from the control estimate, specification or schedule. It may be favourable or unfavourable. A change occurs when any factor including design, but not limited to design, varies appreciably from the control. Thus a change in process sequence or addition of an extra pump or deletion of a pump, or an increase in the price of materials, or delay in construction, all represent changes. Similarly, a more complex design than that estimated for, represents a change.

Recognition of deviations can best be made by those parties directly connected with the details of the project. An estimator can notice a change from the assumptions originally made. A design engineer knows when the scope is changed, or when equipment not originally felt necessary has to be added. The project manager is not only constantly aware of pressure for change, but should be aware also of general price increases. The important point is that everyone must conscientiously be on the lookout for deviations to the project and that it must be a cooperative endeavour since no one person can identify all the changes that occur. Thus it is the responsibility of everyone involved in the project to bring to the project management's attention any change from the accepted baseline of the project. This must be done by the individual who first becomes aware of any change, as soon as they become aware of it, by making up a change request form and submitting it to a change control group meeting for approval and further action. One example of such a change request form is shown in Figure 8.11. This form contains the following information:

1. It identifies the change, describes it and gives the cost account, work package or cost control number it affects.
2. It gives the reason for the change.
3. It identifies who is initiating or requesting the change and provides for that person's signature.
4. It gives a first descriptive appreciation of the consequences of the change and the segments of the project it affects.
5. It gives a rough estimate of the effect on the project schedule.
6. It gives an order of cost estimate of its effect on cost.
7. It can optionally give a code number to identify the cause of the change for post-project analysis, for example customer request, late design change, error/omission in design, legal, environmental reasons, increase in economic return.

CHANGE REQUEST   Number: ....

                  Revision: ....

PROJECT: Date: ....

ITEM AFFECTED: Name:

                 Work package:

                 Item No(s):

                 Change requested by:

DESCRIPTION OF CHANGE:

REASON FOR CHANGE:

                                          Code:

ITEMS/AREAS AFFECTED BY CHANGE

INITIAL ESTIMATE OF COST/SAVING*   FIRM ESTIMATE:

EFFECT ON SCHEDULE:

REMARKS:

CHANGE APPROVED/REJECTED* - CONTRACTOR'S SIGNATURE: ....

                                          DATE:

                              CLIENT'S SIGNATURE: ....

   *delete one   DATE:

Figure 8.11   Change request form

Additionally, it provides space for a firmer estimate of cost and time, and a record of approval or rejection of the change.

Change control board meeting

The above change request forms would be submitted to a change control board chaired by the project manager and made up of key managers of the project. This should meet frequently, at least once a week in the formative stages of the project, and be a limited attendance 'stand-up' meeting concerned more with communicating changes than problem-solving.

At this meeting, which should not take more than half an hour, those parties working directly on design, estimating and control, table anticipated and potential changes known to them, that have not previously been tabled, or that they have changed since last being tabled.

Subsequent to this meeting, the cost control or estimating representative assesses the guestimated costs, properly estimates those changes having a significant effect, allocates a serial number to the change and passes the form to the project manager. The representative also prepares a summary report showing the effect on the estimate of all probable and potential changes to that date. The base estimate as revised by the changes can be considered to be the current most probable cost of the project.

Thereafter it is the project manager's responsibility to ensure that all groups affected by the change know about it. More importantly, the manager must review the change in conjunction with only the relevant people concerned and come to a joint decision on the acceptance or rejection of the change, or send it back for consideration of other alternatives. The project monthly report should then include a list of changes arising in that month with their probable cost, and a summary of changes to date on the project.

Such a system has been found to have the following benefits:

1. It provides a realistic and current most probable cost and schedule for the project and thus avoids periodic drastically changed forecasts.
2. It identifies potential changes of questionable value, which in turn can be eliminated by good control procedures.
3. It identifies areas where corrective action should be initiated to counter adverse changes.
4. It establishes a disciplined approach to change in cost factors.
5. It makes all personnel more aware of the effect of change and its economic impact on the project.
6. It provides a means subsequently to analyse all changes as to cause and effect, so that future projects can be better planned and estimated.
7. It stops the acceptance of changes requested verbally and requires those requesting a change to make it legal and official by signing for it. If they are reluctant to do so then the need for the change is highly questionable. This removes a common cause of conflict in project work, as very often over the

long life of a project, even with no intention of deception, memories fade and people forget about changes they requested informally.

Integration of the change control system with other project systems

The change control system must be integrated with the other project systems as changes will affect the project plan, estimate, manpower plan and budget. The effect of every change must be reflected on the project baselines for control. It must be re-emphasized that it is useless and positively damaging to effective control to compare actual progress, resource usage and cost to the planned value if these planned values have not taken into account changes that have occurred. Thus the change control system must be integrated with the control and information system, at the very least, at the cost account level, as shown in Figure 8.12. (See p.210.) The consolidation process will then keep the higher level work breakdown and organizational breakdown elements, plans and budgets up to date.

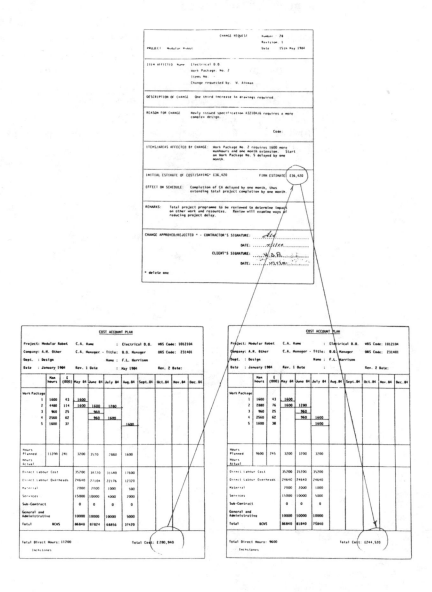

Figure 8.12   Integration of changes into the control and information system

Chapter 9

PROJECT MANAGEMENT INFORMATION SYSTEMS (PMIS)

One of the secrets of effective project management, planning and control is an integrated project management information system based on the following:

- The use of a 'structured' approach to the project, its organization and its systems.
- The use of the 'earned value' approach to 'performance analysis'.
- The use of modern project management computer software and database management systems.

All project managers must be backed up by effective project information systems, as it is impossible to manage a complex entity, such as a project, by the 'seat of the pants', without planning, budgeting, analysis and reporting systems to assist managers in their function. If project managers do not have this back-up, their planning and decision making will be too slow, and will not be used to help them organize and control the project. Without a good information system they cannot control their project, will not know until too late what is happening, and must spend a lot of their most valuable and scarcest resource, time, on simple supervision and the collection of information. Any information they do receive will inevitably be too little, too late.

Primary and secondary information modules

Any project management information system will be made up of a number of sub-systems or modules. The modules used on any project will vary with the industry, the requirements of the individual project and the company. These information modules can be arbitrarily divided into primary and secondary modules, simply on the basis that the primary modules are essential and should be used on every project, whilst the secondary modules may be used on only some projects. However, opinions on which modules should be primary, and which secondary, if any, will vary, with no correct division as such; it will all depend on the circumstances.

Primary modules will include the following:

- Structuring and coding the project.
- Change control.
- Design.
- Estimating.
- Materials management.
- Planning.
- Budgeting, or cost management.
- Quality.
- Data acquisition i.e.
    accounting, pay-roll;
    measurement;
- Analysis and reporting.

Secondary modules will include the following:

- Risk analysis.
- Contract administration.
- Correspondence.
- Safety.
- Work packs.
- Contract brief.

Within any individual project information system, several modules may be combined into one, for example budgeting, analysis and reporting may be combined with the planning module in a modern software package. Although the above list of information system modules may seem large, all the primary and most of the secondary modules will exist explicitly or implicitly on every project in some form or another. They may not be described anywhere, but the functions they represent will be carried out and some sort of data files will be maintained, even if only in a cardboard folder.

However, the effectiveness of these individual modules and the total project management information system will vary considerably. All too often the project manager has to accept the existing company systems, which are not designed to cope with the dynamic requirements of project management. As a result the project management information system may be a 'hotch-potch' of existing purchasing, accounting and financial systems, which are not integrated in any way, and whatever computer-based project planning package the company purchased in the past. This is inadequate for the management, planning and control of projects and is a recipe for project failure.

Examples of the kind of problems that arise are as follows:

- Structuring and coding will be carried out, but only in a limited manner and it will not be used to integrate all the project systems.
- In some cases, budgeting will not be carried out, thus there will be no expenditure plan, and cost control will be severely limited.
- Change control will be simplistic and ineffective, leading to the breakdown of project control.
- Analysis and reporting may be limited in usefulness, leading to project failure.
- The information system may be too slow for effective control.
- The modules will in all probability not be integrated, with all that entails.

All information system modules are interrelated to a greater or lesser extent, particularly the primary modules, as shown in Figure 9.1. Each module produces data and information that are used in other modules, or uses information produced by other modules, or very often both. Thus as outlined previously, integration of these information system modules into an integrated project management information system (IPMIS) is of great importance for effective project management, planning and control.

Design of the project management information system (PMIS)

In order to ensure that the individual information system modules are effective and that they are integrated, the project management information system needs to be consciously designed. This design and the implementation of the system is much easier today than even a few years ago. The following factors contribute to this:

- The modern methodology of project control is more established.
- Computer hardware and software is cheaper, more powerful and easier to use.
- Project management software packages, including project planning and specialist modules such as materials management and cost management, are more sophisticated, cheaper, carry out more functions and are much more widely available.
- Communication between computers and software is much, much easier.

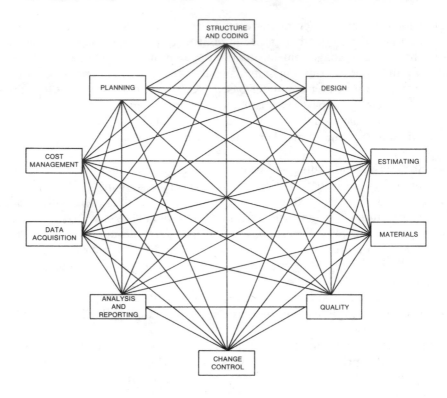

FIgure 9.1   Interactions between primary information modules

- Exprcience in the design and implementation of such systems is more widespread and help can be obtained from package suppliers and consultants, often using template systems.
- Database management information packages are widely available, used by many firms and easy to use, with most project management software packages designed to include or interface with them.

The PMIS and database management packages

Ideally, the integrated project management information system should be a database management information system, with all files on a database common to all the information modules. Project planning packages are then only one of the modules of the total system, as shown in Figure 9.2. However, moving from a hotch-potch of information modules to an integrated database approach may be too large a step for a company, although there are several states of nature or steps, that can facilitate integration:

- The use of aWBS approach and coding in all of the modules, even though

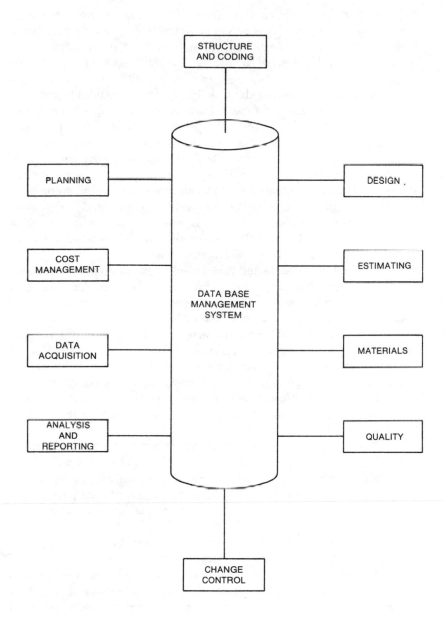

Figure 9.2   Database and the primary information modules

they may be independent entities. The mere fact that all modules use the same structures and coding is an essential half-way house to integration. It does mean that although integration may have to be implemented manually, or at the keyboard and it is difficult to keep up to date, integration is possible.

- Partial integration involving the linking of several modules in one software package. The modern project management packages have come a long way from the old concept of a work scheduling tool. They now combine several of the primary modules into one package, and many specialist project packages are available, for example cost management and materials management. Facilities for dealing with C.Spec. concepts, analysis and reporting are increasingly incorporated in the planning packages. In addition most now either interface to, or contain database management information systems or spreadsheets.
- Partial integration through the use of output files produced by one module as input for one or more other modules.
- Files, input and output data and tables used by each system, although not integrated, are produced by a file manager or database package using the same type of format. Database management systems, the simplest form of which is a simple file manager, can be used to set up data input screens, file and table structures, and output reports, without necessarily linking all the modules into one large database. All the modules use data and text files in a tabular form. Such files are made up of records, that is rows in a table, say one for each activity, work package, cost account, purchase order or drawing. Within each record, columns or fields hold data for that item, such as scheduled completion, vender code, draughtsman's name or actual labour cost.

    Creating, maintaining and organizing such files on an independent module basis is relatively easy with such packages. Thus the use of a file manager or database package to set up and operate individual modules is of value in itself, even without considering how it facilitates partial communication between modules and total integration into a database system.
- The next step is, of course, to move to a relational database approach which links all the modules into an integrated project management information system (IPMIS). The widespread availability and ease of use of these database packages have made the adoption of an IPMIS a reality and not a dream. The primary modules in such a system generally cover the factors described below.

Structure and coding

Although the modern planning and cost management packages include structuring in their initial project organization segment, structuring and coding must be implemented in the first phase of the project. The structuring of the project into its WBS, or WBS and OBS elements, cost accounts and work packages, and their coding, establishes the framework for the integration of the project and its information systems. All the information modules should use this structure and coding, not just planning and cost control.

Although it may not be possible to establish the full structure and coding of the project in its earliest stages, the first few levels of structure and coding can be established at the first stage, both in the work and organizational dimensions. Thereafter, it can be expanded into lower level elements, cost accounts and work packages as the project develops. In addition, where other coding systems are used, for example in a drawing register, they must always be related to this structure and coding, using data tables if necessary. This module is very much the organizational module for the project and its information systems and as such, it is central to the design of the integrated project management information system.

Design

Although the planning and control of the design phase is part of the project planning, the detailed planning and control of the design involves a large amount of data and information which is normally handled in the design information module. The planning and control of design may thus be carried out totally in the planning module, shared between the planning and design module or done in the design module alone. This planning will involve the normal sequential type development of the design plan.

The design module may thus contain three elements:

1. An interface with any computer aided design (CAD) system.
2. The detailed planning and control of the design phase, interfaced with the planning module.
3. The output data and information to be used in other modules.

The design module thus takes information from any CAD modeller used, or from the general design process, and generates detailed information. The output data to be used in other modules will include the following information:

- Equipment registers.
- Drawing registers.
- Bill of materials/material take-off.
- Descriptions and specifications.

The detail used extends to individual pieces of equipment and drawings, thus detailed design planning and control will generally be based on a tabular presentation of milestone type schedules, using a standard planning template for each item. As such it takes the form of, or is integrated with design and documentaion control and the drawing register. This maintains the records of documents and drawings, the persons responsible for the drawings, dates required, dates produced, the work package or cost account to which it belongs, the list of people to receive the drawing and other data pertaining to the design and the drawing.

The output information will be structured and coded to the level of the work package whenever possible. However, if stucturing and planning have not progressed to that level then it should be linked to whatever stage structuring and coding have reached. Every effort should be made to reach the cost account stage of coding in the design phase. This ensures that for each cost account the following is identified:

- The equipment required for its completion.
- The relevant drawings.
- The material requirements.
- Descriptions, specifications and any special requirements.

Change control

Change control can be a separate module or form part of one or more of the other primary modules, but in either case it has links with all the information modules.

Estimating

Although there will generally be project estimates established before the design stage, the definitive detailed estimate for planning and control can usually be made only after, or overlapping the design and materials management stages. In addition, during the design and estimating stages, the structuring and coding of the project can be extended to the cost account level and often also to the work or planning package level.

The estimating module will take information from the design, and possibly the materials management module and hold the estimated cost for the project and its component parts. Whether or not computer-assisted estimating is used, the estimating data will also include the estimated man-hours per labour category, material requirements and manufacturing or construction equipment usage for the work to be done on each work package or cost account. It will therefore produce much of the basic data for the planning database or CTR catalogue, that is, such data for each work package, planning package or cost account as follows:

- Man-hours for each category of labour.

- Labour rates and costs.
- Material usage.
- Material rates and costs.
- Overheads.
- Equipment usage and costs.
- Services required.

Materials management system

Innumerable projects are delayed due to the late delivery of materials or equipment, and yet many project plans show only a single arrow or bar entitled 'delivery of equipment and materials'. It cannot be emphasized enough that the management, planning and control of this phase of a project is as important as that of construction and design, irrespective of the size of the project. The materials management information module must extend to cover all the firms supplying material and equipment to the project to include them in the global project control system. They are no different to the other contractors, subcontractors or functional departments working on the project, and are part of the overall project organization. Delays in delivery can be kept to a minimum by effective, organized planning and control, and unpleasant surprises can be avoided.

The materials management information module is thus a critical part of any project's management information system and must extend from the equipment specification and material take off from drawings at the design stage, to the issue and usage of this equipment and material on the job. It interrelates with all the other primary modules and could be considered as an alternative central element of the project's information system. It covers both of the following items:

- Equipment – discrete items such as pumps, computers, etc. used on individual work packages.
- Material – bulk quantities usable on several work packages, such as piping, or cable.

The procurement of these categories of materials can be represented by a standard planning template. This can be displayed as a bar chart or network for each purchase order, but is generally contained in a milestone table or file, as for the drawing register, and shown in Figure 9.3. Entries for each of the milestones include 'Scheduled', 'Actual' and 'Forecast'. Other information can be included in the file or related files, such as prices, quantities, and details of vendors for each purchase order or requisition.

Various reports in the materials management or procurement control cycle can be produced from these files as required, for example individual supplier performance, late invitations to tender, tenders requiring further information from design, variations in forecast delivery dates and dates required on site, or

Equipment/Materials Milestone Schedule

Project: Simple Example

Date: 25-Ja-91
Revision: 2

Requis. Number	Descrip.	Cost A./ Work P.	Drawing Numbers	Design Complete	Spec./ M.T.Off	Enqu. Sent Off	Quotat. Received	Purch.O Placed	Intermed. Inspect.	Final Inspect.	Fabric. Complete	Received On Site	Required On Site
0013897	Elect.Mo	42-321	EM24649	29-Ma-91	27-Ap-91	3-May-91	17-My-91	24-My-91	5-Jul-91	16-Au-91	30-Au-91	13-Se-91	27-Se-91

Figure 9.3 Equipment/materials milestone schedule

all purchase orders for one work package or cost account. Nowhere is reporting by exception more important than in these procurement reports. A full report on all purchase orders, or work package information on a large project would be as thick as a large book. Although such a report needs to be reviewed at times, it's more likely that in the office of a busy manager its destination would be the waste paper basket.

Procurement reports need to be structured, so that individual managers receive only the reports relevant to their area of responsibility, and filtered so that information, not just data is given to the manager. Thus the thick pile of computer output would be reduced to, hopefully, only one or two sheets detailing critical items showing delays or other problems. That is, the manager would receive exception reports showing only those items requiring management action.

The materials information module will thus have 'linkages' to all the primary modules:

1. Design
   Design provides the initial input regarding equipment, drawings and material take-off.
2. Estimating
   Materials management provides information on actual material and equipment prices, either to be used in the definitive estimate or for comparison with estimated prices.
3. Planning
   Planning provides information on 'required on site', whilst materials management provides planning with information as to 'avaliable on site'. As changes occur in both modules, such as slippage on progress on site and delays in the delivery of materials, information must flow back and forth between modules.
4. Cost management
   Estimating and materials management provides input on estimated materials and equipment costs for each cost account and work package to the cost management or budgeting module. When combined with schedule information, this gives the time-phased expenditure budget for these elements of the cost breakdown structure. Materials management also provides information on commitments and cash flow.
5. Job cards
   Information for job cards for each work package, activity or task, is produced from the material information system. For example, in addition to the drawings required, purchase order numbers and material requirements for each job card or work package will be produced by this module.
6. Data acquisition
   Information on actual prices and material usage is fed back, not only to the cost management module, but also to the material module, to monitor actual usage against estimated, ordered and stock. Many projects have run

out of stock, or used more than ordered, and therefore stock usage and control must be controlled. Sometimes this occurs because changes, variations and additional work take bulk material, such as piping, but are not taken into account in the ordering system.

7.   Analysis and reporting

Cost management or budgeting

All projects have some form of cost management information system, however, not all are integrated with the project schedule and resourcing. Sometimes the methodology used does not include budgeting, that is, time-phased expenditure plans for work packages, activities or cost accounts, etc. An expenditure budget for the elements of the cost breakdown structure is essential for the financial control of the project, and it must be integrated with the project schedule and resource budget. Without an expenditure budget for the project activities, work packages, cost accounts and WBS/OBS elements, it is not possible either to be in control of costs, or to be fully in control of the project as a whole.

The project information systems should include a budgeting or cost management module which takes the estimating, purchasing, sub-contract, schedule and resource information and produces a time phased expenditure budget for all the elements of the project. The budgeting module may be a stand alone module or part of the planning module. Most project planning packages have simple labour cost budgeting facilities linked to their scheduling and resourcing, but these do not usually include all the elements of the cost breakdown structure, except through some modification of the available fields.

Increasingly such packages are incorporating C.Spec. analysis and reporting facilities to varying levels of sophistication. In addition, one of the commonest specialist software packages produced is a C.Spec. module, for example Artemis Cost, Open Plan Cobra and Primavera's Parade. These cost management modules are linked to their project planning packages and incorporate full C.Spec. analysis, forecasting and reporting facilities. They thus include full WBS, OBS and CBS structuring, with cost accounts and work packages, and their coding, plus C.Spec. analysis and reporting facilities. Nevertheless it must be emphasized again that structuring and coding does not apply only to planning and cost management, it must pervade all the project systems and information modules.

Quality control and assurance

Quality control and assurance are significant parts of any project and, just like any other element of the project, must be managed, planned and controlled . The quality assurance and control system module is an integral part of any project's system, whether it is simply a file of Clerk of Works reports or a full B.S. 5750/I.S.O. 9000 system module. A typical QA plan sets out the formal checklist and test procedures to be followed for each material delivery, each job card according to its discipline and each sub-system as it reaches completion. There are internal checklists and test procedures set out by the contractor, followed by those defined by the client and finally those issued by the inspecting authority. The QA information module will contain the data on inspections and sign-off of completed work. If job cards are used, they will only be shown as completed when the required inspection is signed off.

Data acquisistion

The effectiveness of the data acquisition, or monitoring modules of the PMIS are critical to its success. Without fast, accurate and correctly assigned data and information on what has actually been accomplished on the project, and what resources and expenditure this has taken, control of a project is impossible.

There are often problems in obtaining this information as it comes from many sources, and is dependent on the firm's accounting and other standard systems, which may not be project-oriented. The accounting system may collect data on its own set of cost codes, which cannot be transformed to the coding system of the project and therefore there may be only a limited number of cost centres on which control can be exercised; in the extreme case there may be only one, the project itself.

In addition, collecting accurate information from the point of work on a large number of small coded items is often impossible. For example, the use of a crane in an area may be difficult to assign to individual work packages, or even cost accounts. Similarly, personnel may go from one work package to another during the course of a day, and the assignment of their man-hours to individual work packages may be difficult, and very often is done arbitrarily by a foreman at the end of a week. Thus the design of the monitoring or data acquisition module is important, and in the worst case scenario it may determine the structure and coding system used.

Three types of data need to be collected:

1. Actual values, e.g. costs, man-hours, actual start and finish of jobs.
2. Earned value, e.g. valuation of work done, percentage complete, budgeted cost/man-hours of work performed.
3. Non-quantitative information, e.g. textual reports, comments, reasons, fears, small indications of problems, e.g. hunches.

In addition to the information collected in other modules, such as design and materials management, the principal information producing modules or systems are as follows:

- The firm's accountancy, payroll and time-keeping systems.

- Progress measurement systems.

The firm's accountancy and payroll systems will collect the man-hours and cost information, and the value of commitments, invoices and cash flows. This will include input from many of the other information modules. Projects, including construction ones, are beginning to catch up with practices common in production work for many years. This involves the use of point of work data collection systems, such as job cards and work packs, and electronic time keeping with facilities for automatic data collection.

The measurement of work done will include quantity surveyor valuations, other measurements of work completed, actual starts and finishes of activities, milestones achieved and estimates of work completed. However, estimates of work completed should always be kept to a minimum and apply to only small packages of work. Once such data have been collected they need to be consolidated and allocated to the structures and coding used, then communicated to the other system modules, particularly analysis and reporting.

Analysis and reporting

The analysis and reporting module is the interface between management and the project control system. As such, how analysis is carried out, and what reports are made to whom and, when, can decide the effectiveness of project control. It must be remembered that one of the causes of project failure is 'The use of superficial status/progress reports'. Thus conscious thought and care must be given to the design of the analysis and reporting modules.

Although some modules, such as design and materials management, will contain their own analysis and reporting facilities, particularly of detailed activities, the principal analysis and reporting functions are generally incorporated with the planning and cost management modules. However, the analysis and reporting functions take data from all the other information modules and analyse them to produce management reports on progress and performance, both for the past and as projections for the future. Although emphasis in the literature tends to be on the quantitative and graphical output, written reports, comments on problems, fears, hunches and other non-quantitative information are just as important.

The analysis must make use of the three sets of data produced by the planning and data acquisition modules:

1. The baselines for control, i.e. the project schedule, resources and expenditure budgets.
2. The actual schedule progress, resource usage and expenditure.
3. The earned value obtained by this resource usage and expenditure.

It must use these three sets of data to extract management information for decision-making and action, using both variance analysis and performance analysis, based on earned value.

No matter how sophisticated the analysis is, it must also be remembered that one of the causes of project failure is 'insufficient use of status/progress reports'. It is an unfortunate fact that sometimes senior management does not read the project reports, or fully understand the implications of what it does read, and urgently required recognition of problems and corrective action are delayed until too late to be effective. Thus the way in which information is presented to management can make a significant difference to understanding it. Information should be presented in such a manner that the following characteristics apply:

- It is easily understood.
- It is in as simple a form as possible.
- It highlights problems, e.g. exception reporting.
- It is relevant and meaningful.
- It is timely.
- It covers period to period analysis.
- It is cumulative to date.
- It identifies trends and projects these trends into the future.
- It is consolidated, but traceable as to the cause or source of problem.
- It is personalized.

The personalization of analysis and reports is important to reinforce personal accountability, motivation and the contractor/consignee concept. Each manager of a cost account, WBS and OBS element, as well as the project manager should receive reports on their own and the group's progress and performance, and how it affects the project as a whole. Without this personalization, the whole concept breaks down; with it, performance can improve significantly. This personalization is made automatic, and requires little effort, when the project is structured and coded in two or more dimensions.

Planning and scheduling

Modern computer software packages for project planning and control, and other specialist software for project management applications, began with the introduction of Artemis on a Hewlett Packard mini-computer in 1976. In addition, small project planning packages began to come onto the market for CP/M based micro-computers and the Apple 2.

Since then, there have been significant developments in computer hardware, software, project planning and control methodology and the integration of project management information systems. There is now a bewildering array of project planning software packages available on many different computer systems. Unfortunately there is no standard approach to all aspects of project planning and control in these packages, and a review of them would necessitate almost a complete book. Each user must evaluate the packages available in the light of their own particular requirements and choose that package which best meets their needs.

It is important that the choice of which project planning package to use is not made simply on how effectively it carries out the project planning function, in isolation from the other important requirements. Therefore the planning package must be evaluated on the basis of how it satisfies the following requirements, as well as its basic role of planning:

- The firm's IT strategy.
- The firm's chosen methodology of project planning and control.
- The package's database interfaces.
- The package's role in relation to the other project management information system modules.
- Its ease of use.
- Its scheduling effectiveness, particularly in resource limited situations.

The firm's IT strategy

The firm's IT strategy will influence the following factors:

- The choice of hardware.
- Networking and communication between computers.
- The database management system and spreadsheet used.

The choice of hardware

The hardware platform or platforms used for the project planning module should conform with those supported by the firm within its general IT strategy. Previously when centralized computing was the norm, this would not have applied. Today when distributed computing is much more widespread, it is possible to have many of the standard project planning packages on many forms of centralized or decentralized computing. Platforms used include the following:[1]

- Mainframes e.g. IBM on VM/MVS.
- Mini-computers e.g. DEC VAX under VMS.
- Workstations under UNIX.
- Personal computers, ranging from the simple 8086 machine, through to the extremely powerful super-micros available today.

Networking and communication between computers

Where multiple personal computers are used for project management information systems, it is generally necessary to network them together, both for the
exchange of information and to reduce the cost of software. Although the price
of a PC based planning package varies from several hundred to several thou-
sand pounds or dollars, the cost mounts up when individual packages have to be
purchased for many personal computers, even with the discounts available for
bulk buying. Networking can reduce this cost. In addition, a common practice
is to use relatively cheap, but effective packages on PCs for distributed planning,
such as SuperProject or Timeline, and link them to a more powerful package for
central use, for example Artemis on a mainframe or mini-computer.

The firm's database management information system

If the firm's computing services support and use particular database languages
or systems and spreadsheets, then it is logical to use project planning packages
which use or can interface with these systems. For example, if the firm uses
Oracle or dBase 111 or 1V for general application work, there are advantages in
choosing planning packages which use or interface with these systems.

Support for the user's methodology of project control

The project planning module used must be designed to support the methodology of project control that the user wants to implement. Often the opposite
happens, in that the methodology implicit in the planning package determines
the user's methodology. In some ways this can be an advantage in that modern
packages are increasingly leading the way towards a more professional methodology of project control. Nevertheless the user should decide on the methodology it wants, and purchase a planning package to support it, and not vice versa.

In all but the smallest project, the trend in serious project management is to
use a structured methodology as outlined, to handle the general project, the
portfolio of projects and the very large project. Planning packages available
vary considerably in how they deal with this structured methodology. Some do
not take a structured approach, but most take one of the following options and
support structuring, but to very varying extents:

- Structuring is implicit to varying extents, but not central to the design of
  the methodology used.
- Structuring is explicit to varying extents, with some packages having it
  fully developed in associated C.Spec. packages.
- Structuring is central to the methodology used in the package and is fully
  developed within it, generally with C.Spec. analysis and reporting
  included.

A planning package which supports a structured approach to project planning and control, that is, project control, will have the following facilities:

- Outlining of activities, as described previously.
- The ability to handle multiple projects and sub-projects, with common and separate resources. Although structuring can handle these factors, this ability is useful in handling multiple and large projects.
- Structuring the project in at least two dimensions, plus the usual sorting/ selecting facilities available on all packages.
- Significant coding of these dimensions.
- Graphical display and printing of the work and organization breakdown structures.

Although the graphical display of the WBS may appear to be a luxury, it is very useful, particularly in the early stages of the project. In the structured approach, creating the WBS is a critical early step in the management, planning and control of a project, and the ability graphically to build and display the project WBS means it can be done quickly and communicated easily.

It is important to recognize that structuring and coding of a project should start well before its detailed planning. The planning package structuring and coding facilities can thus be used in the project definition stage to establish the summary WBS and coding, and then to expand them as the project is developd through its life cycle. Similarly the structuring can also be used during the establishment of the project organization structure, that is the OBS and its coding.

These codes can be used in the other modules, or the database can be used to link other coding systems, for example drawing codes, purchase order codes, to the WBS/OBS codes, using data tables. These WBS/OBS codes can be generated by the package, particularly if it is used in these early stages, or manually input, for example if the structures were coded prior to the use of the structured planning package.

Database interface

No project planning package covers all modules of the project management information system, and all modules must be integrated. Therefore it is essential that the planning package chosen has an integral database management information system and/or an interface with standard data base systems and spreadsheets, preferably that used and supported by the firm. Different packages interface with different data base systems to varying extents. The following examples outline only some of these systems and the situation is constantly changing as packages are revised and up-dated.

1. Packages with proprietary integral database.
   - Application system (IBM)

- Artemis
- Cresta
- Qwiknet Professional
2. Packages with third party integral database:
    - Panorama – Oracle
    - Open Plan – dBase/Recital
    - Prestige – Oracle/Ingress.
3. Packages with full export/import to third party databases. There are many of these, e.g. SuperProject V2.0 can export or import data in the format of:
    - comma separated values
    - Lotus 1-2-3 spreadsheet
    - Supercalc spreadsheet
    - dBase 111
    - Multiplan SYLK
    - Fixed ASC11.
4. Packages with limited export and/or import to third party databases,e.g. Instaplan Version 2 can:
    - import/export – ASC11
    - export to Lotus 1-2-3
    - export to dBase 111.

Other modules

Although the database management system plays *the* central role in the integrated project management information system, the planning module can also play a central role. This is because in addition to its vital planning role, it can carry out or consolidate the functions of several of the information system modules. These functions typically include the following:

- The planning and control of the project expenditure, i.e. cost management.
- The control analysis of progress and performance of schedule, resources and cost.
- The management reporting function.

Cost management

Although planning packages were originally designed to schedule the work and the manpower, they are now increasingly incorporating 'cost management' facilities. This trend arises from the recognition of the need to integrate schedule, resources and cost and the convenience of doing this in one module or package. There are now three options for the handling of cost management:

1. The planning package handles the schedule and resource plans, and interfaces with the firm's project financial module through the database.

2. As above, but the interface is with a C.Spec. 'companion' package to the planning package, e.g. Artemis Cost, Open Plan Cobra and Primavera's Parade.
3. The planning package includes major cost management facilities, including C.Spec. analysis and reporting.

There are problems in including a full cost management module within the planning package:

- Cost management requirements and treatment vary from firm to firm, and the package would have to be very flexible to be able to handle all these variations.
- A full treatment of cost management would necessitate a large package.

As a result some packages work on the basis that to provide a link to the database is the best way of tackling these problems. Despite this there are advantages in including cost management capabilities within the planning package. It is relatively straightforward to convert the resource plans produced in the planning package into an expenditure budget for the labour element. Almost all packages have some labour costing facilities, which vary from the very primitive to a full treatment of all labour costs. A complete expenditure budget for all elements, cost accounts and work packages can be developed using consolidated values for materials, sub-contracts and other costs.

Schedule, resource and expenditure budgets and control analysis must be integrated, and the planning package can be more easily developed to achieve this integration, as it is already at least partially developed. Otherwise the separate cost management module must include this integration, and this is one of the reasons for the introduction of the 'companion' C.Spec. packages, which use a standard methodology of cost management, analysis and reports.

Control analysis is already built into these planning packages and there is a growing tendency for them to incorporate earned value, performance analysis facilities, as well as variance analysis. In some packages this is applied to the schedule, resources and the limited labour costing facilities, but in others it covers the full range of consolidated costs. Extensive reporting and graphical capabilities are also included in the planning packages and these can produce the individual and consolidated reports for management, including the standard C.Spec. reports.

Which approach to follow and which package to use depends on the methodology of project control adopted, whether full or limited C.Spec. analysis and reporting are required, the design of the integrated project management information system and the cost management facilities included in the planning package. These cost management capabilities included in the package, or as a companion module, are continually being developed and improved. It is likely in the future that separate cost management modules will be used only to collect and consolidate costs and input them to the integrated budgeting, analysis and reporting facilities included in the planning packages.

Control analysis

Packages vary considerably in the emphasis given to the control function, or as it is generally called, 'tracking', yet control is just as important as planning. Therefore planning packages should be evaluated as much in terms of how effectively they can be used to analyse and control progress and performance of schedule, resources and costs, as to how effective they are in planning these factors.

The planning package must establish the essential baselines for control of schedule, resources and cost, and keep them up to date through the change control system. This will necessitate the saving of the original definitive baselines, the revised baselines developed as the project progresses, including the reasons for these changes, and the ability to compare actual progress and performance against any or all of these baselines.

Actual values, progress and performance must be input to the planning package from the data acquisition process, and be analysed and consolidated to produce management information for action. This analysis should include variance analysis, and earned value analysis and increasingly, full C.Spec. analysis functions. The implications of deviations in progress and performance in terms of schedule, resources and expenditure and the necessary corrective actions must be forecast and the projects plans revised to maintain the baselines as effective control tools.

Reporting and graphics

The planning module should provide the bulk of the management reports required for schedule, resources and cost, including the standard C.Spec. reports and any other reports required by any level of management. These should be filtered, consolidated and sorted to provide personalized detailed and summary reports for all groups, elements and managers.

The ability to produce these reports through their C.Spec. reporting capabilities and their flexible report generators is a significant advantage of modern planning packages. Not the least of their facilities is the ability to produce multi-coloured graphical reports. Although these may be considered by some people to be simply 'pretty pictures', they are extremely useful in several ways:

- Graphical analysis can give information which is not apparent from tabular data and calculations.
- An effective graphical output can show a large amount of information and analysis.
- They are invaluable for communicating the results of analysis, particularly to senior management.

Ease of use

Project planning packages can vary considerably in how easy they are to use. Some of the most powerful are essentially development systems, or language based toolkits, designed to make it easier for users to develop their total IPMIS, as well as carrying out the project planning. They give increased power and flexibility, but require programmers with some knowledge of the high level languages used.

Steps have been taken to make all packages easier to use, with good 'HELP' facilities. Many of these advances arise from developments associated with the PC market and the increasing use of workstations. One of the most valuable of these is gaining increased usage in project planning packages, that is 'graphical user interfaces' (GUI). These include GEM, Apple Macintosh, Microsoft Windows, Presentation Manager and proprietary GUI developd by the package suppliers.

These GUI generally use the following:

- A mouse and pointer environment with pull-down menus, making the package much easier and faster to use, both for the regular and occasional users.
- Multiple windows to enable different aspects of the project to be viewed at the same time.
- A mouse and pointer to 'draw' the network on the screen.

The drawing of the networks on the screen and the ability to see the network displayed does speed up the modelling and establishment of task relationships. Tasks, that is, in the UK context activities, can be created and linked using any of the standard relationships, and activity details added in a window. Activities can be moved around on the screen to change the shape of the network, and the screen can be scrolled around the larger network. However, using the structured approach, hierarchical planning and discrete cost account planning modules, simplifies the need for the scrolling of larger networks. Thereafter the network can be printed in total or in part. All in all, it is impressive to see the speed in which a network model can be created using a graphical user interface.

Scheduling effectiveness

Whereas some specialized packages use Gantt charts, normally in their linked form, the standard planning package generally uses the precedence diagram method, or offers options of the precedence method (activity on node) or the arrow diagram method (activity on arrow), combined with Gantt charts, milestones, S charts, etc.

It is necessary to evaluate the packages available as to their scheduling effectiveness, particularly in resource limited conditions, as well as such factors as the size of the project they can handle and their speed in carrying out the necessary calculations. Although most packages will give similar results in the straightforward time scheduling of the work, they can give very variable schedules when resource limited scheduling is carried out. Even the time scheduling results can vary from package to package if there are unusual relationships between activities, such as some 'ladder' type relationships; also if there are Start to Finish relationships between activities and the package used supports only FS, SS or FF relationships.

The main differences in the schedules generated by the various packages arise because of the way they handle resource levelling. These can result in significant differences in the completion time of a project. For example in one project, which was subject to litigation, different packages gave a six week difference in scheduled completion times. This is illustrated by one series of benchmark tests of a number of packages, using the same network which contained one or two unusual relationships. This should have given a scheduled project completion time of 65 working days in a resource limited situation. The results obtained from ten packages ranged from 66 days to 105 days. In one package, simply changing the order of activities in the activity list changed the scheduled completion time from 83 days to 71 days. In another, using five different priority criteria, the results were 66, 66, 73, 99 and 100 days.[2]

Notes

1. Scopec International, *A Guide to the Selection of Project Management Software*, presentation to the Association of Project Managers (Scotland) February, 1989.
2. Adrian Dooley, a series of articles on benchmark testing of software packages, *Project Manager Today*, commenced October 1989 and continued monthly thereafter.

Chapter 10

THE CONTROL CYCLE – CONCLUSION TO PROJECT CONTROL

The modern planning and control cycle

The traditional planning and control cycle as shown below, assumes that a project is planned, the work is executed to this plan, and control action is taken to keep the project progressing to plan, or to revise it if necessary.

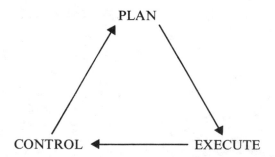

PLAN

CONTROL ◄——————— EXECUTE

The modern planning and control cycle follows the same general lines, but as real life is a good deal more complicated than the traditional cycle assumes, there are more stages to the cycle. In addition, running through the cycle is the constant theme of integration through structuring.

This modern planning and control cycle is shown in Figure 10.1, and involves the following steps or elements:

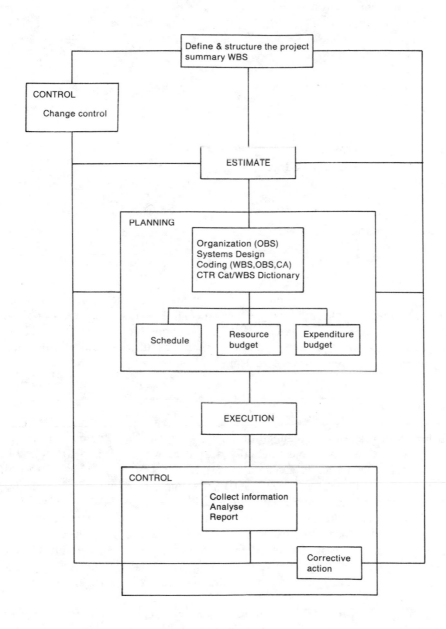

Figure 10.1   The modern control cycle

1. Project definition and summary work breakdown structure.
2. Change control system.
3. Estimating.
4. Planning:
   - organization
   - systems
   - coding
   - CTR catalogue
   - baseline plans for:
       schedule
       resources
       expenditure budget
5. Execution.
6. Control:
   - data collection
   - analysis
   - reporting
   - management decision-making and executive action.

In many projects this is a multiple cycle, because of the inadequacy of the information available at the start of the project fully to define, estimate and plan it. However, these steps make up the basic planning and control cycle which is applicable to every project, and the elements of it will be outlined before examining the more complex case of multiple control cycle projects.

Project definition

Before a project can be planned or executed, it must first be defined, as this determines 'what' the project actually is and the work required to achieve its objectives. Various terms are used to describe this project definition such as project scope, statement of work (SOW), statement of requirements, specifications, contract brief or documentation, etc.

The project specification may be different for different phases and companies involved in a project. For example, the project definition for a construction contractor may consist of a fully defined project design; for an architect it may consist of a design brief; and for the company's Board of Directors, it may consist of a technical, marketing and financial rate of return, outline project proposal.

Defining the project is probably the most critical element in the project control cycle as it determines everything else that follows. If a project is incompletely or confusingly defined, it can lead to a completed project that is very different from that the client or project sponsor thought they were going to get, and want. At the very least, a poorly defined project can lead to additional cost and delays in completion. Therefore considerable care must be taken in defining a project and to obtaining the agreement of all interested parties to this definition.

The project definition should include the following factors:

1. The objectives of the project.
2. The project strategies, including the contracting strategies.
3. A statement, or scope of work.
4. A summary project work breakdown structure and its initial coding.
5. Specifications.
6. A summary schedule showing the proposed start date, target completion date, milestones and WBS elements.
7. Indicative budgets or estimates, and any financial constraints.
8. Operating, maintenance and safety policies.

The statement of work, or technical scope of the project etc., depending on the industry or jargon used, describes the work required for the project and what is going to be its end product. In conjunction with this description, the first two or three levels of the project work breakdown structure should be established. This will include the project's WBS dictionary and coding. This ensures that each important WBS element of the work is defined, as well as the project, and that the work required for each element is determined at the very first stage in the project control cycle.

Change control system

All too often, as a project progresses through its life cycle, changes are made which affect the overall cost, schedule and economics. Many projects start life as an economic proposition, and before anyone realizes it, the cost has increased by anything from 20 per cent to 100 per cent, without any conscious decisions being taken. Therefore as soon as a project is defined, even in the most elementary way, a system to monitor and control changes must be established, as described previously (p.203).

A change control system performs two functions:

1. It gives to management the control of changes such that before a change is implemented, a conscious management decision must be made, based on justifiable criteria.
2. It monitors and reports to management the general impact of changes.

This change control system will thus become operational initially to control changes to the project definition, and will be structured on the basis of the summary project work breakdown structure and its coding. As the project progresses, the change control system will expand to cover all the elements of the control cycle, and will be structured on the basis of the WBS, OBS and their merger into cost accounts, and their coding.

Project estimate

The project estimate contains most of the information required to plan the project in the project dimension, including schedule, resource plans and expenditure budget. Effective control also requires the comparison of actual costs, resources and times with those used in the estimate and plans based on it. Yet in many projects, the schedules, resource plans and budgets, and the actual outcomes of these factors, cannot be directly related to the estimate. This in turn creates the problem that estimating rates cannot be confirmed, because the feedback of actual performance cannot be directly compared to the estimate.

The principal reason for this state of affairs is that the estimate and the plans are structured differently, with each using a different breakdown of the project work. Often, the structure and breakdown of a project estimate bears no relation to how the project is planned or how the work is carried out. Among the reasons for this are the following:

1. 'It is more convenient, or the estimate can be done much easier and quicker that way.' This frequently used to happen when in a tendering situation, estimates had to be prepared quickly.
2. Estimates may be prepared on a rule of thumb, or statistical basis, e.g. parametric estimating.
3. The client has specified the format of a tender, perhaps on a bill of quantities basis, which is not easily related to how the work can be planned or carried out.
4. Bloody-mindedness, or resistance to change on the part of the estimator.

Whatever the reason the results can be catastrophic for the project. It is critical that the estimate can be related to the plans, and to the control data and reports, and vice versa. Thus the structure of the estimate must match the structure of the project, the plans and the control system, that is, they should all be structured on the basis of the project work breakdown structure. If the estimate is structured on some other basis, it is necessary to restructure or transform it to match the work breakdown structure, and to make the information contained in the estimate useable in the planning process. This can usually be achieved using spreadsheets or specialized transformation programmes.

Thus the project estimate should be the pricing of the elements of the project work breakdown structure, based on the definition of the work involved in these elements in the project definition stage. As more detail is involved, this often requires the extension of the summary WBS to more levels of breakdown. However, consistency is maintained in that the consolidation of these lower levels of breakdown will match the summary elements established in the definition stage and used in the change control system from the start. This enables the coding, dictionary and CRT catalogue to be prepared for the WBS elements.

Project planning

The estimate provides the data necessary for the project schedule, resource and budget plans, but there are a number of other elements required to carry out the modern planning and control process. These are necessary to ensure integration, two-dimensional planning and control and the design of the project systems. They include the following:

1. Designing the project organization
   This includes establishing the relationships between groups, defining the organization breakdown structure and coding it. It also includes the merging of the WBS and OBS to identify the work assignments and responsibilities of organizational groups, i.e. the cost accounts, or 'who does what', and the disaggregation of the project's objectives on the same basis.
   This will include the preparation and issue of the project coordination procedures and responsibility matrix. This will identify the key individuals from the organizational elements, responsibilities and interrelationships. This is an essential step to ensure communication and coordination, particularly, but not only between client and contractor.
2. Design of the project systems
   The project systems can then be designed and integrated using the code of accounts based on the WBS, OBS and cost accounts. This will also include contract coordination procedures between client and contractor and other internal coordination procedures.
3. CRT catalogue/WBS dictionary/activity database
   The cost, resource and time requirements for all elements, cost accounts and activities will have to be determined before planning can commence. This may be formally constructed on a CRT or WBS basis, or it may be in a database, spreadsheet or on the back of an envelope. No matter how, a CRT catalogue, WBS dictionary or some form of database holding roughly the same type of information will be required at this stage.

These essential steps may be carried out during estimating, before or during planning, and before or after contracts are let. Unfortunately these steps were often implicit, or left to the accountants and other staff groups to carry out, instead of being very much the concern of project management. They are vital steps in the planning and control process and planning and control will be ineffective without them.

These steps and the planning of the schedule, resources and expenditure are based on the project structures that have been developed from the initial summary work breakdown structure of the definition stage. It is thus extended in the estimating and planning stages and combined with the organization breakdown structure and coding. Thereafter the project is planned on a hierarchical, two dimensional basis, integrating schedule, resources and budgets using these structures as previously described.

Control

Data and information are collected as the project work progresses, on the code of accounts, and evaluated as described previously under performance analysis (p.176). Reports are then produced for those involved relating to their areas of responsibility. Thereafter action must be taken to deal with the deviations and problems highlighted, or the previous work will have been done for nothing.

Multiple control cycles

The control cycle described identifies the modern planning and control process for any project. However, it is very likely that it will only apply in its basic form to a developed project at a stage where contracts could be placed, and not to the total project life cycle. The reason for this is that a project cannot generally be fully defined in terms of the work required to complete it until a considerable amount of work, time, resources and money have been expended on the project.

The problem is that there is simply not enough information available at the early stages in the project life cycle to define, estimate and plan the project with any degree of detail or accuracy. In these early stages of a project, statements are often made regarding completion dates, costs and rates of return. These can only be targets, or expressions of hope, as the information on which to base them is simply not available to make reliable estimates of any of these factors. Nevertheless, in order to ensure efficient and effective working, the project must be planned and controlled from the very first stage of the project life cycle.

The total project life cycle, as outlined in Chapter 4, has the following stages:

1. Conception.
2. Definition.
3. Design.
4. Procurement
5. Execution (e.g. manufacturing, fabrication, programming, construction).
6. Commissioning.

In addition, many projects have contract tendering processes between many of the stages, through which contractors are employed to carry out the subsequent stage or stages.

Many projects cannot be fully defined, estimated and all stages planned until the design stage is completed. There can thus be three stages in the project definition process, and often three or more planning and control cycles, within the overall planning and control cycle:

1. The 'conceptual' definition of the project produced at the end of the conception stage.
2. The definition of the project requirements produced at the end of the definition stage.

3.   The fully detailed definition of the project produced at the end of the design stage.

In spite of this, each stage of the project must be planned and controlled, and all stages must be planned and controlled in one integrated overall project control cycle. As a result of this information problem a multi-stage, or phased control cycle must be adopted for such projects, and this will incorporate a rolling wave approach to both planning and control, as shown in summary in Figure 10.2.

In this multi-phase approach, the conception stage of the project life cycle will result in the following:

- Level 1 plans and estimates for the project as a whole.
- Level 2 or 3 plans and estimates for the definition stage, which is in effect the 'execution' stage for these plans.

The Level 1 project plans will be used to establish the overall project planning and control cycle, whilst the Level 2 or 3 plans will be the basis of the phase control cycle for the definition stage. In addition as soon as the first conceptual definition of the project is crystallized, no matter how tentative this is, it is imperative that the change control system is established.

The output from the definition stage will produce the plans for the execution stage, that is the design stage. This will have its own phase control cycle, within the overall project cycle and change control system. This process will be repeated, with some overlap, for the subsequent stages of the project life cycle, as is outlined in more detail below.

Conception phase

The conception phase in a project takes an idea and turns it into a formal project proposal. It will define the project conceptually, develop the project's objectives and initial ideas on strategy, and roughly define what is required to complete the project. It will also prepare an initial Level 1 summary plan, a Level 1 approximate estimate of cost and the resources required to complete the project, based on experience of other projects; all of which will be structured and coded to one or two levels of a work breakdown structure. This stage evaluates alternatives, strategies and the economics of the project proposal. It thus involves an iterative process which evaluates different alternative proposals and strategies, based on the approximate estimates of cost, resources and time developed in the process.

The planning and control cycle for the conception phase is thus somewhat different from the basic cycle. The conceptual definition of the project is followed by estimating and planning stages as before, but the various project alternative proposals, their rough estimates, plans and overall economics are then evaluated in the 'control' stage. This involves an iterative process as the alternatives are compared and refined, until one or more conceptual definition,

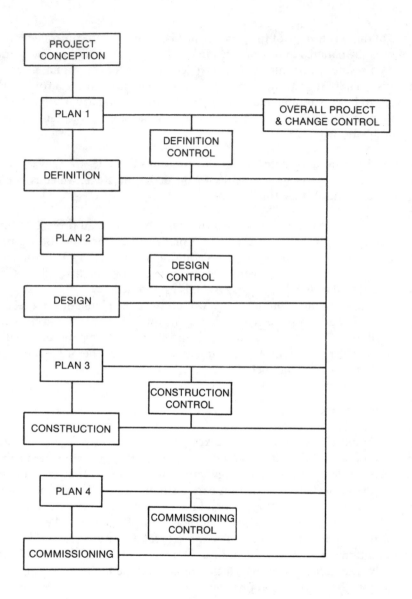

Figure 10.2   The multi-stage project control cycle

plan and estimate are put forward to the decision-making body for approval to proceed. This control element of the conceptual cycle thus includes a revision option, a rejection or 'no-go' option and an approval or 'go' option which will trigger the move to the formal definition stage.

The conception stage will also include the planning and estimating of the resources and cost of the definition stage, to Level 2 or 3. In addition, it may also include a tendering process to employ consultants or contractors to assist in the preliminary design work that may be necessary to develop the conceptual project proposal into the formal definition of the project.

The output from this conception phase will then include the first summary, conceptual or approximate, of the following:

1. Project definition.
2. A summary project work breakdown structure.
3. Project objectives and strategy.
4. Estimates and plans for the overall project at a Level 1, i.e. summary basis.
5. Estimates and plans for the definition stage of the project at a Level 2 or 3, i.e. on a detailed basis.

Definition stage

In the second definition stage of the project life cycle, the project requirements will be defined, as detailed in the basic planning and control life cycle. This will take the project to the stage at which design work can start, that is, the designers will know what they have to design. In a contract situation, it will give the architect a brief for the building, or, for example, contracts can be let for the design of the modules for a North Sea oil platform.

An estimate and the second stage of plans will be produced for this definition and the 'go, no-go', revision decision process repeated. Where design, or design and build contracts are involved, there will be a tendering process towards the end of this stage. When the tenders are received, there may also be another 'go, no-go', or revision decision made, if tender prices are significantly different to the estimates. The work in this development stage will have to be controlled against its input stage plans, and change control will have to be maintained, within the overall project control cycle.

The output from this stage will be that detailed as for the basic control cycle, with the plans and estimates being more or less as follows:

- Level 2 for the project as a whole.
- Level 3 for the design stage.

The execution stage will still be somewhat uncertain, as it cannot be fully defined, estimated or planned in detail until substantial parts of the design phase are completed.

Design phase

The design phase will follow the same pattern and as design work progresses, plans and estimates for the subsequent stages can be completed in more detail. In some industries, where design and execution are overlapped, procurement, fabrication or construction will be started part way through the design stage. In others, where execution, construction or building are based on completed designs, the tendering process will be repeated as before. Again, there may be a 'go, no-go', or revision decision made after tenders are received. This stage will be subject to its own control cycle, set within the overall cycle and change control system. Output will include the detailed design, the definitive estimate and plans for the following:

- Level 3 for the execution stage.
- Level 2 for the commissioning stage.

This process is repeated for subsequent stages, with the various phases tending to overlap.

Summary

The rolling wave project planning for such projects thus follows a pattern as shown below:

1. Project
    - Level 1 at the end of the conception phase
    - Level 2 at the end of the definition phase.
2. Each stage:
    - The Level 3 or detailed plan for each stage following the conception stage, is developed towards the end of the preceding stage. Thus the crest of the wave, i.e. Level 3 planning, with Level 4 short-term detailed planning or work packs occurs within each stage as it proceeds. In general the detailed planning for each stage will start part way through its preceding stage.

Conclusion

In the 1960s project planning was revolutionized by the introduction of computer-based network methods, such as the critical path method, PERT and precedence diagramming. Unfortunately in the following years, developments in project planning and control stagnated with little new being added to the basic concepts of these network methods. Although the C.Spec. methodology was introduced to US government projects in the late 1960's, there was little acceptance of it in general project work.

In the last few years this picture has changed and another revolution has taken place in how project planning and control are carried out. Not the least of these changes is that project planning and project control are no longer looked on as separate entities, as implied by the use of the term 'project control' to cover both planning and control. Project control is no longer simply concerned with the knowledge and application of planning techniques, such as network methods or Gantt charts to prepare a project schedule; it now requires the combination of these techniques with a structured methodology, which embraces the organization, planning and control of a project, the human element and integrated project management information systems.

A catalyst in the changes that have taken place is the widespread availability and use of distributed computers, easy to use dedicated project software packages and relational database systems. However, it is the widespread adoption of this structured methodology of project control, backed up by these integrated project management information systems that has revolutionized project management, planning and control.

Structured methodology of project control

The methodology of project control used is much more important than which planning technique is used. There are several effective methodologies of project control in use today, such as C.Spec., PRINCE and the cost, resource and time methodology. They all show the following characteristics:

- Organization, planning, control, systems and the human element are 'integrated'.
- The project is structured in one, two or more dimensions.
- Planning and control tends to be structured, two dimensional, hierarchical, multi-level, rolling wave, modular and personalized.
- There is an emphasis on personal accountability and responsibility right down to the lower levels of management.
- Planning tends to distributed, but integrated.
- Performance analysis is based on earned value.
- The control cycle is multi-stage, and the project is structured in the initial stages.
- There is an integrated project management information system (IPMIS).

Total integration

The modern project plan is an integrated set of three plans, that is the work schedule, the resource or manpower plan and the expenditure budget. This integrated 'plan' covers all activities, groups, companies and stages of the project from its conception to its completion, and beyond. This plan, and the consequent control function, are integrated with the organization of the project, the project management systems and the people involved to give the concept of 'total' integration. This total integration is essential to the effective management of a project, and its lack has been one of the principal reasons for the failure of many projects.

Structuring the project

Central to the achievement of this integration, and in fact the basis of the modern approach to project management, planning and control, is the structuring of the project in one, two or more dimensions to provide a framework for integration. This structuring performs many functions, including the following:

- It is an aid to the organization of the project.
- It is the basis of the design of the project management systems.
- It establishes the hierarchy of plans and control reports.
- It is an aid to the man-management of the project.

This approach provides a formal and systematic method of structuring a project and its organization, coding the project elements and activities and integrating all its systems. It has developed along two lines:

- A single dimension work breakdown structure which breaks a project down into its principal elements.
- A two-dimensional approach which combines the work breakdown structure and an organization breakdown structure to identify the individual work assignments of organizational elements on WBS elements.

Thereafter, other structures, such as the cost breakdown structure, may be used in conjunction with either of these two approaches.

The classical two dimensional approach originated in the C.Spec. methodology developed by the US government in the late 1960s, but found little acceptance outside of government projects until the late 1980s. The single dimension approach was adopted by large industrial projects, as a somewhat simpler derivative of the C.Spec. approach. However, in the late 1980s, the wide availability of low cost, but effective project software supporting a multi-dimensional approach led to a merging of the two methodologies.

Integral to these structures is the use of a significant coding system to identify uniquely each element of work and the structural relationships. The use of these structure based codes extends throughout the project management systems, and are critical to their integration.

Structured planning and control

The planning and control of the project follows the structures used, and is modular, that is, based on the WBS and OBS elements, and the assignments or cost accounts defined by the intersection of these structures in the two dimensional approach. In the single dimension approach it is based on the WBS elements and work packages, with individual discipline plans also produced.

Large, monolithic plans are no longer used; like dinosaurs they are slow and should be extinct. Instead, project plans are made in a hierarchical, multi-level manner, with the level of detail being consolidated up the hierarchy. The number of levels may vary and they may correspond to the levels used in the structures, but a common hierarchy used in many projects is given below:

- Level 1 – Summary plan.
- Level 2 – Intermediate detail plan.
- Level 3 – Detailed individual element plans.
- Level 4   Short-term plans often involving the use of job cards.

Within this hierarchy, the problem of the lack of information at the start of a large project to plan it in sufficient detail, particularly the later stages, is handled by using the rolling wave concept. This uses the Level 1 or Level 2 plans to integrate all stages of the project, whilst developing the Level 3 and 4 plans for later stages as the necessary information becomes available.

Personal accountability and responsibility

Planning and control have also become much more personalized, with each manager, group and company having their own plans and control reports, within the overall framework created by the levels of planning and the project structures. These modular and personalized plans and control information are used to reinforce the delegation of personal accountability and responsibility to each manager and group involved, This combined with the contractor/consignee principle for in-house work, greatly enhances motivation and teamwork within the project group.

Distributed, but integrated planning and control

Within the context of the above personalized planning, accountability and responsibility, both planning and control now tend to be distributed to these managers and groups. At the same time, they are integrated within the framework of the structures and hierarchy of plans.

Performance analysis

Whether or not the C.Spec. methodology is adopted, there is now a widespread adoption of performance analysis based on the use of earned value, as well as the more traditional variance analysis of progress. Thus each manager and group has individual measurement of performance of both time and cost, which gives greater control and increases motivation.

Control cycle

The control cycle is recognized as a multiple control cycle, using the rolling wave concept and hierarchical planning. Integral to this cycle is a change control system which is implemented as soon as a project is first defined. In addition, it is recognized that structuring and coding of the project should be initiated in the first conceptual stage of the project.

Integrated project management information systems

No project can be effectively managed without a project management information system to plan, control and integrate the people and the work. This information system will consist of many information sub-systems, of which planning is only one, and it is essential that these sub-system information modules are integrated. This integration is much easier than it was even a few years ago, with a relational database forming the core of an integrated project management information system. Within this system, the modern planning software package is playing an increasing role, in that it can consolidate several information sub-system modules into one, for example cost management, earned value analysis and reporting.

PART THREE

Chapter 11

HUMAN BEHAVIOUR
IN THE PROJECT
SETTING

The bulk of this book has been concerned with the organization of projects and project management systems. One system has not yet been covered and without the effective working of this system, all the other systems will fail; this is the 'people system'. Management is about obtaining results 'through people', and thus how the project manager deals with people and how these people deal with one another can make a significant difference to project performance. Effective project organization, a structured methodology of project planning and control and good human relations are all necessary for good performance on projects, but none of them are sufficient on their own. In addition to professional skills in organizing, planning and controlling a project, in order to be successful a project manager must develop his skills in managing people as these are critical to project performance, which in reality is actually people performance.

The five critical areas

The critical areas of human behaviour in which a project manager must have expertise are as follows:

1. Leadership
2. Achieving power in a fluid situation.
3. The motivation of individuals and groups.
4. Developing teams and teamwork.
5. Managing conflict.

The project manager requires these skills to handle the human problems which arise because of the characteristics of projects, the fact that the normal patterns of human behaviour are accelerated and accentuated in project work and because of the particular problems associated with the forms of project organization used. Among the problems that adversely influence human behaviour is that the forms of project organization that are necessary to manage a project are specialized, often complex, handle multi-discipline, multi-company undertakings and conflict with conventional organization theory in many ways.

Most other branches of management follow the majority of the textbook principles of organization theory:

1. The structure is hierarchical.
2. The lines of authority are based on a superior–subordinate relationship.
3. Subordinates have only one superior.
4. There is a division of labour by task specialization.
5. There is a limited span of control.
6. There is a division between line and staff.
7. There is a parity between responsibility and authority.

The forms of project organization used often ignore all of these so-called principles of management and 'break the rules'. Disregard for these principles does mean that the project organization has organizational complexity and an inherent conflict situation, but in large projects, involving different departments and companies, there is a new set of circumstances. In order to bind these diverse elements into one organization, committed to complete a project to its time, cost and performance objectives, and effectively to manage it, a new set of ground rules has had to evolve.

The man-management of project work requires a modification of the conventional human relations approach. In this, many of the cherished beliefs as taught in business schools and preached by human behaviour consultants have to be reconsidered, and the approach used must be based on the harsh reality of the project environment. The remainder of this book is devoted to the principal points, strategies and tools that a project manager can use to manage the human side of project management. As such, it endeavours to take an applied and realistic approach to the specialized nature of the human problems in the project setting.

Leadership

The quickest way to change the performance of an organization is to change its leader. Leadership is critical to high performance on projects, as it is with almost any human endeavour. There is some debate over whether there is a difference between management and leadership, or between managers and leaders. One of the problems is due mainly to the definitions used for these factors. The conventional definition of management is 'The achievement of results through others'. The definition of leadership is much less established, but most definitions follow the general lines of that below:

> The human behaviour process by which the activities of one person influence the behaviour of others to support goals desired by the leader.

There is very little difference between these definitions for management and leadership. However, some people argue that:

> Managers and leaders are very different kinds of people. They differ in motivation, personal history and how they think and act.

The problem arises from the conventional definitions of leadership, in that it is much more than 'getting followers to follow'. Leadership involves the following important factors:

- A mission, or vision of a future state of nature, or set of goals, normally involving change.
- A high personal commitment and drive by the leader to these goals.
- Actions to achieve these goals, normally involving a conceived strategy.
- Mobilizing, inspiring and maintaining commitment by others to the achievement of these goals.

Thus maintaining the status quo, put rather unfairly as the ongoing management of operations, may not require much leadership, but changing the status quo does. Management of an existing planning system or an organizational unit requires less leadership than the introduction of a new methodology of project control, or the development of teamwork among a group of managers starting work on a new project. Thus emphasis on leadership is much higher in the management of change, or in project management, than in the management of ongoing operations; this is the prime difference between management and leadership. Some types of management and some situations require more leadership than others.

Leadership is critical to the successful completion of a project, and indeed to the effective introduction or improvement of project management. A leader can lift the performance of an organization to a new level if he or she conceives and believes it is possible, is totally committed to it, takes actions to achieve it and inspires the people in the organization to the achievement of this higher level of performance, that is, makes the followers believe it is possible and makes them committed to this vision. Leadership, or management style is how the project mobilizes this commitment, but this vision is as much, if not more what leadership is about than merely getting others to follow.

Leadership style

Leadership style has been the subject of much research, and conventional belief identifies two independent dimensions to a manager's leadership style or behaviour. These two dimensions go under many names, such as :-

Task-oriented	Employee-oriented
Initiating structure	Consideration
Autocratic	Social orientation
Despotic	Human behaviour approach
Directive	Participative
Production-centred	Team-oriented
Concern for production	Democratic
Dictator	Socio-emotional orientation
Strong leadership	Concern for people
Managing	Non-directive
Theory X	Permissive
	Theory Y

The project manager who is task-oriented is characterized as a strong, competent, dominant leader who centralizes decision making, problem solving, planning and control. Conventional theory indicates that with such a leader the following will result:

- Production, or goal attainment will be higher than with the employee-oriented approach, at least in the short term.
- Decisions will be made more rapidly, although implementation may be slower.
- Emergencies and crises will be tackled more effectively.

However, in addition:

- Personal needs and interests of employees will have low priority.
- Employee morale may be low.
- Hostility may be high.
- Employee creativity and initiative may be stifled.
- If the strong leader leaves, the organization will tend to fall apart.

The employee-oriented project manager is characterized by a high emphasis on participation and teamwork in decision-making, problem-solving, planning and control. Conventional theory indicates that with such a leader the following will result:

- Personal needs and employee interests will have a high priority.
- Production and goal achievement will be higher in the longer term, than with the task-oriented approach.

- Employee creativity and initiative will be increased.
- Morale and employee satisfaction will be high.
- Commitment will be high.

However, in addition:

- Decision-making will take longer, but implementation may be faster.

Thus both the task-oriented and employee-oriented approaches have advantages and disadvantages. The theories of leadership style tend to integrate the two dimensions in a form that has been popularized by Blake and Mouton as the managerial grid,[1] using the terms 'concern for people' and 'concern for production' to describe the two dimensions. This identifies four principles or extremes of management style:

1. A high concern for people and a low concern for production – the (1,9) manager, i.e. the employee-oriented manager.
2. A low concern for people and a high concern for production – the (9,1) manager, i.e. the task-oriented manager.
3. A low concern for production and people – the (1,1) manager or adminstrator.
4. A high concern for people and production – the (9,9) manager.

In between these extremes, managers can be anywhere in the grid, depending on the balance between their concern for people and production. The principal attention of the theory and what is recommended as the most effective leadership style is the (9,9) style, sometimes termed the 'Hi-Hi' leader, who combines a high task and a high employee orientation. This is identified as the ideal leader who can get the best results and can flexibly use both dimensions of leadership.

Despite the popularity of this approach, there are problems with the concept, as shown by the following quotations:

> Despite abundant testimonials about the effectiveness of such 'ideal' styles as (9,9), however, empirical research does not necessarily support the claims.[2]

> 'The idea that leaders who are high on both consideration and initiating structure will be the most effective has been the subject of a sizeable body of research.
>
> In a wide range of organizations the hypothesis has failed to win support. In all but a very few cases when leader behaviour did relate to criteria, either consideration alone or structure alone predicted as well as the combination posited by the theory.
>
> ...it does question the view that a really effective leader must be adept at dealing with both socio-emotional and productivity aspects.[3]

Care must therefore be taken when applying conventional beliefs and theories to applied situations, such as project management. Luckily there is also a body of applied research applicable to project management which does give some guidelines to an effective leadership style.

Employee-oriented approach

Research work to determine those factors which contribute to the success or failure of projects reveals the following:

- The lack of project team participation in decision making and problem-solving strongly affects the perceived failure of projects.
- Project team participation in determining schedules and budgets is associated with project success.
- The lack of team spirit and sense of mission within the project team also strongly affects the perceived failure of projects.[4]

Therefore it can be concluded that participation and teamwork, both factors that are given a high emphasis in the employee centred approach, contribute to preventing project failure and achieving project success.

However, research also shows the following:

- Participation increases employee satisfaction, but not necessarily performance. Despite conventional belief, no direct link has been established after decades of research. The objective of the employee-oriented approach appears to be to make people happy and satisfied at work, but not necessarily to obtain high performance in the achievement of the task. This is supposed to arise naturally out of this job satisfaction, but it does not necessarily do so. This is summed up in the following comments on the results of field experiments in participation:

  Compared to low-participation managers, high participation managers had better performance in six studies, worse performance in four studies, and there was no clear difference in seven studies.[5]

  Teams tend to develop complacency and euphoria and do not necessarily achieve the highest performance they are capable of. They tend to need 'someone around to crack the whip'.[6]

  Lack of direction and control results in low productivity and a failure to meet deadlines.[7]

Task oriented approach

Applied research in project management has also shown the following conclusions with regards to leadership style:

The statement that the most effective project managers are non-directive, human relations-oriented leaders as opposed to directive, managing, task-oriented leaders is mostly false.

The research described in this paper supports the concept of a leader who is task-oriented with a back-up of social orientation for most project efforts.[4]

In very favourable or in very unfavourable situations for getting a task accomplished by group effort, the autocratic, task-controlling, managing leadership works best. In situations intermediate in difficulty, the non-directive, permissive leader is most successful [8]

The project manager must have a high task orientation and a competent autocrat does achieve results. Nevertheless, the manager will not achieve high performance in the attainment of the project's goals if people are alienated, demotivated, uncommitted to the project's goals, hostile and there is not at least a cooperative working relationship.

The project manager's prime objectives must be the effective achievement of the project's objectives through high performance, and not just to make people happy and satisfied at work, except in so far as this contributes to the achievement the manager's task. Thus the employee-oriented dimension of leadership style is essentially supportive to the task-oriented dimension of project leadership. It must also be recognized that motivation, commitment and teamwork can be achieved by the directive, task-oriented leader in many ways, and the participative human behaviour approach is only one of them.

This concept of a high task-oriented leadership style, with a social back-up, has to be moderated in the matrix and multi-company setting. It can be effective when the project manager is in charge of a dedicated project team, or organizational unit, where individuals and groups are directly responsible to the project manager. Yet it is more than likely to bring about conflict with those over whom the project manager has limited or indefinite authority, such as in the matrix organization.

This is particularly relevant in the multi-company situation, where the project manager's power is defined by the contracts and the manager's personal and political power. Acting directively with those people who do not recognize your authority or power can be counterproductive and lead to conflict. Therefore, the leadership style that can be used is contingent on the project manager's power and the situation.

Thus to sum up:

- The project manager must have a high task orientation; in management grid terms a (9,?) manager.
- As a means effectively to achieve the project's objectives, the project manager should also encourage participation and teamwork, but as sup-

portive to the task orientation above. In management grid terms the project manager should be something like a (9,6) or (9,7) manager.

- This must be modified by what 'power' the project manager has, and the situation. The lower the power, the higher must be the participation emphasis.

Power

The simplest definition of management defines it as 'obtaining results through people'. In a similar vein, the simplest definition of power defines it as 'the ability to get people to do what you want them to do'. Therefore management can be redefined as simply 'The use of power to obtain results'.

Power is thus essential to management and without it you cannot manage. Whether power belongs to an individual, a group or is widely dispersed does not change the fact that it is power that gets things done, that is, it is power that achieves the following:

- Takes decisions
- Commits resources
- Controls
- Takes action
- Rewards
- Punishes
- Sways minds
- Generates enthusiasm
- Gets others to follow
- Changes the course of events.

It is essential to all achievements, to management and to leadership.

It is no wonder that 'insufficient authority and influence strongly influences the perceived failure of projects.' For example, in an emergency or crisis, or more particularly when there are small signs of the beginning of an adverse trend that the project manager believes requires urgent corrective action, but of which others are unconvinced, which will get faster results?

- Requesting actions as a plaintiff.
- Persuading others to take action from a position of weakness.
- Negotiating with equals.
- Giving instructions, i.e. directing, or requesting action as a superior who must be obeyed.

The level of power of the project manager influences the leadership styles that can be used. The higher the level of power, the more task-oriented the manager can be; the lower the level of power, the more participative the manager must be. The level of power, or more particularly in this case, of authority, also interacts with the organization structure used. The form of matrix is determined by, or determines, the authority of the project manager. In the functional matrix, this authority is low, in the project matrix it is high, and in the balanced matrix it is somewhere between the two, and often uncertain.

In the multi-company situation, the project manager typically has limited and insufficient authority to give directions to all those involved. Thus, as noted earlier, in the matrix and the multi-company situations, there exists an authority gap whereby project managers' responsibility exceeds their authority. Yet the project manager needs some measure of power over all those concerned if he is to manage the project and exercise leadership to achieve the project's objectives. Thus project managers' power must be considerably in excess of their positional authority.

It is important to differentiate and to understand the difference between power and authority. Authority is often termed legitimate power, which is a misnomer, as it wrongly implies that all other forms of power are illegitimate. Authority is in fact the legal power which pertains to a manager's position in the organizational hierarchy to give subordinates instructions which they must follow or be disciplined. It thus also includes the power to reward or punish, sometimes termed coercive power. Authority is, however, only one source of a manager's power and can be considered as only a sub-set of that power.

The many sources of power available to a manager can be viewed on three levels:

1. Positional superior–subordinate power
   This includes the following:
   a) Legal authority: the superior has the right to give instructions to his subordinates, and they accept they have duty to carry out these instructions.
   b) Reward power: the superior has the power to award financial rewards, promotions and attractive jobs, and the subordinate does what the superior wants in order to obtain these rewards.
   c) Coercive power: the superior has the power to punish or discipline the subordinate, to the extent of dismissal and the subordinate does what the superior wants in order to avoid these punishments.
   d) Contract authority: a special case of positional power which arises from contracts and purchase agreements in mutli-company or even matrix organizations. These agreements give the client some measure of authority over the other party, and often this works both ways.
2. Personal power
   This includes the following:
   a) Expert power: people do what the power holder wants because he or she is recognized to have special knowledge or expertise.

    b)   Referent power: people do what the power holder wants because of admiration, loyalty, friendship, respect, attraction or other forms of personal relationship, e.g. charismatic leadership.

3.   Political power

    This is power based on the power holder's skill in and use of the many activities of politics to gain power.

Positional superior–subordinate power is unidirectional, that is, it operates down the hierarchical pyramid and it is exercised by a superior over subordinates. All other forms of power are multi-directional, and can be exercised down, up, sideways and diagonally across the hierarchical tree. For example, a subordinate can have real power, often termed influence, over a superior.

Positional superior–subordinate power, or more specifically authority, can operate diagonally downwards, but this can lead to problems and conflict. In other words someone of higher hierarchical position can give instructions to someone of lower position, who is not in that manager's group. However, if the manager relies only on positional authority, that subordinate need not necessarily carry out these instructions, and the subordinate's own superior may resent it.

The term 'level of power' used above is used deliberately, for as in the martial arts, the manager tends to progress to the higher levels of power as abilities increase. For example, a newly appointed manager may have only positional power; with increasing experience expert power may develop, as well as referent or leadership power. However, at the lower levels of management, political power is generally also at a lower level. It is only when managers start to climb the hierarchical tree that they become players in the arena where politics takes place and they may gain political skills and power. Political power is the highest form of managerial power and can be considered the 'black belt' of management.

Any manager who relies solely on superior–subordinate authority is of very limited effectiveness, particularly at a senior level. It is only necessary to have seen different people holding the same position in an organization to realize what a difference varying levels of personal and political power can make to a manager's effectiveness.

Project managers' positional power is always limited in the matrix and multi-company situation, and therefore they must rely on their personal and political power. The new project manager in a first appointment in that role has little personal power and therefore must consciously develop it in the years ahead. The successful experienced project manager can have considerable personal power, which may have been enhanced over the years by rewarding subordinates by the use of upward influence. The project manager therefore tends to have loyal followers who move with the manager from project to project. However, such personal power has to be enhanced by political power.

Political power

Politics has a negative image and has acquired a bad name over the centuries. Few managers will freely admit to being skilled political operators or are willing to talk about the extent of politics in their organizations. Yet the New Collins Concise Dictionary of the English Language (1984) takes a prosaic view of politics and defines it as:

> Any activity concerned with the acquisition of power.
>
> Manoeuvres or factors leading up to influencing others.
>
> The Art and Science of directing and administering states and other political units (i.e. any organization).

Thus there is nothing intrinsically immoral about activities aimed at achieving power, and politics need not necessarily lead to ill-feeling, double-dealing or conflict. In reality, the art of achieving power, that is politics, is just as much a function of management as planning, decision-making and controlling, and is necessary and normal in management. This is because straightforward superior–subordinate authority is very limited and totally inadequate by itself for the achievement of results in the larger hierarchic organization.

Although the term 'politics' has become associated in many people's minds with underhand activities, this only represents the dark side of politics, which in turn is usually associated with conflict. The light side to power and politics is similar to socialized power motivation. In this the manager uses power and politics to achieve results for the benefit of others, the organization and the common good. Inhibitions, ethics or scruples restrain the negative use of power and the type of political activities used. Teamwork, participation and Theory Y concepts can co-exist with the light side of power and politics. This is just as well, as this light side of politics is an essential complement to a manager's superior–subordinate authority. This means that in project work the project manager's political activities are generally directed towards the achievement of the project's objectives and not self advancement.

The project manager thus must be able to use those activities which make up politics, as shown in the political toolkit of Figure 11.1, except hopefully those of deceit and deception, to achieve the project's objectives. The project manager is in a strong position to use all of these activities because of the manager's centrality in the project organization. The tools are available and are important to enable the manager to manage the project.[9] In particular, one of the most important and strongest tools to achieve power in the matrix and multi-company situation is the project planning and control system.

The project plan, that is, the work schedule, the resource and expenditure budgets, is an important source of power for the project manager. The planning process is an effective way of obtaining the participation of people in other groups and companies, and their commitment to achieving the targets outlined

1. Gaining support from a higher power source or sources
    - Sponsorship
    - Lobbying
    - Co-option
2. Alliance or coalition building, i.e. gaining support from peers, or near-peers.
    - Exchange of favours (IOU)
    - Bargains
    - Bribery (in one form or another)
    - Establishing a common cause
    - Combining for mutual support or defence
3. Controlling a critical resource
    - Money
    - People
    - Expertise
    - Reporting
    - Centrality or gate-keeping
    - Information
4. Controlling the decision process
    - Selection of criteria of choice and constraints
    - Selection of the alternatives short list
    - Controlling the information about alternatives
5. Controlling the committee process
    - Agenda, content and order of
    - Membership
    - Minutes
    - Chairmanship
    - Calling of meetings
    - Pre-agenda negotiations
6. Use of positional authority
    - Rewards
    - Coercion
7. Use of the scientific element
    - Planning
    - Control
8. Deceit and deception
    - Secrecy
    - Surprise
    - Hidden objectives
    - Hidden agendas
    - Two faces
    - All things to all people
9. Information
    - Censoring or withholding
    - Distorting
10. Miscellaneous games
    - Divide and rule
    - Whistle blowing
    - In the same life boat
    - Red herring game
    - White knight game

Figure 11.1   The political manager's tool kit

in the plans. This commitment can be achieved, even if participation is limited, provided the plans are 'accepted' by those concerned. Plans commit the people involved to the achievement of their time targets, with the resources specified, at the cost budgeted. Once plans are accepted, the project manager has the implicit power to hold them to their own commitments and to take action if they are not met.

Similarly, the application of the contractor/consignee concept and of distributed accountability and responsibility gives the project manager power to hold other managers accountable for the achievement of their goals, which are clearly specified. Even more importantly, these managers normally then accept their commitment to meeting these goals, and recognize the role of the project manager in this process. In essence they concede a measure of power to the project manager, knowingly or unknowingly.

The project management information system is also a source of power for the project manager. It enhances the manager's planning power and, since the project manager is responsible for reporting progress to senior management, this gives him or her the ear of these higher power sources, and thus enhances his or her general power. The project manager is also at the centre of the information system and has the power to call, chair and minute meetings. These factors are recognized sources of power. Thus the planning and control system can give the project manager the major source of political power over all the diverse individuals, groups and companies working on the project, if the manager knows how to use it as such.

Motivation

The performance of individuals is a function of their ability and their motivation. Motivation can influence an individual's performance both positively and negatively, and in the twentieth century there have been many theories advanced on motivation in the organizational setting. Some of these are philosophies, some of them are very popular, most are very moralistic and sometimes they are not backed up or confirmed by applied research in hard managerial situations. What is certain is that the organizational person is a complex being and no one stereotype, or motivational factor applies to all people, for all of the time.

The following discussion provides a brief outline of some motivating theories and factors which have applied research back-up and are of practical use in the project setting:

- Participation – the project as a motivator.
- Expectancy theory – the reward system.
- Achievement, goal theory and target setting.

Participation

During the 1960s and 1970s participative management based on organizational behaviour concepts was very much the fashion and was considered to represent good practice. Those who did not adopt these concepts were looked down on pityingly and were considered to be old-fashioned or even immoral.

The participative approach to management and motivation could be said to have evolved as a reaction to the adverse effects of scientific management. The scientific approach to management, that is, in management grid terms the (9,1) manager, which involves an emphasis on planning, direction, control and work study, incorporates Theory X concepts of human behaviour and has been found wanting over the years.

As is implicit in the name, participative management involves the participation of the subordinate in decision-making and a reduction in the use of direct authority. Subordinates or groups set or largely contribute to the setting of their own objectives. The senior manager does not take decisions unilaterally or autocratically, but meets with the group, shares the problem with them and encourages them to participate in determining the solutions. This emphasizes the role of the senior manager as less of an autocratic boss and more of a teacher, professional helper, colleague or consultant. In turn it assumes that the individual can then derive satisfaction from performing a job effectively and have a high level of motivation.

The concept of a manager's role *vis à vis* the other manager's as being a teacher, professional helper, colleague and consultant on the lines of a professional to clients, does hold some validity. In inter-group and inter-company relationships, authoritative management is often difficult, if not impossible, and therefore there must always be an element of participative management in project work. However, in the late 1970s and the 1980s doubts began to be raised about the validity of the human behaviour approach as an all embracing philosophy of management. Although it was recognized that these concepts can and do represent relationships between some individuals and groups, it was questioned whether the fully participative approach leads to high performance and whether it is applicable in its basic form to the reality of people, and of life in the typical hierarchic organization.

The following comments were made at this time:

> In discussion of this concept, two of its propositions should be clearly distinguished. One, of a factual – that is, testable – nature is that participation leads to increased productivity: 'Involve your employees and they will produce more', management has been told by a generation of industrial psycholgists.
>
> ... it is interesting that the factual proposition has not held up in much of the research. Studies by Fiedler (1964) and others have indicated that participation is not necessarily correlated with satisfaction or productivity. These relationships depend on the work situations in question.[10]

If the human behaviour, participative approach is implemented on its own, you are not guaranteed results in terms of task achievement, and it is results that count. Thus there is a danger that implementing this approach to management can result in a well adjusted, happy and contented organization, but not necessarily one which will produce the best results. Thus the participative human behaviour approach, in management grid terms the (1,9) manager, has also been found wanting.

Nevertheless, participation can increase employee creativity, initiative, morale and satisfaction, and can generate commitment to the project and its goals. Commitment can be defined as follows:

> A strongly held attachment to, personal association with or belief in something, such as values, a cause, a person, or a project and its objectives.

Commitment is an emotional state and can motivate people to extreme self-sacrifice. Thus although participation on its own does not necessarily increase performance, it is a motivating factor that project managers should use to achieve their objectives.

People need meaning in their organizational life, to feel they are part of events and to have some influence over them. If you treat people like children, they will certainly behave like naughty children; if you treat people as adults, they 'may' behave like responsible adults. People do generally work better if they are given respect, are involved with decisions which affect their life and work, and are treated in a participative manner, although this does not apply to everybody and not all the time. Participation when combined with a task-oriented approach is an effective motivator. This is not the wishy-washy, 'Charlie Brown' style of management, which was sometimes the result of the participative movement, but a combination of leadership, and the scientific and human sides of management.

Participation can be used to build a strong commitment to a project, such that it almost becomes a living entity to which people owe loyalty and to which they are committed. Many professionals and supervisory people feel alienated by the nature of their work and their failure to see how it fits into the company or project picture. The many layers of management in a large organization leave those at the lower and middle levels feeling a sense of powerlessness and remoteness from decision-making, and it is difficult for them to equate their own personal needs with that of the organization. This leads to a loss of involvement and commitment to the project and its objectives.

Participation, when combined with the delegation of accountability and responsibility to contractor/consignee situations, cost account, WBS and OBS element managers, and a structured approach to project control, can overcome these problems and can lead to a high level of personal commitment and satisfaction. Everyone on the project can become associated with its success or failure. They can see how their contribution fits into the complete picture, and if they work a little harder, they can see what effect it has on the progress of a job.

This commitment to the project can lead to the development of what could be termed a project attitude of mind, in which people's interests are subordinated to the project and they associate themselves with it. This project attitude of mind is a way of thinking that penetrates throughout the organization and unites all involved towards the accomplishment of the project's objectives. There becomes an acceptance that it is no longer enough to say 'our department's effort was satisfactory but the project was delayed because of someone else.' No single individual's or group's effort is satisfactory unless the project is a success, and every effort is made to assist other organizational elements to carry out their tasks successfully. This involves removing departmental blinkers and cooperating by helping one another to complete the project successfully in terms of all its objectives. Thus participation can generate commitment to the project and the project itself can become a strong motivator.

Expectancy theory and the reward system

Most managers in the project setting have personal goals and are ambitious, that is, they want to advance their careers. As a result, they will exert considerable effort if they think that these efforts will lead to promotion, more money, power, recognition, praise, more scope, or a better assignment. This applies to all levels of management, although the actual personal goals may vary with the individual and the level of management.

This describes expectancy theory, in which the individual is motivated by the belief that increased effort will result in higher performance, which in turn will be rewarded by the fulfilment of personal goals. Expectancy theory of motivation does not apply to all individuals in all types of organizations, and is subject to several constraints. However, applied research on expectancy theory, as expressed by the reward system, has confirmed it is an effective motivator 'for some of the people, some of the time'.

In general, the reward system can motivate individuals to higher performance if the following are true:

- The individual values highly such rewards as advancement, more money, more scope, power, a good assignment, a good assessment.
- The individual believes that a high level of personal, or team performance will be recognized, produce results and will bring these rewards.
- The individual has an opportunity to perform.

Thus expectancy theory can be made to work through the reward system, particularly when it is linked to clear-cut individual objectives and performance measurement. This motivational factor can be combined with an emphasis on individual accountability and responsibility as expressed in the contractor/ consignee principle, cost account, WBS and OBS element managers, and structured and personalized project planning and control.

The 'equity' of the reward system is also important, as nothing demotivates people faster than 'inequity'. If promotions and pay rises are seen to be fair and just, then motivation is increased. If they are based on nepotism, fawning and favouritism then all but the chosen few are demotivated.

Achievement, goal theory and target setting

MacCelland's achievement motivation theory is a well-established concept which states that the need to achieve is a strong motivator. It is generally accepted that for the majority of the kind of people engaged in project work, achievement is an important motivating influence. Indeed, project work is designed for achievement; 'I built that!' In addition, it has been established, both in theory and in practice, that setting people specific difficult, but achievable targets can motivate many people to a higher level of performance than just the simple admonition to 'do your best'. Achievement and target setting can be combined with the project planning and control system to give an extremely effective motivator in project work.

A large amount of research has shown that if people are set difficult targets they will exert themselves to achieve them. The 'acceptance' by people of the reasonableness of these targets and feedback on their performance are critical factors in the effectiveness of these motivational factors.[5] Whether or not these targets are set participatively or autocratically appears not to be critical, as long as they are accepted by the individual. Participative target setting, of course, facilitates their acceptance, but tends to result in easier targets being set. Autocratically set targets are often accepted because of respect for positional authority, but if targets set autocratically are viewed as too difficult, they will not be accepted, or achieved.

In practice, this describes the planning process, where involvement of those who are to carry out the work is vital to the acceptance of, and commitment to the plan. Therefore one of the objectives of the project manager is to use the planning process as a motivational tool in project management. Again, the contractor/consignee principle, cost account, WBS and OBS element managers, and the structured and personalized planning and control system can be used to establish personal targets for each manager and group and to motivate them to a high level of performance.

Research has also shown that knowledge of how a person is performing can enhance the motivational effects of target setting. Thus feedback on performance is essential. In other words, project control information is another motivator, but it must be related to the individual and to their personal targets. At this stage the recognition of achievement is important, through praise, rewards, and positive reinforcement, that is, expectancy theory.

One of the dangers inherent in the use of target setting for motivation is the danger that individuals will focus completely on their own targets to the detriment of cooperation with others, and the overall project targets. Thus it is essential that the individual's target must be a building block in the overall project organization's targets and joint responsibilities must be defined and targeted. This is what planning is all about. The matrix of responsibilities also defines individual and joint responsibilities, and the overall structured plan integrates the individual's plans and targets.

Summary

Thus in the project setting, participation, the project as a motivator, expectancy, as expressed by the reward system, achievement and target setting can all be used to increase motivation. These factors interact with the organization structure of the project and the structured methodology of project planning and control, such that there is synergy between the scientific and human sides of project management effectively to motivate individuals and groups to achieve higher performance and the project's objectives.

Conflict – Hostile – Neutral – Friendly – Teamwork
◄──────── Cooperation ────────►

Figure 11.2   The conflict/teamwork dimension

Team development

When individuals, groups and companies interact and are interdependent, as in project work, overall organizational performance depends not only on how these organizational elements perform as individual entities, but also on how effectively they work together. This is largely determined by the nature of the interpersonal relationships between these elements, which are described by such terms as conflict, cooperation and teamwork.

The conflict/teamwork dimension

When there is interdependence between individuals and groups, there must always be some degree of cooperation between them. However, the nature of this cooperation can vary considerably and it is this which, to a large degree, determines the performance of the organizational unit. At one extreme, the nature of this cooperation, or in other words the relationship between the individuals and groups, can be very hostile, that is, conflict. At the other extreme, it can be very friendly and supportive, that is, teamwork. By definition, conflict and teamwork cannot co-exist, and between these two extremes there can be many varying degrees of cooperation. Thus the nature of relationships between individuals and groups can be considered to be on a continuum or single dimension, which at one extreme has conflict and at the other teamwork. In between these extremes, the nature of the relationships, or degree of cooperation, can vary between hostile, neutral and friendly cooperation, as shown In Figure 11.2.

Initially when people come together, relationships are somewhere in between the extremes of this dimension. The exact initial position on this conflict/teamwork dimension is dependent on the people themselves, the nature of their previous relationships, and a number of structural causes of conflict. In an ideal world, relationships would start at the cooperation point and then move to teamwork. This is the phase theory of team development, which has been identified by many researchers.

In practice, the relationships between those involved in an organization can move back and forth towards either extreme on the conflict teamwork dimension. In most organizations relationships tend to be grouped somewhere near the middle ground in some form of cooperation, and the full benefits of teamwork are not achieved. However, in a significant number of project organizations, relationships between individuals and groups approach, or are at the conflict extremity.

Teamwork	Conflict
Members of the group are committed to the group's/project objectives.	Members of the group have divergent objectives.
Communication is 'open'.	Communication is guarded, censored or withheld.
There is mutual trust between members.	Distrust and negative stereotyping is mutual.
Mutual support exists between members.	When a group member has problems, other members stand aside or take advantage of that member's predicament.
People express feelings and ideas.	Feelings are hidden, and ideas are withheld.
Disagreements are expressed and worked through.	Disagreements lead to power struggles and win–lose battles.
The group atmosphere is relaxed, comfortable and informal.	The atmosphere is cold, strained unpleasant and formal.

Figure 11.3   Characteristics of Teamwork and Conflict

The term 'team' is often used to describe any group of individuals, or managers of groups or departments, for example management team, or project team. This is often misleading as there are differences between a collection of individuals, or managers, comprising a group or organizational unit and a 'team'. For example, the term 'team' describes the characteristics of the relationships within the group, and not all groups are teams. This is best understood by looking at the factors that characterize teamwork, and the lack of it, between individuals, groups and companies who make up an organizational unit (see Figure 11.3).

When there is interaction and interdependency between individuals, groups and companies involved in a joint undertaking, such as a project, cooperation is essential to efficient working. The more this cooperation approaches teamwork, the more effective the organization is likely to be. The more this cooperation approaches conflict, the less effective the organization will be. Therefore one of the objectives of the project manager should always be to lead the individuals, groups and companies, who make up the project organization towards total teamwork.

Developing teamwork in a small group is much easier than developing teamwork between groups and in a large organizational unit. Often small groups form effective teams within themselves, and are committed to their individual group's objectives, which may or may not be the project's objectives. At the same time they are hostile to other groups outside of the ring fence which delimits their team's boundaries. The larger the organization, or more precisely the organization unit, the more difficult it is to develop total teamwork throughout the organization, and the more likely there is to be conflict between groups.

Developing teamwork requires first of all that those individuals who interact together and who are interdependent, and form a distinct group, be identified and a group 'entity' established. This applies to the formal and informal organization, and includes the functional, mixed, matrix and horizontal groups that exist at all levels in the project organization. Once these 'family' groups are identified, team development can commence. It is also essential to identify key integrating superiors, whose functions are to lead, manage and integrate the groups, both in terms of work output and human relations.

However, in a large organization, it is particularly important to apply team development to those individuals who have overlapping group membership. These include the formal group superiors, among others, and are what Likert[11] termed 'linking pins'. These individuals link the groups together and if team-work can be established between linking pins, then it is very likely that their respective subordinate groups will work together in the same manner. Conversely, if there is conflict between these linking pin senior managers, it is very likely there will be conflict between their respective subordinates.

For example, in a building project, if the client's representative, the architect and the construction manager work as a team, then their respective organizations will also work together in the same manner. Similarly, if the project manager and the functional manager work as a team, the problems of the matrix organization are much reduced. Thus this linking pin concept is particularly relevant in the matrix and multi-company project situation. The relationships between the senior managers of the different groups, departments and companies involved in the project, set the tone and nature of the relationships of all those working on the project.

Team-building

Team building, or development, is very fashionable today, there are many consultants specializing in it and the processes involved are much more crystallized than previously. Team-building interventions may involve the following activities:

- Role analysis and psychological matching of team members.
- Team building through organizational development, training courses, management games and in particular the use of problem solving team-building workshops.

The role analysis approach

The study of teams has shown that team members carry out various roles that facilitate the working of the team and its development. Traditionally they have been divided into 'task roles', which help the team to accomplish its objectives, and 'building and maintenance roles' which help establish and maintain the teamwork relationship between members:

Task Roles	**Building & maintenance**
Iniator	Harmonizer
Informer	Gatekeeper

Information seeker	Encourager
Clarifier	Compromiser
Summarizer/Coordinator	Observer/Commentator
Reality tester	Follower
Procedural technician	
Energizer	
Elaborator	
Consensus tester	

Modern research, such as that carried out by Belbin[6], and Margerison and McCann,[12] has taken this concept a stage further and has crystallized the roles required in an effective team. It also uses a battery of psychometric and other tests, which enables peoples' preferences for various roles, mental ability, personality and character to be determined and measured, as detailed below:

- Individual's role preferences can be clarified, together with the expectations and obligations of these roles.
- Individuals can be counselled and matched to their preferred roles.
- Balanced teams can be designed on the basis of the roles required and by matching group members to their preferred roles.

Unfortunately, in a matrix or multi-company situation in project work, it is difficult to design a balanced team based on preferred roles. Nevertheless an understanding of the different roles involved in teams and of the role preferences of the members of the project group are of use in tackling the difficult problem of team building.

Stages of team development

It takes time to develop a team from a new group; it does not happen overnight. Such a group progresses through a number of phases in which mutual trust and respect grow and it develops into a team. This development may include the following phases:

- Evaluation/immature group.
- Experimentation/risk taking.
- Consolidation/intimacy.
- Mature team.

When a new immature group comes together on a project it is usually at the neutral cooperation stage in the conflict/teamwork dimension. There is then a period when people get to know and evaluate one another in relation to personalities, abilities, personal goals and the power structure. If these are found acceptable, there will be a period of experimentation when people start to expose their feelings and to take risks in terms of more open communication and trust. If these experiments are successful, they respect the other members and feel they can trust them, they move on to a group consolidation phase and there is more intimacy and the growth of friendship, that is, friendly cooperation. At this stage, disagreements are aired more freely and attempts are made to work them through without emotions being raised. Once this stage is passed, they can move on to a mature teamwork phase with all the characteristics of a team.

If an adverse reaction occurs at any stage, team development may stall and the group will remain at that stage of cooperation, revert to an earlier stage, or even start down the slippery road to conflict. This process of team development can be accelerated by the use of organization development interventions on team building and action-learning type courses on teamwork.

Team-building through organization development

Organization development (OD) can be defined as:

> For me, the essence of OD is using the action research model to apply behavioral science and management techniques aimed at organizational improvement, including both institutional effectiveness and the quality of life of the members of the system.[13]

It tends to have the following characteristics:

- An emphasis on the work team as the key unit for addressing issues and learning more effective modes of organizational behaviour.
- An emphasis, though not exclusively so, on group, intergroup, and organizational processes in contrast to substantive content.
- The use of an action research model.
- An emphasis on the collaborative management of work team culture, including temporary teams.
- An emphasis on the management of the culture of the total system, including intergroup culture.
- Attention to the management system ramifications.
- A view of the change effort as an ongoing process.[14]

OD is not a 'quick fix' solution, rather it is a longer term effort to improve the way people work together in a group or organization, and their effectiveness. Team building is an important part of OD, and its activities are concerned with the following:

- Diagnosis.
- Task accomplishment.
- Building and maintaining effective interpersonal relationships.
- Understanding and maintaining group processes.

- Role analysis and negotiations.

It emphasizes working with the total group of individuals who interact and are interdependent. This includes 'family' groups of a superior and his subordinates, and special groups, such as task forces, project groups and groups of interlocking pins. The type of interventions used include the following:

- Diagnostic meetings
  This involves an evaluation of the functioning of the group and the identification of any problems.
- Sensitivity training
  This helps individuals learn about themselves and the effect of their behaviour on others.
- Team-building meetings
  These concentrate on how the group can develop teamwork, and generally involve problem-solving, team-building workshops.
- Role analysis and negotiations
  This involves the processes defined previously and negotiations, or horse trading on roles, power distribution and behaviour.
- Intergroup interventions and organizational mirror interventions
  These interventions are similar to the above, but are concerned with the resolution of problems between groups.

Team-building through organization development can be effective over time, and can change the behaviour of managers and lead to effective teamwork.

Team building courses

In order to shorten the process of team-building, many behavioural consultants run team-building courses and management games, which can either be external to the organization, or in-house. These generally concentrate on the following areas:

- Developing team skills through action learning and personal experience.
- Sensitivity training.
- Problem-solving, team-building activities.
- Counselling, coaching and reviewing activities and behaviour observed in the process.

These can be effective, but are preferably run in-house and should involve the total group, or linking pins, including in particular the senior manager or managers. At present, outward bound or wilderness survival courses are very popular in this context.

Application to project work

Unfortunately, in the project setting, it is generally not possible to design a balanced team based on role analysis, or have the time for the OD approach. Individuals are assembled from different groups, departments and companies for a temporary undertaking, and teamwork must be developed quickly. The project manager has sometimes little say in which people from other departments in the company are allocated to the project, and little or no say on the people from other companies. However, an important tool in team-building is the problem-solving, team-building workshop, and the project start-up requirements are made to measure for the use of this intervention. These workshops do lead to the development of teamwork and they underpin both the OD approach and the team-building courses.

The concepts underlying the use of these workshops in team-building are best described in the following quote:

> When a group engages in problem-solving activities directed towards task accomplishment, the group members 'build something together'. It appears that the act of building something together also builds a sense of camaraderie, cohesion and esprit de corps.
>
>   Team building occurs as a natural by-product of learning to solve problems in a group setting.[14]

The main ingredients involved in a group building something together are as follows:

- Get the right people together for ...
- a large block of uninterrupted time ...
- to work on high priority problems or opportunities that ..
- they have identified and that are worked on ...
- in ways that are structured to enhance the likelihood of ...
- realistic solutions and action plans that are ...
- implemented enthusiastically and ...
- followed up to assess actual versus expected results.[15]

In a project start-up situation, it is necessary to communicate the project objectives, its scope and the responsibilities of those involved. It is also necessary for people to come together to develop the project's organization structure, plans, communication channels and information systems.

These requirements are often handled by holding an extended project start-up meeting involving all the key people working on the project, that is, the linking pins. This start-up meeting can be turned into a problem-solving, team-building workshop, with or without the use of behavioural consultants, or other aspects of the team building courses. It would involve the key project members from the groups, departments and companies taking a three to five day residential break to carry out these required activities. This type of start-up meeting is valuable in itself to carry out these essential start-up requirements, but it is also invaluable in getting people to know each other and in the development of teamwork.

Before there is a chance of teamwork being developed, it is also necessary to create conditions conducive to teamwork. All too often in project work the conditions created are more conducive to the development of conflict. This subject will be discussed in the following chapter.

Notes

1. R.R. Blake and J.S. Mouton (1985) *The Managerial Grid 111*, Gulf Publishing Co.
2. P.L. Hunsaker and C.W. Cook (1986) *Managing Organization Behavior*, Addison Wesley Publishing Co.
3. J.B. Miner (1980) *Theories of Organizational Behaviour*, The Dryden Press.
4. B.N. Baker, D.C. Murphy and D. Fisher (1983) 'Factors affecting project success', in D.I. Cleland and W.R. King (eds) *Project Management Handbook*, Van Nostrand Reinhold.
5. G.A. Yukl (1981) *Leadership in Organizations*, Prentice Hall.
6. R. Meridith Belbin (1981) *Management Teams: Why They Succeed or Fail*, Heinemann Professional Publishing.
7. P.J. Duffy and R.D. Thomas (1988) 'Project performance auditing', *From Conception to Completion*, 9th World Congress on Project Management.
8. F.E. Fielder (1965) 'Engineer the job to fit the manager', *Harvard Business Review*, September–October.
9. F.L. Harrison (1988) 'Conflict, power and politics in project management', *From Conception to Completion*, 9th World Congress on Project Management.
10. H. Mintzberg (1983) *Structure in Fives: Designing Effective Organizations*, Prentice Hall.
11. R. Likert (1961) *New Patterns of Management*, McGraw Hill.
12. C. Margerison and D. McCann, *How to Lead a Winning Team*, MCB University Press.
13. D.D. Umstot (1980) 'Organization development technology and the military: a surprising merger?', *Academy of Management Review*, 5(2).
14. W.L. French and C.H. Bell Jr (1984) *Organization Development*, Prentice Hall.
15. C. Bell Jr and J. Rosenzweig (1978) 'Highlights of an organization improvement program in a city government', in W.L. French, C.H. Bell Jr and R.A. Zawacki (eds), *Organization Development: Theory, Practice and Research*, Business Publications.

Chapter 12

CONFLICT IN THE PROJECT SETTING

The 'reality' of the project environment

An underlying assumption of behaviouralists is that 'individuals are well balanced human beings who work unselfishly together towards a common objective.' The human behaviour, or fully participative approach to management is a highly moralistic approach and it would be wonderful if all individuals, groups, companies and even nations behaved as it assumes. Unfortunately, not all, or perhaps not even the majority, do. In practice, the reality of people, and of organizations tends to be somewhat different to their assumptions, and in the real world, unless the project manager is very lucky or skilful, the following scenario is likely to exist:

- The level of trust, mutual support, respect and open communication is generally low.
- Teamwork, except in small groups, is rare.
- Hostility, and even hate, between individuals and groups is not uncommon.
- Conflict is widespread.
- Political manoeuvring to achieve power exists in almost every organization.
- Political conflict among senior managers is widespread.[1]

These facts of life may be considered a jaundiced and cynical view of management, but unfortunately they represent a view of life in many organizations, and the situation they describe is all too common. Thus a significant problem in the achievement of participation and teamwork in the project organization is the existence of conflict between individuals and groups. In particular, it is useless to attempt to develop teamwork if there is conflict in the organization, and unfortunately conflict exists in many project organizations, as it does in many companies.

The consequences of conflict

Conflict is where but for the restraints of civilization and society, blows would be struck. The depth of feelings or hostility that exist in the business setting as a result of conflict is often astonishing. Conflict between individuals and groups in an organization prevents participation and makes it impossible to create or maintain an effective team of all those working in the organization, which is the only way of achieving their ultimate performance potential.

Conflict leads to a lack of respect and trust between groups, a lack of harmony and cooperation, and a breakdown in communication, with information being distorted, censored or withheld. Each group will tend to reject ideas, opinions and suggestions arising from the other groups, and feelings or emotions will run high, with a greater chance of mistakes being made by people whose judgement is clouded by stress. Groups will tend to have unspoken objectives, different from those of the organization, such as to 'get' the other group, block anything they propose, achieve dominance over them and show them in a poor light to senior management. Organizational objectives will be subordinated to the group goals, which concentrate on achieving dominance or victory over the other groups. This accelerates the breakdown of communication between groups, and creates unfavourable attitudes and images of other groups.

There will be a polarization into a 'we/they' attitude, instead of 'all for one and one for all'. Decision-making and problem-solving will be slow and difficult, differences will not be worked through in an open manner and there will be win/lose situations leading to more hostility and conflict, lowest common denominator compromises, or submission of disputes to higher levels of management for arbitration. In general conflict is detrimental to overall performance and will make it impossible for a commitment to the organizational objectives to develop.

Alternatively, conflict between groups can actually enhance the cohesion and team spirit of the individual group. Group loyalty will increase, internal differences will be buried within the group and there will be a greater commitment to the group's objectives, but not necessarily to the organization's objectives. The individuals in the group will tend to close ranks against a common enemy, that is the other groups.

Within these groups there is a more purposeful atmosphere, and probably more autocratic leadership patterns, more structuring and organization, more in-group loyalty and conformity for a solid front to the 'enemy'. The group within itself tends to be more effective in achieving its own objectives where coordination and interaction with other groups is not required. Though this may be advantageous for the individual group, it will prevent the development of total teamwork and thus lead to poorer organizational performance.

Thus it is true that conflict between individuals and groups in an independent situation can lead to increased performance. However, when those individuals and groups are interdependent, conflict will always prevent participation and teamwork, and thus will always result in reduced overall performance. People, groups and organizations rarely achieve their true potential performance because of the effects of conflict.

Disagreement or conflict?

A number of researchers have studied conflict in project management, for example Wilemon,[2] Butler,[3] Thamhain and Wilemon,[4] and Kerzner.[5] For example, Thamhain and Wilemon in a sample of 100 project managers identified the following rank order for potential sources of conflict experienced by project managers.

1.   Schedules.
2.   Project priorities.
3.   Manpower resources.
4.   Technical conflict.
5.   Administration procedures.
6.   Cost objectives.
7.   Personality conflicts.

Although disagreements over these factors are identified as the content of conflict, it can be argued that in general they are not the actual sources of conflict, except perhaps for the last factor, personality conflicts. A misconception about conflict is that it is caused by disagreement between people, that is, disagreement over schedules, project priorities or as Pfeffer calls them 'heterogeneous beliefs about technology'.[6]

It is almost impossible to have an organization without disagreements arising between the people involved and these disagreements lead to heated discussion and arguments. It would be foolish to imagine that people and groups can work together without disagreements occurring. In fact, it is highly desirable that you have these differences and disagreements exist , as without them performance would be low and the organization would be mediocre and complacent or consist of a group of 'yes men'. Disagreement in a healthy organization is essential for efficient and effective problem-solving and decision-making, and need not by itself lead to conflict.

If you have teamwork, or at least a cooperative working relationship, disagreements can be worked through and good relationships between the individuals and groups maintained. However, as relationships move from co-operation to the early stages of conflict, disagreements tend to be resolved by bargaining and compromises are made. The danger then is that resentment about having to give up too much in the compromise will push relationships into conflict.

The important point is that such disagreements over issues are not the causes of conflict, but are what conflict is observed to be about. Differences and disagreements can occur over a million and one topics, and in one organization can lead to raging conflict and major power struggles involving the whole work force. Yet in another organization, these very same disagreements are worked through and teamwork prevails.

Where these disagreements do lead to conflict, they are not generally the real source of that conflict, but merely the symptoms of the underlying conflict 'disease', caused by other factors. They are thus what conflict is about, but not the 'source' of the conflict. In a healthy organizational relationship people can walk away from disagreement over an issue and resume a cooperative or teamwork relationship. Where conflict exists this is not possible; emotions are raised to high intensity and disagreement is not limited to the subject directly involved, but extends to everything proposed by the other party. Basically, if A says it is white, B will say it is black. The following factors differentiate conflict from disagreement about an issue:

- The intensity of emotion generated and sustained over a long period.
- The disagreement or conflict extends beyond the issue concerned into all of the interrelationships between the two parties.
- There are one or more underlying sources of conflict.

It is thus necessary to probe deeper to determine the source or sources of such conflict. It is not disagreement over these million and one topics that causes conflict, it is the breakdown of relationships between people and groups. Conflict occurs between people and is caused by people, and there are a large number of factors, that cause, are the source or accentuate conflict. These fall into three classifications, as shown in Figure 12.1.

1. Factors primarily associated with problems caused by the structure of the organization, i.e. organization problems.
2. Factors arising out of people's self-interests.
3. Factors primarily associated with problems caused by individuals, i.e. people problems.

Organization structure and conflict

The organization structure of a project can increase or decrease the potential for conflict, and thus conversely the potential for teamwork between individuals and groups. Organization design is thus of great importance, and can on its own

Problems with the organization structure

Large organizations	Temporary nature
Large organizational units	Large functional departments
Tall hierarchies	Problems of integration
Bureaucracy	Clashes of cultures
Over-centralization	Functional orientation
Authority/power problems	Confrontation of managers
Complexity	Dual subordination
Uncertainty	Defence of territory

People's self-interests

Personal motivations	Competition
Incompatible objectives	Peer competition
Forms of contract	For scarce resources
	Survival

People problems
'Normal people'

Differences in:	Dependency
Personalities	Lack of interpersonal skills
Abilities	History of conflict
Motivation	

'Problem people'

Extreme ineptness in interpersonal skills	Management style not conducive to teamwork
Insecurity and stress	Autocratic
Peter Principle	Permissive
Professional as a manager	Administrator (1,1)
The managerial rogue	Clashes of styles

Figure 12.1   Sources of conflict

impel people into conflict, or teamwork, despite individual attitudes or desires. Problems in the organization of projects which accentuate the tendency for conflict, or teamwork, were covered explicitly and implicitly in Chapters 2 to 4 on the organization of projects. The following summary covers the main points of those factors which contribute to the generation of conflict.

The size and shape of the organization structure

The larger the organization, and the organization units, the taller the management hierarchy, the more centralized it is, and the more bureaucratically it operates, the more likely there is to be conflict between the managers and groups involved. The size and shape of the organization structure used can impel people towards conflict due to the uncertainty and complexity of the structure, problems with authority, the existence of large functional departments and the remoteness of key integrating superiors, among other reasons.

Problems due to weak, inadequate or uncertain power

Modern writers on power and politics, such as Pfeffer[6] and Mintzberg[7] identify the dispersion of power as the principal factor leading to politics in an organization. The same principle applies to authority gaps, weaknesses in the organization structure and weak superior power, whether it is positional, personal or political power.

Pfeffer's model is particularly applicable to the analysis of conflict and power in an organizational unit. It states that the following factors produce conflict in an organization:

- The environment.
- Interdependence.
- Hetrogeneous beliefs about technology, i.e. differences over how to achieve goals.
- Differentiation, i.e. functionalization.
- Scarcity of resources.

If this conflict concerns matters which management considers to be important and power is dispersed, then conflict escalates to the political level. In addition to the problems created by the authority gap of the project manager, a weak key integrationist superior in any position can accentuate conflict. A weak superior will simply not have the power to prevent conflict occurring, or to manage it, if it does. This is often coupled with a superior who has only positional power and who often 'to maintain his authority' must exercise coercive power. The manager who is continually disciplining subordinates, almost certainly lacks personal or political power. If this superior is also insecure, for any reason, he or she will feel threatened by subordinates, peers and superiors. The tendency is then for this manager to employ the 'dark' side of politics to strengthen his or her position and to weaken the others in this conflict situation, purely for defensive reasons. Thus factors such as the authority gap of the project manager, combined with the nature and complexity of the organization structure are strong sources of conflict in project management.

Dual subordination

The matrix organization has many of the above problems, not the least of which is that of dual subordination. Unless both project and functional managers accept this arrangement and deal with it sensitively, conflict will be accentuated.

Functionalization

The mere fact that separate groups are formed, reinforced by the specialist nature of these groups, creates divisions in the organization and sets people apart. These divisions can then lead to problems with large functional groups, as described in Chapters 2 to 4 on organization:

- Accentuation and clashes of cultures.

- Difficulties in integration, both of work and people.
- Functional orientation.
- Confrontation between matrix and functional managers.

However, the mere fact that there are separate differentiated groups causes problems which lead to conflict. Not the least of these is the age old concept of 'defence of territory'. A basic human motivation is the motivation to defend one's territory. A manager's sphere of influence, area of technical expertise, responsibilities and subordinates can be considered his or her territory. When another manager encroaches on this territory, the manager springs to its defence and conflict arises. This occurs instinctively, but it is also stimulated by the fear that this encroachment may only be a prelude to a permanent takeover of territory.

This problem exists with any hierarchial organization, but it is particularly widespread in the matrix organization. The project manager must be involved in the management, planning and control of all the groups involved in the project. Functional managers may resent this invasion of their territory and the subversion of their subordinates, as they see it, and act defensively or counter attack. The problem is compounded when responsibilities and authority are unclear. Thus this primitive motivational factor can lead to conflict in organizations involved in the highest technology work, and is accentuated by the organization structure used.

The people factor

Although structural problems can influence people towards conflict or teamwork, the people factor can dominate this influence. In other words, even if the form of organization structure is heavily biased towards encouraging teamwork between individuals and groups, problems with individuals can lead to conflict. Conversely, even if the organization structure points towards conflict, individuals and groups can still develop teamwork.

People problems leading to conflict in project management can be classified under two headings:

- Individual and group self-interests.
- Problem people or personality problems.

Individual and group self-interests

Behavioural theories tend to assume that all managers are 'social beings who are totally unselfish and primarily concerned with the organization's interests'. It would be nice if such a paragon of virtue could be called the 'normal' manager, but it is highly debateable whether this is so. None the less, it would probably also be wrong to take the cynical opposite approach that all managers are cold, calculating beings, concerned solely with self interest.

Most managers are at least partially motivated by self-interest, and it would be foolish to imagine otherwise. There is nothing intrinsically immoral about this, particularly if these self-interests are, or can be, aligned with the organization's interests. Even if they are not aligned and they are purely selfish, this is still understandable and very human. Yet when the self interests of managers differ, there can be conflicts of interests, or incompatible objectives, and they in turn lead to conflict.

Incompatible objectives

Often individuals and groups, both small and large, have their own objectives which may be incompatible with other groups' objectives and with those of the organization as a whole. These objectives may be openly displayed, but in a conflict situation they are more often hidden. Typically in such a case they are self-advancement or adversary type objectives, such as to gain dominance, discredit and even eliminate another group.

Sometimes these incompatible objectives arise from the difference in cultures in functional and project groups, but often they arise between large groups in projects because of the form of contract used. This can create conflict between client, contractor and subcontractor, etc. over time, cost and quality unless the contract is designed to avoid this sort of problem. For example, the client will want the lowest cost, fastest completion time and highest quality, which are incompatible objectives in themselves. The contractor will want to make a profit, which may mean claiming for all the extras or changes, thus increasing the cost; it will want to complete the project in the most cost-effective time to itself, and it will want the minimum quality to meet the contractual specifications. At least, this is likely be the view of each party of the other's supposed objectives. The most extreme example of this is the basic cost plus or re-imbursable form of contract, where incompatible objectives, defence of territory and conflict are the norm. It seems strange that many such contracts seem to be written deliberately to create conflict between the groups involved.

Sometimes the problem is not so much that the objectives are incompatible, but more that they are invisible. It is not unknown for the organization's objectives not to be communicated adequately to all those involved, and not to be broken down into individual and group objectives, coordinated with the organization's. Sometimes the organization's objectives are not accepted as their own by individuals and groups. Occasionally, the organization has no clearly defined objectives. Whatever the reasons, where incompatible objectives exist in an organization, or objectives are unclear, do not exist, or are not accepted, this will very likely lead to conflict.

Competition

People vary as to how strong a motivator is the 'desire to win', that is competition. Traditionally, cultures may be differentiated, for example the English may stress 'good losers', whilst the Americans may emphasize 'winning at all costs'. Whether these stereotypes represent reality or not, the desire to win, or perhaps in some people, the desire 'not to lose', is a strong motivator for most managers. Belbin[8] describes such competitive senior managers as 'shapers', and comments on their proneness to aggression, producing reciprocal reactions from other group members, and the fact they have no hesitation in pursuing their goals by illicit means. In business, management and organizations, winning is everything for many managers; to come second is to fail, and thus beating your competitors is the 'name of the game'. All too often, coming second actually means that the manager does not survive very long in that organization.

Competition is a stimulus to performance, both in athletics and in management, but it is also a source of conflict. Competition with others does spur individuals, groups and organizations to higher performance and greater teamwork. Thus competition between groups will lead to greater teamwork within the group and, if the groups are independent and do not interact with each other, higher organizational performance. On the other hand, if groups are interdependent and interact with each other, then competition between groups is likely to lead to conflict and lower organizational unit performance.

Three common areas of competition contribute to conflict in a project:

1. Peer competition.
2. Competition for scarce resources.
3. Competition for survival in a harsh environment.

Human nature being what it is, there will always tend to be competition between peers for rewards, promotion, recognition, credit, 'glory', getting their own way, power and dominance. In a healthy climate, this can lead to increased performance, but if any of the other sources of conflict exist, and in particular if there are people problems, then this competition will greatly accentuate conflict. The higher the level in the hierarchy this competition exists, the more serious will be its effect on, and of conflict.

When resources are scarce there will always tend to be competition for them, both in the interdependent and the independent situations. The two most common resources over which there is competition and thus conflict are money and people. If the availability of funds is limited, senior managers will compete and fight to get their 'share'. Similarly, managers will compete to get 'adequate' staff for their projects, both in number and in quality. Empire building is a common facet of many organizations and each manager may compete to build up their organizations. Managers will also compete for scope to expand, achieve and for the opportunity to perform.

Although this scarcity of resources applies to most organizations, the fiercest competition over this factor occurs when a firm or project meets a harsh environment: a very tight project; project managers competing to manage a scarce project; or when rationalization, retrenchment or closure is threatened. In this situation it is conflict over survival, and almost literally blood can flow. Which groups suffer redundancy, which groups are eliminated, if groups are merged, who goes and who becomes the new group's manager, are all justified sources of conflict, from the individual's point of view.

In less dramatic terms, this source of conflict occurs in the matrix organization where several projects or tasks are resourced by common functional groups. Each task or project manager is in competition with the others to get the best people working on the project in sufficient numbers to meet the objectives. Conflict can thus arise between task managers, and between them and the functional group managers over the quality and quantity of resources of people and money assigned to the individual project or task.

Thus people's self interests, as expressed in what motivates them, incompatible objectives, and competition, are an understandable source of conflict. It is up to the project manager to ensure that people's self-interests are aligned with the project's and that they are best served by cooperation and not conflict.

People problems

Conflict, almost by definition, involves raised emotions or ill feelings, but up to now the sources of conflict discussed have been based on substantive self-interest or structural problems. It has been presumed that as two parties come into conflict over substantive issues, emotions become aroused and ill-feeling grows between the parties involved. However, this process operates in the opposite direction too.

Organizations are not staffed with 'rational, cognitive persons abstracted from such emotions as anger, hate, envy or pride'. Emotions exist, emotional ties do link individuals and groups in an organization, and they cannot be ignored. They may be positive and thus encourage teamwork, but they may also be negative and encourage conflict. Thus an significant source of conflict is that which is given the generic name of 'personality differences', which could be more appropriately termed 'people problems'. Conflict need not be based solely on substantive self-interest, it can be based on emotions, that is ill-feeling by one party, or between parties, or as the theorist would term it, socio-emotional relationships between parties. The way people deal with one another is one of the most important sources of conflict and destroyers of teamwork.

In practice, when conflict is primarily based on emotions, substantive issues are brought into the conflict, but resolving them does not resolve the conflict, as they are merely side issues, or symptoms. Thus conflict, based on emotions, personality differences or people problems, is very difficult to deal with.

The term 'personality differences' is a rather inadequate description of the feelings or emotions generated from a breakdown of human relationships. It may cover the following emotions or reactions:

- Aggression
- Anger
- Annoyance
- Antagonism
- Dislike
- Envy

- Fear
- Frustration
- Hate
- Jealousy
- Neurotic hostility
- Resentment

Although terms like hate in the management setting appear to be extravagant, it is unfortunately true that feelings can and do develop to this intensity. The full range of human emotions can be generated by the way people relate to each other, often without any substantive self-interest being involved. Once any one of these emotions is felt by one or more of the parties, then relationships are on the slippery road to conflict.

It must be recognized that even if every manager was a competent, well-balanced human being with no special likes or dislikes, there would be problems with personality differences. It must also be recognized that managers are human beings, each with their own full share of human failings, likes and dislikes, and variable competency and motivation. Thus in addition to the personality differences and problems that arise with well balanced human beings, it is unfortunately necessary to add the many causes of conflict from personality, ability and motivational sources, that arise with 'normal', real-life human beings. If this were not enough, it is also true that many organizations have their share of fools, incompetents, rogues, neurotics and other 'problem people', who multiply the sources of conflict. Only one such catalyst is sufficient to lead to conflict and the breakdown of teamwork.

Sometimes the personality differences arise for no more reason than one party takes an instant dislike to the other party. People are different and have differing personalities which sometimes clash for no apparent reason. Often the starting point of conflict caused by personality problems is simply resentment at another person's actions, attitude, tone, look or words. This resentment is followed by a reduction or withdrawal of cooperation, and relationships have then started to move away from teamwork and towards conflict.

Often the mere fact that these individuals and groups are interdependent leads to personality differences and conflict. Individuals and groups in an organizational unit are dependent on one another for their performance. Some people may simply resent being dependent on someone else and react against it. More commonly, when there are problems or set-backs, the tendency is to blame the other person, or group involved. Sometimes this may be justified, sometimes it is not, but the net result is the same: antagonism, personality differences and conflict. A common result of this factor is 'negative stereotyping', that is, each group comes to believe the other group is composed of morons, fools and incompetents.

Negative stereotyping and conflict may arise from a history of conflict built up over a number of years. This source of conflict is very difficult to eradicate as it may have been incorporated into each group's culture. Any new member, even a group leader, would find it very difficult to break with tradition and participate with the enemy. This is the 'Hill billy feud' or 'Romeo and Juliet' syndrome which typifies many interdepartmental relationships.

Varying ability and commitment can also contribute significantly to personality differences and conflict. Managers and their subordinates in an organizational unit may vary in their managerial and technical abilities; they may be good at some activities and not at others; their speed of working, or understanding of new ideas may vary; finally their motivation, energy and commitment to the organization's objectives may vary. When any such variations are significant, there is the potential for conflict. The individual at the lower level of these factors may feel insecure and threatened because of it, and thus act defensively. The higher performing individual may feel superior and hold the others in contempt, and show it. The result may be an intellectual elite which forms a close-knit team, and excludes those it feels do not meet its standards in any of these factors.

Problems in interpersonal relationships that are not based on structural or substantive self-interest issues, generally arise because of the following:

• A lack of interpersonal skills in the otherwise competent manager.
• The existence in the organization of difficult or problem people.

Lack of interpersonal skills

Many managers lack skill in dealing with interpersonal relationships and can 'put people's backs up', cause offence and resentment, and start relationships on the path to conflict, quite unconsciously. It is surprising, or perhaps not so surprising, what a difference the choice of the following routes can make to interpersonal relationships:

1. You communicate with people with sensitivity and tact, and take into account their feelings.
2. You use the wrong word, are a bit abrupt when under pressure, do not listen, or you show your feelings in a look.

This does not mean to say that one need be soft or easy going, or even participative. Consider the subtleties of the English language as applied to a strong leadership style. The dictionary or thesaurus associates strong with hard, harsh, tough, firm, unyielding, callous, etc. Yet there is a world of difference between leadership styles based on these descriptions, for example strong and harsh.

Nevertheless this lack of interpersonal skill causes many of the interpersonal difficulties that exist in organizations. As a general style of management, sensitivity training, that is, training to stimulate openness, to break down inhibitions and to develop the skill of honest feedback, has had its heyday,[9] as it tends to develop ineffective Theory Y managers, yet used selectively it can improve the way managers deal with their fellow human beings. Thus specialized training can make a significant difference in reducing the incidence of this source of conflict. The same cannot be definitely stated when describing personality problems caused by the actions of difficult or problem people.[10]

Problem people

Although conflict due to personality differences can occur with almost anyone, 'difficult' or 'problem people' are particularly prone to be the source of conflict. Many organizations can identify managers who have problems in one way or another in their interpersonal relationships. They are generally not team players and they can generate interpersonal differences and conflict across the complete span of their relationships, that is with peers, subordinates and even their superiors.

These problem managers, in addition to having one or other of the problems already outlined, often have one of the following problems:

- Extreme ineptness in interpersonal skills, often deeply based in their personality; this includes fools, incompetents, neurotics and sometimes extremely intelligent 'Apollo' types.
- Insecurity and stress.
- A management style not conducive to teamwork.
- They are 'managerial rogues'.

Ineptness in interpersonal skills

Although many managers have a lack of interpersonal skills, there are some who are particularly inept in this area. This ineptness is due to, or has become part of their personality. In such cases it is likely that no amount of training or psychotherapy will change their manner of dealing with people. If this type of training is pressed too far, there is a real danger of mental breakdown in this type of situation.

It might be thought unlikely at first that any effective organizations would have fools, incompetents or neurotics in its management. Yet, it is not altogether uncommon to have such problem people, sometimes at the highest levels, and if present, they act as a catalyst for interpersonal problems. However the opposite can also apply in that groups made up of extremely clever people, that is with high scores in mental ability, have been found to be difficult to manage, prone to destructive debate and have difficulties in decision-making.

Insecurity and stress

Insecurity and stress are related and can be sources of conflict. Most organizations have their share of managers who feel or who actually are insecure. Insecure managers are generally frightened to expose themselves to the risk of failure, of 'being found out', act defensively and are resistant to change. Thus in an interdependent situation where there is continuous change, and authority and responsibilities are unclear, the insecure manager is always likely to come into conflict with the agent of change, that is the project manager.

Sometimes this insecurity is entirely justified if the manager's survival is personally threatened. It may be that the project workload in the organization is falling and there is the danger of redundancy; the manager may be under the threat of discipline; or may be out of his or her depth with new methods and technology, or may be being stalked by a powerful enemy. The manager may have incurred a superior's displeasure and if this superior is a rogue, the manager's life may be being made very difficult.

More often it is because the manager is unable, or feels unable to cope with the demands being made. Managers may feel role conflict, be unhappy with the ambiguity in their role, and be out of their depth in a rapidly changing situation. Their greatest fear is being found out to be incompetent. They feel barely able to cope with the present situation and if there is change, they would be totally lost.

This can occur with two of the common phenomena in management:

- The Peter Principle.
- The professional who has difficulties in the role of a manager.

The Peter Principle is that 'a manager gets promoted to his or her level of incompetence'. Unfortunately this frequently does happen, and such a manager will always tend to be insecure, act defensively, be resistant to change and be a source of conflict.

The phenomenon of the problems of the professional as a manager is more complex. Many professionals encounter problems when they move from a role as a specialist technologist to that of a manager. This can occur in two stages: first when the professional becomes a functional manager in his or her specialism; and second when he or she becomes a general or project manager. Professionals generally are promoted on their professional ability and not necessarily on their potential management ablity. This can lead to problems related to role identity and role conflict when taking a position as a functional manager. The professional, although a manager, will still sometimes tend to identify more closely with the role of a professional specialist, than that of a manager.

Such professionals often find it difficult to overcome problems caused by the lack of compatibility between their purely professional role and the non-technical requirements of the managerial role. This can lead to professionals as managers having difficulty in dealing with people, in organizing, planning and controlling activities, and in handling the financial aspects. This may lead to conflict with others and within themselves. When professionals move into the general or project manager roles, their problems are compounded, unless they shed most of their professional background and culture, and this is often difficult.

The insecurity source of conflict and other personality problems are made worse when the person involved cannot handle the stress involved in their job. The textbook defines stress as:

> A non specific response of the body to any demand made upon it. It is manifest in the psychological, emotional and physiological reactions to internal or external environmental conditions to which the individual's adaptive abilities are perceived to be overextended.[11]

Stress can affect an individual mentally, emotionally or physically. Some stress can stimulate a person to higher performance, but increasing stress will reduce performance, increase the potential for conflict and even kill.

Extra-organizational factors can cause stress in an individual, which will affect work performance and the likelihood of conflict. However, within the organization there are two principal sources of stress:

- Workload.
- Conflict and politics.

A heavy workload can cause stress in a conscientious or insecure individual. This work overload can be either quantitative, that is, too much work to handle, or qualitative, that is, the work is outside the person's ability.

However, the principal cause of organizational stress is the sources of conflict outlined in this chapter, the conflict itself, and the power politics arising from it. Thus a vicious spiral can be created, whereby stress can be caused by those factors causing conflict and this stress in turn can lead to further conflict. It should be noted that one survey of over 2,500 managers identified the political climate of the organization as the principal cause of stress.

Management style as a source of conflict

The employment of a leadership or management style in dealing with subordinates, peers and near-peers in other groups that is inconsistent with the organization culture, the people involved, the situation and the power of the manager, can be a significant source of personality differences, destroyer of teamwork and creator of conflict. People associate an autocratic, despotic style of leadership or management with the generation of this type of conflict, and this does occur in many organizations. Take for example the arrogant use of power by the autocratic manager, who treats subordinates 'like dirt'. The manager's attitude is 'I am the boss and you are my subordinate, so jump when I say so.' The explicit use of naked authority or power to enforce compliance can be counterproductive and is unlikely to generate commitment and teamwork; fear is a poor motivator.

Yet, it is the manner in which power is used that largely determines whether it results in enthusiastic commitment, passive compliance or resistance by those concerned. Strong leadership, the exercise of authority and power, autocratic management, and firm control need not be contradictory to participative management, motivation and teamwork, but can actually be complementary to them. It is the combination of these factors which leads to effective project management. To obtain the best results, power must be exercised in a manner that is more implicit than explicit, and which recognizes respect for the individual.

People do not like living, or working, in an uncertain disorganized world; they actually welcome leadership, accept legitimate authority and established power, and need control. People accept recognized authority and power, not simply through fear, but through respect for it. Thus the exercise of power need not break down participation or teamwork, and in fact if not exercised, uncertainty, confusion and conflict can be created. Also, autocratic management is accepted in the appropriate situations, for example when time is short, decisions are difficult or are of extreme importance, or when there is respect for the ability, power and leadership of the autocratic manager. The necessity or legitimacy of control is also recognized and accepted by most people, and control does perform essential monitoring and motivational functions in project work.

Nevertheless if a strong leadership style is employed, the leader must have the necessary power, and the people involved must recognize and accept it. If these conditions are not met, as may occur in the matrix or multi-company situations, the management style used must be tempered by the situation and the actual power of the manager, if conflict is to be avoided.

It is not only the autocratic manager who can generate such personality differences. The weak, indecisive manager and the bureaucratic manager can be sources of conflict just as much as the autocratic manager. If leadership is indefinite, the senior manager lacks or does not exercise power and employs a weak participative management style, subordinates and others will feel they are becalmed, rudderless,and leaderless, and tend to try to establish their power. This in turn leads to politics and conflict. The bureaucratic manager, who acts more as an administrator, who minutes everything in detail and uses memos to communicate, with copies to all and sundry, instead of face to face, two-way communication, can also generate personality differences which lead to conflict.

A clash of management styles between the various groups and companies working on a project can also cause conflict. This can occur because of two strong leaders competing for dominance, but it is also a result of the fact that different groups or companies with different management styles have to work together. Consider the simple case of individuals from four groups, or the groups themselves, working as one organizational unit and each group taking a different corner of the management grid. One group is totally turned off (1,1); one is at the extreme of concern for people (1,9); one is at the extreme of concern for production (9,1); and the other combines task and people (9,9). Without a very effective and sensitive integrationist manager, there are bound to be misunderstandings, bewilderment, and conflict between these individuals and groups.

Another source of conflict due to management style occurs with what could be termed the management 'rogue' who has a personalized power orientation.

The managerial rogue

The term 'rogue' is used to describe a manager who is ruthless, unprincipled, determined to gain advancement and has few scruples as to how it is achieved, and has a strong personalized power motivation. Behavioural theorists identify two sides to power motivation, a light side and a dark side, or to give them their theoretical textbook names, socialized power motivation and personalized power motivation. Socialized power motivation can enhance the effectiveness of an organization, in that the senior manager uses his or her power to achieve results for the benefit of others and the objectives of the organization. Social norms restrain the negative use of power and it is still possible to have participation and teamwork.

This is not the case with personalized power motivation which almost invariably leads to conflict. The senior manager with personalized power motivation tends to operate as a bully, has a strong detrimental effect on individual motivation, and conflict within and between groups is the norm. Personalized power motivation is characterized by a desire to dominate others, beat the competition, keep subordinates weak and dependent, practice divide and rule politics to maintain dominance, and to use power for personal gain. As one authority states, 'they are often rude, sexually exploitive and greatly concerned with acquiring status symbols.' They often employ typical bully-type methods: encouraging toadies and spies; rewarding favourites; and punishing those who resist those methods. They generally manage through 'force, fear and favour'.

The impact of such managers on their own organizations can be disastrous. Subordinates and other managers will endeavour either formally or informally to develop a power balance and political in-fighting becomes endemic. This manager becomes isolated except for 'yes men' and favourites, and not only does he or she get minimal performance and compliance with direct instructions only, but sabotage will also occur. Communication operates on a one-to-one guarded basis, new ideas are suppressed either because they are slapped down or because they are simply withheld, and risk taking is diminished. It is only because of the subordinates' inherent acceptance of positional power, their commitment to the organization's goals, their desire to survive, and admittedly the ability and energy of the superior manager that the organization achieves any results. In addition, such managers are normally expert in the use of their reward and coercive power to motivate subordinates.

However, motivation is considerably reduced, as fear is a poor motivator, and participation and teamwork are non-existent within the manager's group. Outside of the manager's positional power sphere, other managers reject this manager's attempts to increase positional authority or power, and teamwork between groups is limited to isolated individuals, that is one-to-one type situations or very small groups.

The managerial rogue and politics

One of the unfortunate facts of life is that these rogues tend to reach senior management positions and thus have a significant impact on the extent of the use of the dark side of politics in an organization. The hard working, head-down straightforward manager who is not involved in politics will always tend to be trumped by the effective political operator. In some ways this is justified in that as a manager advances to middle and senior management, involvement in the light side of politics is necessary to be fully effective. Thus senior managers should be both effective managers and effective political operators.

Whereas the light side of politics may be to acquire power to manage the organization more effectively, or more bluntly 'getting your own way', for the good of the organization, in the dark side of politics, the manager is concerned with defeating the opposing forces in order to get his or her own way for personal or group objectives, often unrelated to the good of the organization. When this conflict climbs the hierarchical tree and enters the political arena, woe betide the organization. Political conflict draws everyone to one side or another, and diverts management time, energy and ingenuity away from achieving the objectives of the organization, to achieve victory over the enemy.

Political conflict can be defined as the combination of a struggle between opposing forces, combined with the activities of opponents to acquire power to defeat the 'enemy'. Typically alliances and coalitions are built up by the opposing individuals and groups, until conflict extends throughout the organizational unit, not just those who are initially directly involved in the conflict. Individuals who endeavour to stand clear of this political conflict and support neither party, usually end up being treated unfairly by one of them or both.

The situation may deteriorate to such an extent that the two factions in an organization who are locked in combat, will concentrate all their attention on in-fighting to the extent that they ignore greater external threats to the organization's existence. The organization can fail or be taken over without these factions being aware of the threats until the very last moment. Typically ethics or scruples are lost, political games dominate, divisive objectives are maximized, winning becomes all important and deviousness prevails rather than teamwork. Unfortunately this struggle for power, particularly among senior managers, and the consequential organizational political manoeuvring appears to be a characteristic of many large hierarchical organizations.

Managing the rogue manager

Rogue managers tend to be difficult to handle as subordinates and almost impossible to work with as peers without conflict and politics. One such rogue in an organizational unit is enough to destroy teamwork and bring about political conflict, and the higher such a rogue advances up the hierarchical tree, the more disruptive is the impact. Yet as superiors, particularly as chief executives or the head of an operational unit, they can sometimes be very effective in achieving results as they are often hard driving, personally competent autocrats, in managerial grid terms (9,1) managers. In addition, so-called troublemakers may be classified as rogues, when in fact they are individuals who do not accept the status quo. If managed correctly this type of troublemaker can be a high performer.

Thus, in deciding what action to take to deal with such rogues, it is first necessary to determine whether the particular attributes of that individual are effective or counterproductive to the achievement of the project's objectives. There are typically only two options:

1. Get rid of the rogue, if you can.
2. Manage the rogue, and take the risk.

The management of rogues, as a subordinate, peer or superior, is a high risk strategy which involves the following:

- Gain the rogue's respect, if only as a dangerous person to cross or have as an enemy. As Machiavelli stated, 'You have to be both a 'fox and a lion'[12] or as the Scots would say 'Wha' dare meddle wi' me.'
- Align the rogue's objectives so that they are compatible with yours and the organization's. This involves the 'life boat' strategy from the politician's toolkit, that is ensure that you are both in the same life boat, and that the rogue knows that you will sink or swim together. This involves increasing the rogue's interdependency with you and those managers with whom he or she must interact, such that he or she is dependent on them for the achievement of personal goals.
- Decrease the rogue's interdependency, such that he or she is the head of a more or less independent organizational unit, and thus does not have to interact or be interdependent with anyone who is not a direct subordinate.[9]

This last strategy is much the most effective way to use competent rogues and where they can contribute most to the project's objectives. This is particularly so if there is a troubleshooting role or where there is a crisis. Rogues are most effective in a short-term management of change role under pressure, and least effective in the management of ongoing operations which require interaction with their peers. This may not be very pleasant for the rogue's subordinates, but it can result in high organizational unit performance.

The management of conflict

The traditional theory identifies five modes of managing conflict:

1. Withdrawal
   Retreating or withdrawing from an actual or potential disagreement.
2. Force
   Exerting one's viewpoint at the potential expense of another, often characterized by competiveness and a win/lose situation.
3. Smoothing
   De-emphasizing or avoiding areas of differences and emphasizing areas of agreement.
4. Compromise
   Bargaining and searching for solutions that bring some degree of satisfaction to the parties in dispute.
5. Confrontation
   Facing the conflict directly, which involves a problem solving approach whereby affected parties work through their disagreements.

These modes of resolving conflict are more applicable to the resolution of disagreements than to the resolution of conflict for the reasons outlined below:

- Their use and success in resolving disagreements is dependent on the nature of the existing relationships between individuals and groups.
- They tackle only the symptoms of the conflict disease and not the underlying sources of conflict.

For example, the following modes of disagreement resolution are only applicable when the existing relationships are as shown:

Relationships	Mode of resolution
Conflict	– Withdrawal
	– Forcing
Cooperation	– Smoothing
	– Compromise
Teamwork	– Confrontation

Withdrawal and force are used in the conflict situation, and though they resolve the differences they increase the underlying sources of conflict. Smoothing and compromise are effective in the cooperative stage of relationships and if reasonably balanced they can be effective. Confrontation works when there is teamwork and only then. The management of conflict involves identifying and tackling the underlying sources of conflict, and not the symptoms. The most effective way of managing conflict is to prevent it happening in the first place by the following means:

- Create conditions conducive to teamwork.
- Recognize the first signs of the deterioration of relationships and take action to reverse the movement.
- Manage the organization in such a way that teamwork is encouraged and conflict is discouraged.

This is not always possible and once conflict is recognized, it is necessary to identify the underlying sources, whether they be organization structure, personal self-interests, personality or people problems. This is achieved by auditing the relationships, the organization and the people involved and comparing them with the models outlined in the text. Thereafter it is a case of eliminating the sources of conflict by restructuring the organization or other management action to change the nature of relationships, deal with problem people, create conditions conducive to teamwork and lead the people from conflict to teamwork.

Conclusion – from conflict to teamwork

The leadership of the project manager and other senior managers in the project is critical to the achievement of the project's objectives through high performance. Inevitably this involves a high degree of task orientation; it is results that count, not making people happy and satisfied at work, except in so far as this contributes to the achievement of the task. The project manager must thus be a professional in the 'scientific' aspects of project management, that is the organization, planning and control of the project, combined with the necessary analysis and decision-making. The project manager must have a high personal motivation to succeed, and possess leadership and drive. In order to be able to have the power to carry out this leadership, the project manager must be able to use all the tools available to enhance his or her positional power by personal and political power.

However, unless project managers can also combine this scientific side of project management with the human side, they will be unable to motivate all those involved in the project to achieve high performance and will be in constant conflict with their peers and near-peers, particularly in the matrix and multi-company situations. Teamwork, or at the very least, a cooperative working relationship, is essential in project work, as it is the performance of the organization as a whole which is critical to success, and not just individual or group performance.

Among the most important of the project manager's tasks is the combination of the following:

- The task achievement leadership of the organization.
- The motivation of the individuals, groups and organizational units.
- The welding of these entities to work as a team to achieve the project's objectives.
- The management of conflict, or more precisely the moving of relationships in the conflict–teamwork dimension towards the teamwork extremity.

Therefore not only must the project manager exercise leadership in the achievement of the project's objectives, but must also 'lead' the people and groups involved towards being an effective, highly motivated team.

The following attributes are required of the project manager:

- A vision that teamwork is possible and desirable.
- A high personal commitment to its achievement.
- A conceived strategy to achieve it.
- The ability to take the necessary steps to implement it.
- The ability to create a climate in the organization by words and deeds that inspire the people involved to follow his or her example.

In this leadership, the project manager must recognize that whatever the shortcomings as a general philosophy and style of management, there is a great deal of truth in the work of the human behaviour scientists of the 1960s and 1970s, and thus the project manager should include the following steps in his or her strategy:

- Treat people as adults.
- Communicate with them.
- Vary management style as to the situation, the people and the project manager's power, i.e. use a contingency approach.
- Deal sensitively with:
    dual subordination
    defence of territory
    insecurity and stress
    professionals as managers
    the Peter Principle.
- Deal with, that is manage, rogues.
- Rotate people between functions to break down functional and cultural barriers.
- Establish close physical contact and social interaction in groups and linking pins, i.e. locate them in the same or adjacent offices.
- Align the objectives and create mutual self-interests, e.g. do not write contracts designed to create conflict.

- Implement the following human behaviour strategies:
  Be aware of small signs indicating a breakdown in human relations.
  Audit the organization.
  Train the people and groups in human relations.
  Implement 'team building'.
  Encourage the establishment of the project as a 'super-ordinate object-ive'.
  Avoid win/lose situations, if possible without sacrificing task accom-plishment.
  Do not make enemies needlessly.
  Apply achievement, goal theory and target setting.
  Back this up with the reward system.

In carrying out these strategies the project manager must combine the organiza-tion structure, the structured methodology of project planning and control and the human aspect to provide effective means with which to achieve high motiva-tion and teamwork. If the project manager can achieve this, there are available many valuable tools to avoid or manage conflict, motivate individuals and groups, and build an effective, high performing total team. These factors can contribute to the following.

Organization structure

The project organization structure should be designed to create conditions conducive to motivation and teamwork. This involves the following:

- The avoidance of large, tall, monolithic, centrally controlled hierarchical organization structures.
- The avoidance of large, internal to the project, functional groups or departments.
- The use of mixed or small functional groups, whenever possible, to avoid functional orientation and facilitate teamwork.
- An emphasis on flat, decentralized, organic organization structures com-bined with a divisional structure and discrete organizational units in the larger project.
- An emphasis on the delegation of personal accountability and responsib-ility to individual managers, groups and organizational units.
- The use of the contractor/consignee concept with the in-company matrix organization.
- The clarification of the overall project organization structure, and, for individuals, groups and organizational units:
  Authority
  Objectives
  Responsibilities.
- The identification of formal, matrix and informal groups as discrete

entities, and their key integrating managers. This establishes mutual self-interests, integration and facilitates team development.

Planning and control

The structured methodology of planning and control is used to reinforce this delegation of accountability and responsibility:

1. The structuring of the project in one, two or more dimensions, clearly identifies the responsibilities of organizational and project element, group and cost account or work package managers.
2. Planning and control is participative and personalized.
   - Each individual manager and group has specified their own unique goals, objectives, and planned baselines of schedule, cost and resources.
   - They each receive their own reports on progress and performance measured against these baselines.
   - They have participated in the setting of these goals and baselines.
   - They know what they have to do to achieve good performance and they receive feedback on their own and their colleagues' performance.
3. This is used to:
   - Encourage commitment to the project and the development of a project attitude.
   - Give meaning to individual contributors to the project.
   - Facilitate motivation through achievement, goal theory and target setting.
   - Give a basis for the supporting reward system.

Notes

1. F.L. Harrison (1988) 'Conflict, power and politics in project management', *From Conception to Completion*, 9th World Congress on Project Management.
2. D.L. Wilemon (1971) *Project Management Conflict: A View from Apollo*, Proceedings of the Project Management Institute.
3. A.G. Butler (1973) 'Project management: a study in organizational conflict, *Academy of Management Journal*, March.
4. H.J. Thamhain and D.L. Wilemon (1974) *Conflict Management in Project-Oriented Work Environments*, Proceedings of the Project Management Institute.
5. H. Kerzner (1984) *Project Management*, Van Nostrand Reinhold.
6. J. Pfeffer (1981) *Power in Organizations*, Ballinger Publishing Co.
7. H. Mintzberg (1983) *Power In and Around Organizations*, Prentice Hall.
8. R. Meridith Belbin (1981) *Management Teams: Why They Succeed or Fail*, Heinemann Professional Publishing.

9. W.F.G. Mastenbroek (1987) *Conflict Management and Organization Development*, Wiley.
10. H. Bisno (1988) *Managing Conflict*, Sage Publications.
11. J.E. McGrath, 'Stress and behavior in organizations', in M.D. Dunnette, ed., (1976) *Handbook of Industrial and Organizational Psychology*, Chicago: Rand McNally.
12. Machiavelli (c. 1540) *The Prince*.

INDEX